THE MISSIONARY LETTERS OF VINCENT DONOVAN

The Missionary Letters
of Vincent Donovan

1957–1973

Edited by John P. Bowen

With a Foreword by Brian D. McLaren

PICKWICK *Publications* · Eugene, Oregon

THE MISSIONARY LETTERS OF VINCENT DONOVAN
1957–1973

Pickwick Publications
An Imprint of Wipf and Stock Publishers
199 W. 8th Ave., Suite 3
Eugene, OR 97401

www.wipfandstock.com

ISBN 13: 978-1-60899-117-4

Cataloging-in-Publication data:

Donovan, Vincent, J., 1926–2000.

The missionary letters of Vincent Donovan : 1957–1973 / Vincent J. Donovan, edited by John P. Bowen. Foreword by Brian D. McLaren.

xviii + 234 p. ; 23 cm. — Includes bibliographical references and index.

ISBN 13: 978-1-60899-117-4

1. Maasai (African people)—Missions. 2. Missions—Africa, East. 3. Missions. 4. Missions, American—Africa. 5. Church renewal—Catholic Church. I. Bowen, John P. II. McLaren, Brian D., 1956–. III. Title.

BT60 .D63 2011

Manufactured in the U.S.A.

This book is dedicated to those Spiritans and other missionaries
who have worked among the Maasai, particularly:

Bill Christy
Joe Herzstein
Gene Hillman (RIP)
Gerry Kohler
Ned Marchessault
and
Pat Patten

And honors the memory of Bill and Rosie Donovan

Contents

Illustrations

Foreword

MY GRANDFATHER, LIKE VINCENT Donovan, was a missionary to Africa. While Donovan was at work in Kenya and Tanzania, my grandfather was at work in Angola to the south and west. As a young boy, I grew up looking forward to his next furlough so I could hear his next installment of stories from Africa. Like most boys, I was especially hoping for stories of elephants and giraffes, of mambas and cobras and crocodiles, and he did have a few of those to share. But most of his stories were about new churches and preaching tours, about training elders and forming Christian communities. Now those subjects interest me even more than giraffes and crocodiles once did.

My grandfather was a Protestant from the era when Catholics and Protestants were, if not spiritual enemies, vigorous competitors for souls. As a child of the British empire, he probably didn't think much about the ways Protestant and Catholic missionaries were unwittingly agents of competing European empires . . . with Protestants winning souls for heaven and Great Britain, and with Catholics winning souls for heaven and Spain, France, or Portugal. I vaguely remember hearing my grandmother once refer to "some Catholic priests" as "good men," which was a surprisingly magnanimous concession from a Protestant who usually spoke of Rome with disdain. My suspicion is that if my grandparents had met Vincent Donovan, he would have won their respect as one of the "good men," just as he is winning the respect of a wider and wider range of readers today.

I am among the steady stream of Christians, both Catholic and Protestant, who at one point had someone ask, "Have you ever read *Christianity Rediscovered*? Based on what you're saying, I think you'd like it." After such a recommendation, I remember picking up the book shortly after it was published. But I didn't "get into it" and eventually lost interest and put it aside. Over the next twenty years or so I had several other people mention the book to me and it wasn't until the second edition came out that I picked it up and read it again, and this time I was enthralled. How could I have missed its value first time around? My lack of connection said more about my readiness than the book's value.

Donovan wrote as a missiologist, a reflective practitioner of Christian mission, and his voice, together with those of fellow missiologists Lesslie Newbigin and David Bosch, were of inestimable help to me and many of my friends in the 1990s and 2000s. We were going through our own rediscovery of Christianity as we faced a post-modern, post-Enlightenment, post-Christendom, post-Constantinian culture in the West . . . a culture that was growing as distant from conventional Christianity as the cultures of the Maasai and Sonjo.

When John Bowen let me know that he was editing Donovan's letters, I was thrilled because *Christianity Rediscovered* left me wishing for more: more of Donovan's insight into Christian faith and mission, and more insight into Donovan himself. As I read the letters, my curiosity was at once satisfied and intensified. The more I felt I was getting to know this fascinating man, the more I wanted to know.

Seven themes especially strike me as I read and reread these letters, just as they had struck me in the book. I encourage you to stay alert for these important themes as you read. Each of them comes across not simply as an argument or thesis Donovan is trying to defend, but rather as an instinct that guides Donovan as his work unfolds.

First, Donovan displays an ecumenical instinct. He kept no secret about the influence on his own thinking of Anglican missionary Roland Allen, and in these pages, one also sees the influence of Lutheran pastor Dave Simonson and others as well. Thoroughly Catholic, Donovan is also thoroughly ecumenical.

Second, Donovan displays a progressive instinct. You'll see this regarding his view of the role of women in the church. His respect for the leadership gifts of women—untypical in his time, and in our own as well—was truly groundbreaking. Similarly, he was progressive in his views of liturgical renewal and adaptation; decades later, too few have showed a similarly innovative spirit.

Third, Donovan displays what I might call an emergent instinct, the sense that Christian faith is not a finished product to be "sold" or "bought" in "as-is" condition, but rather that it is always in process, a work in progress, an unfinished symphony or canvas that is being shared while it is being developed, and will be further developed by those with whom it is shared. I felt this emergent instinct especially regarding Donovan's view of the priesthood. Donovan realized that the very clergy-laity system in which he worked could too easily create an unhealthy dependency and inferiority among the laity and an unhealthy paternalism and superiority among the clergy. So Donovan seemed determined to use his clerical status to empower leaders for their own mission, not to keep followers dependent on him as missionary.

As critical as this instinct made him regarding some facets of the church institution in its current form, he didn't allow himself to become cynical: rather, he maintained hope that the church was evolving, emerging, learning, and growing. He even seemed to hope that through his and his colleagues' missionary encounter with the Maasai and Sonjo, the church at large would itself rediscover values, freedoms, flexibilities, and other treasures that it had forgotten were part of its inheritance. The church, he dared to hope, could be converted to new and better ways even as it sought to convert others.

Fourth, Donovan displays a profoundly evangelical instinct—in the sense that for him the essence of Christianity is not a static, inflexible institution but a dynamic gospel, not a set of untranslatable doctrines but an ever-incarnating message and mission of hope.

Fifth, I'm struck by Donovan's theological instinct. For Donovan the essence of Christianity, the gospel, is a story—a story about the romance of God and all the tribes of humanity. That vision of the gospel seemed to birth in Donovan a different vision of God. The kind of God he believed in and proclaimed was a God who knows, loves, respects, enters, and enlivens each tribe—a far cry from a European colonial God who conquers all tribes, seeking to assimilate them into a homogenous European soup called "Western civilization." This vision of God, radical then and still radical now for many, led to a radically different understanding of the gospel—less a gospel of primitive heathens being saved from God's wrath, and more a gospel of all creation being saved from human sin, including the manifold sins of Western civilization.

I might call the sixth theme a Socratic instinct in Donovan, a great respect for the power of questions. Here's how he put it in *Christianity Rediscovered*:

> Never accept and be content with unanalyzed assumptions, assumptions about the work, about the people, about the church, or Christianity. Never be afraid to ask questions about the work we have inherited or the work we are doing. There is no question that should not be asked or that is outlawed. The day we are completely satisfied with what we have been doing; the day we have found the perfect, unchangeable system of work, the perfect answer, never in need of being corrected again, on that day we will know that we are wrong, that we have made the greatest mistake of all.[1]

One senses in Donovan's letters the spirit of a "forever-young" disciple, dedicated to lifelong learning, always asking questions—including questions that others assume are outlawed.

Finally, Donovan's letters continually manifest a creative instinct. Christianity is not just a tape recording to be replayed or a memorized spiel to be recited. Rather, it is a song to be loved, learned "by heart," deeply taken in and then creatively adapted, sung and played for others in an ever-fresh way. Ministry and mission are, for him, more art than science. I feel this creativity most strongly in the beautiful Maasai creed Donovan helped create. In it, I hear the song of the gospel transposed into a new key, joyfully played in new African instrumentation and with new African rhythms, yet as I listen, I can't help but recognize the essential, transcendent, universal melody of Jesus.

Vincent Donovan's missional instincts are, I believe, the same ones we need as we face a fast-changing world today. Today you don't have to get a Kenyan or Tanzanian passport to enter a different world: you just need to step outside your parish doors. In or around nearly every movie theatre, coffee shop, pub, dinner table, chat room, website, and circle of friends, a new world is being created, debated, resisted, and explored through thousands of conversations. The church in its many forms is sometimes at the table, part of the conversation, but too often, it is absent, huddled in its familiar institutional fortresses and its comfortable mission compounds, plotting its own internal maintenance rather than its external mission. For those who are driven by conscience and vocation

---

1. Donovan, *Christianity Rediscovered*, 146.

to live and share the gospel of Jesus Christ in the new and different world that morphs daily outside our doors, Vincent Donovan can be a kind of patron saint, a mentor, a model.

And John Bowen serves us well in this venture, not only by presenting Donovan's letters to us with helpful notes at every turn, but also by telling us "What Happened Next?" As I read and reread those fascinating—and sometimes disappointing—reflections from Donovan's colleagues, I feel how our progress in Christian mission is so often a "two steps forward, one step back" affair. And I feel encouraged, as I am able, to take my two steps forward as boldly, humbly, and wisely as I can, leaving the backtracking to others.

Thank God for the example—now more fully available to us, thanks to John Bowen—of that amazing missionary pioneer, Fr. Vincent Donovan.

Brian D. McLaren

Acknowledgments

THIS BOOK HAS HAD a long gestation, and along the way I have been helped by wonderful people, to all of whom I owe grateful thanks.

I had been using *Christianity Rediscovered* for some years in teaching evangelism at Wycliffe College in Toronto, and had (like most readers) always wondered what happened after Donovan left Tanzania. Then, in 2006, I had the opportunity to visit Maasailand and to talk with three missionary priests who knew him—Fr. Ned Marchessault, Fr. Joe Herzstein, and Fr. Pat Patten. I am grateful to all of them for their time, patience, and hospitality. I am also very thankful for the help and input of Erin Biggs, my research assistant on that trip and afterwards, and to Sam Waweru, dear friend and driver extraordinaire, who took us from Nairobi to Tanzania and back.

A report I wrote for the Partners in Mission department of the Anglican Church of Canada found its way onto Fr. Ned's website (www.osotua.org), and thence into the national newsletter of the Spiritans. This prompted an e-mail from Fr. Girard (Gerry) Kohler in Pittsburgh,

Bill Christy (left), Girard Kohler (right) and Eugene Hillman (front). Bethel Park PA, 2007.

and twice after that I was able to visit with him and Fr. Eugene (Gene) Hillman (who has since died) in Pittsburgh.

Gerry introduced me to Fr. Bill Christy, who had also been involved in Maasai evangelization, but some years later than Donovan, who generously allowed me to record his stories, which appear in the concluding essay to this book. Through Gerry, I also met Nora Koren, Donovan's sister, and it was she who trusted me with her lovingly preserved collection of her brother's letters and articles.

Gerry, Gene and Nora have patiently helped me with the myriad of questions which have surfaced during the editing of the letters. In what follows, many of the detailed footnotes about the work of the Spiritans in Tanzania are based on information from Gerry and Gene, while most of the footnotes explaining references to life among the Donovan family in the US are from Nora. Without them, this book could hardly have come into existence, and I am indebted to them more than I can express.

Also at the Spiritan Center in Bethel Park PA, I met Fr. Tony Bacher, who showed me a photograph of the "Gothic cathedral" mentioned in the letter of August 1959, and Fr. Joe Kelly, who gave me access to his own archival materials on the church in Africa. I am very grateful to them. The staff of the Center have also been generous in their help and hospitality, particularly Fr. Dave Cottingham, IT expert at Bethel Park, and Mary Winkler, the archivist.

Fr. Paul McCauley of the Canadian Spiritans has gone the second mile in lending me the tapes of Donovan's last retreat (held in Scarborough, Ontario), and Henry Koren's encyclopedic work, *A Spiritan East Africa Memorial 1863–1993*, which gives biographical information about every Spiritan missionary in East Africa during those years. To him also I owe grateful thanks.

Scholars more knowledgeable than I in various areas have helped me with their expertise, and without them this book would be far poorer: Drs. Kim Groop and Mika Vähäkangas of the University of Helsinki; Drs. Alan Hayes, Joe Mangina, Ephraim Radner, and George Sumner from Wycliffe College, Toronto; Dr. Carl Starklof from St. Michael's University in the University of Toronto; Dr. Joseph Schner of Regis College, University of Toronto; Dr. Terrance Tiessen of Providence Theological Seminary, Otterburne, Manitoba; and Dr. Doug Blomberg of the Institute for Christian Studies in Toronto. Dr. Tim Kelton, Assistant Professor in the Department of Family and Community Medicine at the University of Toronto helped me with Donovan's medical references. To all of these, my sincere thanks.

Funding for my trip to Tanzania came from Partners in Mission, of the Anglican Church of Canada, and for the work involved in this book from the Churches' Council on Theological Education in Canada. My thanks are due to both these bodies for their generosity and vision. I am also grateful to Drs. Carl Starklof, Charles Fensham, and Allan Effa (respectively Catholic, Presbyterian and Baptist missiologists) who generously supported my application to the CCTE.

Dr. Bill Burrows gave invaluable guidance in the early stages of this project. Angela Bick provided speedy and efficient transcriptions of the conversations which lie behind much of what I have contributed to this book. Michael Allerton the indexer has been a pleasure to work with. Special thanks to my friend ben weeks for drawing the map of where Donovan served. And finally, my sincere thanks to Dr. K. C. Hanson and the staff of Wipf and Stock, particularly Dr. Robin Parry (like myself, a man from North Wales), for their prompt, efficient, and friendly help.

John P. Bowen
The Feast of St. Augustine of Canterbury 2009

Prologue

THE IDEA THAT "The camera always lies"[1] seems shocking to those of us who were brought up to believe the opposite. But the case for the untruthfulness of photography is persuasive. Who, for example, has been excluded from that smiling family group? After all, the photograph has edges, and who knows what lies outside those edges? Or what about the serene stately home in the background? Maybe it is surrounded by slums—which would spoil the picture, of course, or at least create a totally different one if they were included.

Yet even what is included in the picture does not tell the whole truth. Were those smiling faces smiling five minutes earlier, or is this a brief truce in a running battle? That wife with her hand so lightly on her husband's shoulder: did that touch come easily, or was it done reluctantly at the insistence of the photographer, simply to improve the composition? Did she snatch it away the second the shutter had clicked?

Vincent Donovan's *Christianity Rediscovered* is a snapshot in time. Like all photographs, it has edges, and cannot describe what is outside the edges, wherever they are drawn. Like many photographs, the subject matter is arranged neatly to form a symmetrical whole. And, as with all photographs, we see through the photographer's eye whatever the photographer thinks we should see.

In the last couple of years, two things have happened to shed light on what is outside the frame of *Christianity Rediscovered*. One is that Vincent Donovan's letters from Tanzania to friends and family during the years 1957 to 1973 have come to light, lovingly preserved over

1. Hood, *The Camera Always Lies.*

1

the years by his sister Nora and published here in book form for the first time. These provide us with a much wider range of snapshots of Donovan's life and work. Apart from anything else, they give us more of the context surrounding the stories told in *Christianity Rediscovered*. Perhaps 20 percent of the book is quoted or adapted from the letters.

The other thing is that those who knew and worked with Donovan, including some who were inspired by him to a life of missionary service, and some who had questions about his work, have been sharing their memories of him. They also have their verbal photographs. Sometimes those photographs shed more light on Donovan's own; at other times, it is difficult to see how those photographs can be of the same event. Their comments provide many of the footnotes to these letters, and form the substance of the epilogue: "What Happened Next?" Of course, none of these photographs is provided by the Maasai or the Sonjo (predictably, they are more often the photographed), who would tell yet another version of the story.[2]

WHAT THE *LETTERS* TELL US

Apart from anything else, the letters tell more dramatic stories of missionary life—of encounters with wild animals, of Donovan's clandestine meeting with Julius Nyerere, the future president of Tanzania; of attempts by Christians of other denominations to kill him; of Antoni, heroic apostle to the Meru; and particularly of the reclusive Sonjo people among whom Donovan spent his last five years in Tanzania. These alone make the letters worth reading.

There is more, however. Here we also get a fuller sense of Donovan the man: more of the various communities to which he belonged, more of his personal struggles, more of how he grew into the convictions that he shares in the first book—in a word, more of his world.

The *Letters* fill in some of the historical background to *Christianity Rediscovered*. Few events in the outside world make themselves felt in the first book. Apart from references to the Second Vatican Council (1962–1965), there is little to tie the book to a particular historical context. Yet the period during which Donovan was in Tanzania saw some

2. The story of some of the Catholic Maasai is told by anthropologist Dorothy Hodgson in *The Church of Women*. Her work receives vigorous and detailed criticism from Kohler in the Spiritans' *East-West Newsletter*. Finnish scholar Mika Vähäkangas tells of conversations with Sonjo in "Ghambageu Encounters Jesus in Sonjo Mythology."

world-changing events. Some of these are referred to in the *Letters*: the independence movements in countries around the world, including Tanzania; the Vietnam War; the civil rights movement in the US; the rise to power and the assassination of John and then of Robert Kennedy; the shooting of Martin Luther King; incidents during the Cold War (such as the shooting down of the U2 spy plane); Woodstock; and the Beatles. Some—though not all—of these show up in the *Letters*. (In particular, the death of President Kennedy goes unmentioned.) He refers to listening to the radio and hearing the news (presumably) on the Voice of America (e.g., October 1968).

Through the *Letters*, Donovan becomes a much more three-dimensional human being. He speaks frankly (at least in letters to family) of the pain of being a missionary. There is of course the homesickness: "Never having been homesick before in my life, I found the feeling strange and unfamiliar to me" (December 1962 cf. July 1968). At the same time, there is the poignancy of not being quite sure any more where home is. "It will be my first Christmas at home in twenty years. And do you know something? I'm frightened!" (December 1961). We see too the yearning and pain when death and other tragedies strike at his family and friends, and he is so far away: when his younger brother Jome (Jerome) dies, he writes, "My heart goes out to you, Dad, more than I can say . . . I am crying now, Dad, and I am not ashamed of it" (April 1965). Eighteen months later, when his father also dies, in order to phone home, he has to be flown to Nairobi by the Flying Doctor Service (November 1966). Though letters are always possible, they are not frequent enough—in either direction. He complains to his brother Bill and his wife Rosie, "Everyone else has given up on me but you two, and I can understand why" (July 1964). And Bill in turn tries to encourage people at home to write to Donovan more often (February 10, 1964). In light of these human glimpses, we learn more from the inside why Donovan resonated with the words of Pope Pius XII that missionaries are "social martyrs" (August 10, 1959).

We also learn much more of his communities here. The Donovan of *Christianity Rediscovered* can appear a lonely and solitary hero—and indeed his friends say he was a loner. Yet the *Letters* make reference to a widespread network of colleagues and friends: he names Bishop Kilasaria, Fr. Eugene Hillman, Fr. Ed Kelly, Fr. Fred Trumbull, Brother Francis, Pastor Dave Simonson, Bishop Durning—and there were many others whom he does not name. Indeed, he says the fellowship of other missionaries helps compensate for the loneliness (August 1959). Not least, an attempt to build cross-denominational bridges by conversations with Lutheran missionaries gets off to a shaky start, but then become a great source of fellowship and theological stimulation (June 1961).

The *Letters* give us insight into the distinctive character of Spiritan work in Tanzania. In the Church of Tanzania, the Diocese of Arusha was regarded as somewhat radical. Indeed, one version of the story of this diocese suggests that it was carved out of the larger Diocese of Moshi in part to accommodate the ethos of the Spiritans.[3] As Donovan would reflect later, "Opinions and thoughts from Arusha always caused much commotion, and were inevitably received with much suspicion and fear" (December 30, 1969). Another version points out that Africans had taken over the positions of leadership in Moshi Diocese (the bishop, Kilasara, was a Chagga), so that the Spiritans could say that their work was done. Yet it remains the case that African churchmen were more conservative than the Spiritans. For example: Donovan describes how the first Bishop of Arusha, Dennis Durning, himself a Spiritan, began a program to train and ordain married permanent deacons. The program was later vetoed by the national conference of bishops (September 1968). Donovan's radical ideas may have seemed extreme to traditionalists, whether in Africa, Europe, or North America, but they were hardly surprising as an expression of the vision of this Order or of this new diocese in particular.

Family was very important to Donovan. Several of his letters to family members survive (and appear in chronological sequence among the other letters). They are interesting and often touching and witty. For example, he writes to his older brother Gib, who was upset the first time his daughter went off on the school bus: "I wouldn't have wept, seeing poor little Shari being taken off to school. I would have fought the bus driver" (January 1970). From his family's side, their loyalty to him is unwavering. Particularly his brother Bill's organizing of the Monthly Mission Donations (MMD) Club, whose supporters contributed one dollar a month to Donovan's support, goes on faithfully through the years.

There are also new insights into Donovan the reflective practitioner of mission. In some ways, the emphases which characterize *Christianity Rediscovered* are there from the beginning of the *Letters*. The Spiritans,

3. The Spiritans is the usual name given to the Congregation of the Holy Ghost (C.S.Sp.), to which Donovan belonged.

since their inception in the mid-nineteenth century, have been committed to inculturation.[4] So it is hardly surprising that even in his earliest years in Tanzania, Donovan can write that he expects to "live to see the day when the white priest will no longer be wanted or needed in Africa" (September 1959). That is deeply embedded in his Order's DNA. As early as 1960, he is collecting Maasai melodies and writing Christian songs to them in the Maasai language—"and presto, we had Masai[5] hymns" (August 1960). Around the same time he preaches what he believes is the first Catholic sermon in Maasai. At this point, he is already using the language of "[clothing] the soul of Christianity with the flesh and blood of Africa" (September 1960, February 1965) and "translating" the story of Jesus into Maasai terms (November–December 1960, January–February 1961). He also understands the concept which becomes so central to *Christianity Rediscovered*, of community conversion: "In any other tribe . . . it was not one man who came forward to accept Christianity. It was . . . usually very, very many at one time normally being baptized in the same day" (November 1963 cf. September 1967).

Yet in other ways he espouses early on views which he will strongly repudiate later. For example, when he first moves to Usa River in September 1962 to work with the Meru, he is excited about the prospect of buying land and erecting buildings. "I am trying to get a plot of land on which to start a mission right now," he writes in December of that year. In January 1964, he is excited about the prospect of buying land "where we could put a chapel . . . a dispensary . . . a school, etc." Then, having erected the first church building, he tells the assembled Merus, "the church has come to Meru" (August 1964).

By April 1967, however, he is saying, "I am more and more convinced that every single building we put up . . . puts off the day when the African Church can come into existence in its own." And in March 1967: "Acquiring land seems to be our primary preoccupation. . . . It gives rise to the 'mission compound' concept, one of the most paralyzing concepts a missionary has to deal with." What had happened? Sometime after coming to Loliondo in 1966, he had met up again with Dave Simonson,

4. Their founder, Francis Libermann (1802–1852), had advised them, for example: "Put off Europe, its customs, its spirit. . . . Become Negroes to the Negroes, in order to form them as they should be, not in the fashion of Europe, but allow them to keep what is peculiar to them" (Letter, cited by Spindler in "Libermann, Francois Marie Paul," 399).

5. Donovan consistently uses the spelling "Masai" though most contemporary writers use the form "Maasai."

the Lutheran pastor who gave him books by Roland Allen. Clearly he was thinking along the same lines as Allen before reading him, but the books seem to have catalyzed and focused some of his convictions.

Another example: early on, he is proud of the fact that missionaries need to be generalists. He (and the great majority were men) needs to be "pastor, principal of school, architect, mason, carpenter, painter, plumber, mechanic, judge, doctor, cook, employer, administrator, accountant, diplomat, explorer, lawyer, beggar, [and] priest" (August 1959). But then, by April 1965 he is bemoaning the fact that "many of the priests and other missionaries who were working in East Africa were doing everything but teaching religion." In December 1965, he wrote, "I have been involved in many kinds of work out here, building, transporting, medical, social, educational, and searching out new sections where the church has never entered, but it was in catechetical work that I truly felt I was closest to the heart of the matter." And by April 1970, it is even more focused: "It is a strange feeling to analyze your whole missionary life and to realize that it works itself out into being nothing but a precarious line of bearing hope to others. My only work is to be a bearer of hope, a carrier of hope." Or April 1971: "A missionary's primary job is to bring the Christian message."

Finally, the *Letters* bear witness to the power of theology done "in the trenches" of mission. Certainly he reads widely—not only Roland Allen (a theologically conservative Anglican), but also Küng, Tillich, Ivan Illich, Bonhoeffer and Rahner, among others—but his theological work is never done in isolation from mission. Even when we do not agree with his conclusions, we have to honor his passion to find the best way of communicating Christianity to those who have never heard it before. It has been said that biblical studies is the conscience of theology. I would go a step further and suggest that missiology is the conscience of both. Donovan is a model of a missionary seeking to bring together biblical studies and theology in the service of the church's mission.

THE USEFULNESS OF THE *LETTERS*

Maybe Hugh Hood is overly skeptical in saying, "The camera always lies." After all, those people in the photograph really were there that day, and those buildings were indeed in the background. But he shocks us into realizing that the camera never tells the whole truth, and that we should exercise some hermeneutical suspicion towards what it tells us.

The Missionary Letters of Vincent Donovan, and the comments of those who knew and worked with him, add considerably to the range of snapshots of his work. Not least, they place *Christianity Rediscovered* in a wider context—contexts of the life of Tanzania, the work of the Spiritan Order, events in the wider world, the theological currents around Vatican II, and the life of Donovan's immediate family. The result is a kind of collage, offering rich and provocative insights from an unusually creative period of Catholic missions in Tanzania.

PRINCIPLES OF SELECTION

The letters reprinted here are only a selection of Donovan's letters. The whole corpus is some 50 percent bigger than this, but to print all of them would have made an unwieldy volume. Some difficult choices therefore had to be made, and the following criteria were followed:

- Priority was given to those letters which demonstrate the development of Donovan's thought.

- Conversely, letters which were simply descriptions of (for example) the wildlife he encountered were omitted.

- In some cases, where material was lifted in part or whole from the letters and incorporated into the book, the reference is noted, but the material itself is omitted.

- Some of the letters to family members have been included where they shed light on his character or on the development of his thinking; others have been omitted.

- On rare occasions, letters from people other than Donovan—his Provincial, Francis McGlynn, and Donovan's brother Bill—have been included because they add to the context of his work and letters.

Care has been taken to transcribe the letters of Donovan as accurately as possible. The rough edges and inconsistencies in his style have been maintained rather than smoothed out in the editorial process in the pursuit of authenticity. Readers wishing to study the full text of the typescript of the *Letters* in PDF format are welcome to e-mail the editor at john.bowen@utoronto.ca.

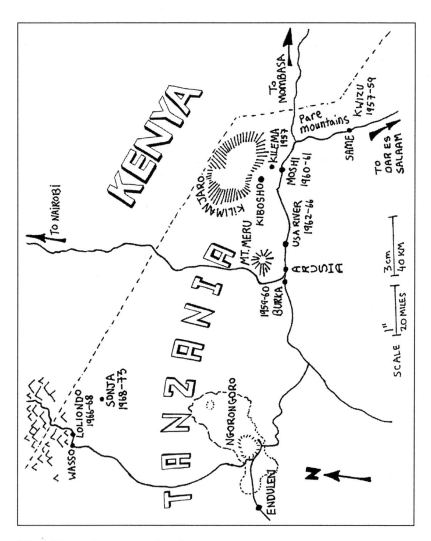

Where Vincent Donovan was based.

8

THE LETTERS

1

KWIZU[1]

(1957–1959)

Kwizu Mission
Jan. 2, 1957

Very Rev. Francis H. McGlynn, C.S.Sp.
Provincial
Holy Ghost Fathers
1615 Manchester Lane, NW
Washington 11, D.C.

Dear Father McGlynn:

The letter you sent to me was held up in Rome for over a month. It came to me when I was stationed in Kilema.[2] I was surprised that, with everyone writing letters about my not going immediately to Africa after the school year in Rome, not anyone told you the reason.

---

1. Kwizu mission was in the Pare district, part of what is now the Diocese of Same, one hundred miles south-east of Arusha.
2. Kilema is in the mountains, five or six miles north-east of the town of Moshi.

I left Rome in early July to go to Switzerland as arranged with you and the Superior General. I got no further than Northern Italy when I received word that I should return to Rome at once. It seems Father Martin had arranged a plane reservation for me in early July for Africa. I went to the R.A.P.T.I.M.[3] agency to pick up my tickets but they informed me that my Visa for Tanganyika had not yet arrived so I could not go. I cancelled that reservation and arranged for the next plane. My Visa still did not come and the process was repeated. All in all two plane reservations and two boat reservations were cancelled before my Visa came, via cable from Africa.

During all that time the British Embassy requested that I do not leave Rome, so I stayed in Rome all during July and August. My Visa finally came on August 30th right after I had cancelled the second boat reservation. I spent all that day on the phone to Genoa, trying to pick up another reservation. I left Rome that night, got to Genoa early in the morning, began haunting the Shipping Office four hours before it opened, got a ticket and got on the boat one hour before the ship sailed away.

It was an exciting voyage. We came to Port Said the very day the Suez Canal Conference opened in Cairo.[4] The passengers were very nervous. Nothing happened. The only disquieting thing about the passage was the ominous presence directly behind us and in front of us in the convoy of two Egyptian Destroyers. We were the only British Ship. Colonel Nasser's soldiers and big guns were in disquieting evidence all along the Canal.

The scalding body of water called the Red Sea, with its 100% humidity, left me a bit sick. We buried one man at sea and two were *in periculo mortis* [in danger of death (Latin)].[5] I always thought 100% humidity meant rain but I found out to my horror it doesn't.

At the port of Aden in Asia I was stoned and surrounded by a hostile mob. Native policemen had to rescue me and escort me back to the ship.

I finally came to Mombasa and made my way up to Moshi in Kilimanjaro. I was temporarily assigned to Kilema to study Swahili. While

3. Raptim is a travel organization for religious and humanitarian organizations.

4. President Nasser of Egypt had nationalized the Suez Canal in 1956, leading to an international crisis and near-outbreak of war. This conference was an attempt to resolve the crisis.

5. Square brackets here and throughout indicate an editorial insertion.

there, during the sick-leave absence of Father Brennan, I became the chauffeur of Bishop Byrne[6] and temporary secretary.

After a time, I began hearing confessions and just recently I preached my first sermon in Swahili. I received the other day what will probably be my permanent appointment—to KWIZU Mission in the Pare Mountains, a bit removed from Moshi and Kilimanjaro. I am under Father Mike Carr and will work with him and Frs. John Walsh, Mangan, McGavran and O'Sullivan. The work is vastly interesting with Witch Doctors for neighbors and Black Magic for breakfast.

Wishing you all God's blessing in the coming New Year and assuring you of my prayers, I remain,

Respectfully yours in the Holy Ghost,
Vincent J. Donovan, C.S.Sp.

[Letter from Francis McGlynn, Provincial of C.S.Sp., January 1957.]

Washington, D.C.
22 January 1957

Reverend Vincent Donovan, C.S.Sp.
Kwizu Mission, P.O. Box 15, Same
Tanganyika, East Africa

Dear Vincent:

When I say I was happy to hear from you, it is putting it mildly. I had been concerned about your long silence, but, as you explain in your letter, it was due to the fact that my letter to you was held up in Rome for over a month.

It comes as a relief to know that the delay in your trip to Africa was due to a series of circumstances beyond your control. I had every confidence that you would carry out the instructions from the Superior

---

6. "With Bishop Joseph Byrne being made Vicar Apostolic of the Vicariate of Kilimanjaro in 1932 [sic] the USA Spiritans received their mandate to the African Mission" (Christy, "History of the American Spiritan Mission in Africa," 1). Joseph Byrne (1886–1961) went to East Africa in 1933 and became Bishop of Moshi in 1953, remaining so until 1959. When he was succeeded by Bishop Joseph Kilasara (see letter of May 1960), the diocese had over 150,000 Catholics, 28 African priests, 164 African Sisters, and 25 African Brothers (Koren, *Memorial*, 332).

General which I conveyed to you, but, owing to the main delays in obtaining your visa, it is understandable that several plane and boat reservations had to be cancelled.

But now that is over, and I am happy to know that you have arrived safely at your mission even though you passed some exciting days in the course of your trip through the Suez Canal.

Part of your letter reads like the Epistles of St. Paul, who also had a taste of being stoned and chased out of town [Acts 14:5, 19]. As you know, we have Father Trahan with us now and he was happy to learn that you are so interested in your new work and that you are already able to hear confessions and even to preach in Swahili. So now that the danger of your travels is behind you, you can settle down to what I know will be a fruitful missionary career.

I heard from Father Martin recently, and in my reply I told him that I had heard from you and was gratified to know that you are now well settled in your permanent work.

With cordial greetings from all of us, I am
Sincerely yours in the Holy Spirit,
Francis H. McGlynn, C.S.Sp.
Provincial

[On October 28 1958, Cardinal Angelo Giuseppe Roncalli was elected Pope, and took the name John XXIII.]

[Letter from Bill Donovan, Vincent's older brother, January 1959.]

731 Gaywood Drive
Pittsburgh 35, Pa.

Dear _____,[7]

A few days ago, I came into possession of a letter Father Vince wrote to a priest in Pittsburgh. The priest is a friend of Father Vince[8] and was able to send him a number of High Mass stipends [offerings] from his parish church. The money Father Vince received as a stipend for these

7. The blank in the original document was so that a personal name could be written in.

8. This was Fr. Donald McIlvane, the assistant priest at Donovan's home parish, who had been ordained the same day as Donovan.

Masses came in very handy for his missionary work in Africa. I would like to quote a few lines from the letter,

> In the past year and a half I have been working among the Masai tribe and the Arusha tribe, who are distant cousins of the Masai, speak the same language, dress the same, and, like them, are primitive in customs and culture. By the grace of God, I have been able to make some inroads among the Arusha for the first time. And so it was decided that I would devote my whole time to them. So I was transferred outside the town of Arusha, and I live alone in a little house that resembles a Pennsylvania miner's shack, among the people of the Arusha tribe. It is an overwhelming job and a tremendous challenge which humbles and frightens me. Please remember me in your prayers. I will need all the help I can get. I don't know how difficult it was for you to get those High Masses for me last year, but I certainly appreciated them. Do you think it would be possible to get me some more this year? They would be a big help. I am completely on my own and must support myself the best way I can. I was even contemplating writing articles for magazines to make some money.[9]

After reading the letter, I gave some thought to the raising of money for Father Vince, to help support him in Africa. Not being able to do it alone, I am turning to his family and friends. I know you are as fond of him as he is of you and would like to help Father Vince if you could. Perhaps you feel as I did at first, that the small amount of money you could send would be of little help. With that thought in mind I am forming a "Father Vince's Dollar A Month Club." A small amount each month from each of us, his family and friends, would give him an amount he could count on each month. You would be helping him and at the same time engaging in a charitable work, which I know Our Lord will not let go unrewarded.

To make it as convenient as possible, I think it best if you send me your dollar by the 18th of each month, if you feel you are able to help out in this charitable undertaking. I will total all the money I have by that date and send a check to Father Vince for that amount. I will take care of all expenses involved and every cent donated will go directly to Father

---

9. US Spiritans did not begin to receive per diem support until after the Chapter meeting of 1970 (see letter of October 1970). For specific projects, missionaries had to raise their own funds from "dollar a month clubs," grants from agencies, and whatever other sources they could find. This meant that it created extra financial difficulty when priests moved from the relatively wealthy towns into unevangelized areas.

Vince. I will also send a list to Father Vince of his benefactors. If you feel that you would like to join this club and are able to do so, will you make a mental note and mail the dollar (or whatever amount, large or small, that you can donate) to reach me by the 18th of each month?

Believe me, it is not easy to beg, and that is what I am doing for Father Vince because he is unable to do it for himself. I know he will remember you in his prayers in a very special way for helping him in God's work with the African people.

Thank you very much and God bless you.
Bill Donovan

2

BURKA[1]

(1959–1960)

March 12, 1959

Dear Relatives and Friends,

I wonder if I could ever tell you how touched I was when I got a letter from my brother Bill, with a check enclosed from all of you for me and my work out here. It is difficult for someone on the receiving end of generosity to let his benefactors know how grateful he is, but I am grateful and I thank you all from the bottom of my heart. Someday in the not too distant future, I trust I will be able to thank you all, personally, face to face.

The places I have been and the things I have seen in these last few years! The strange and intriguing work that I find myself doing in this land so far away from Pittsburgh. If only I could give you some idea

---

1. Burka is just outside Arusha. Kohler comments: "Burka is not so much a village or town in its own right, just a traditional name along the road, picked up by some of the old-time settlers to identify their coffee plantations in the area."

of my life here. It is so different from the work of a parish priest in the United States.

That day, which seems like yesterday, when I watched Pittsburgh disappear out of the back of the train, did I know what it was going to be like then? I don't think so. By the way, someone should write a book or an essay or a poem or something about watching your home town disappear out of the back of a train.

It's a chastening experience. That place that has been the center of your life, the vantage point from which you watched your world go round—it is going to change a great deal before you see it again, and the people in it who have been your whole existence are going to change a great deal before you see them again—if you ever do. This great warm city, vomiting you out of its life, down the railroad tracks, into what?

I wondered too, that day I stood aboard the big ocean liner and watched the shore line of America slip back out of sight. I suddenly realized that my youth was somehow tied to the Statue of Liberty, and I was leaving my youth back there with her. I was leaving America in my late twenties and would possibly return in my middle thirties. Dying will not be an entirely new experience to me. I have already died once, or at least begun to die, there along the rails of the S. S. United States.

And then there was Mombasa, the port on the Indian Ocean, where I set foot for the first time on African soil several years ago [1956], and headed for Mount Kilimanjaro where most of the American missions[2] are. That first ride from Mombasa to Kilimanjaro was a pop-eyed, awe-inspiring ride for me. I guess it would be for anyone. I didn't feel like talking much that day. I wanted to look around and get acquainted with this land that was going to be my home for a long time to come. That first look was rather a depressing experience. The road leads through some of the most desolate land you ever laid eyes on. On both sides of the road nothing but miles and miles of grubby looking earth and thorn bushes as far as the eye can see. This is the *Bush of Africa*. This is the home of the wild animals rugged enough to exist there, the scattered tribes of people barely touched by civilization, who come out and watch the cars go by— naked children, coal black men, and women covered with a skirt around their waists. This is the land where women have the incredible existence

---

2. This is "mission" in the sense of a mission station and church building, at the centre of a parish which might have 40,000 inhabitants. Lutherans as well as Catholics were working in this area.

of spending two days every week walking for water, one day collecting the water, two more days of walking to bring the water back to their homes, two days resting and then starting the whole infernal process all over again. This is the land where I live. I'll tell you more about it and my work here when I write again.

Meanwhile, my gentle cousins and relatives and friends of the fair sex, kiss the water faucets and taps in your houses *for me* at least once a day. And all of you, God bless you and thank you.

> Sincerely yours,
> Father Vince

August 1, 1959

Dear Relatives and Friends,

I want to thank you again for your kindness in sending me money once more. I remember you all in my prayers, and I am thinking of you especially now that your summer season is beginning, and we on the lower half of the globe are entering our cold season. And even though we are only three degrees away from the Equator you would be surprised how cold it can get here.

There are so many things to write about Africa. But there is one thing in Africa which naturally speaking means more to a person like me out here than anything else—and that thing is not even African. I am referring to the other missionaries you find here when you come, the other American Holy Ghost Fathers who are also working in Africa.

The first thing you notice about the priest out here, after being used to the States and Europe, is the extreme youth of the clergy. When I first arrived, the average for pastors out here in all our missions in the diocese of Kilimanjaro was about 36—or priests out of the seminary about ten years. You have a pastor of a very big mission with about 11,000 Catholics who has been out of the seminary about five years. You have a priest in charge of a secondary school, which would be about equivalent to one of our colleges, who left the seminary ten years ago. You have a priest in charge of a Teachers Training Institute who has been out of the seminary just seven years.[3] The Chancellor of the Diocese is out of the seminary only nine years.[4]

Just compare this with any diocese you know anywhere, and you will see how unique it is. One of the causes of this youthful clergy was the war.[5] There are other causes too, but whatever the causes, the results are plain to see. It is apparent as soon as you set foot in Kilimanjaro. There is an arresting, challenging, youthful vigor in the air which is infectious. These priests, as young as they are, are successfully completing tasks which their clerical counterparts in the States would not dream of undertaking before their Silver Jubilees.

Many of them have built churches. Many more have built schools. Several have built their own houses, one of which could have come out of the pages of *Better Homes and Gardens* at half the professional price. One of them from McKees Rocks, without any training whatsoever, designed himself a beautiful, magnificent Gothic Cathedral[6]—and has almost completed it. Most of them are, day by day, handling administrative burdens that would give pause to a Cardinal Spellman.[7] All of them are daily sitting in judgment over family and neighborhood disputes that would tax a lawyer. In some places our fathers have built or are building miles and miles of road through desert sand and living rock, up mountains, down mountains, around mountains and through mountains. And this must all be done through the medium of a strange and foreign language which they never can afford to leave off studying. All this is in addition to their primary work as priests—their pastoral care, hearing confessions, preaching, baptizing, instructing for marriage, running the different societies in the mission, sick calls, visitation of all the houses in

3. Fr. Constantine Conan (b.1920) joined the staff of the Singa Chini St. Patrick's Teacher Training College in 1951. He had been ordained two years earlier (Koren, *Memorial*, 494).

4. Fr. Joseph ("Chick") Brennan (1919–1991), also referred to in the letter of January 2, 1957. He became chancellor in 1950, at the age of 31. (Koren, *Memorial*, 472)

5. During the Second World War, it was too dangerous to ship US missionaries to Africa. There was also a rise in missionary vocations after the War.

6. This was Fr. Anthony Bacher (1919–2009), and the church was in Mawella. Fr. Bacher had turned down scholarships to study engineering and architecture in order to be ordained (Koren, *Memorial*, 476). McKees Rocks is near Pittsburgh PA.

7. Francis Cardinal Spellman (1889–1967) was made Archbishop of New York in 1939, and was named a cardinal in 1946. This was a particularly busy time of building, particularly parochial schools, in the New York Archdiocese.

The church at Mawella mentioned by Donovan in the letter of August 1, 1959. The architect, Fr. Tony Bacher, wrote on this picture, "built without one square foot of blueprint."

the mission, tramping long hours on safari up mountain paths, or bumping even longer hours along the rough indescribable roads through the plains to visit and more firmly solidify the innumerable out missions attached to every main mission.

Pastor, principal of school, architect, mason, carpenter, painter, plumber, mechanic, judge, doctor, cook, employer, administrator, accountant, diplomat, explorer, lawyer, beggar, priest—that is what the missionary is, or must become.

Yes, the first thing I noticed about Africa is the missionary. It would be a little difficult to explain what the comradeship of these fellows can mean to you out here. There is not much recreation out here. Talking to one another is one of the only amusements there is. These guys have developed a knack of consideration and getting along that could be a great lesson for a lot of people in the States. Without it, the "long loneliness"[8] could get a grip on you and make a shambles of your missionary effort.

God love you and bless you.
Father Vince

8. This is the title of the autobiography of Dorothy Day, founder of the Catholic Worker movement, first published in 1952.

August 10, 1959

Dear Relatives and Friends,

Two weeks ago a little African school boy said to me, "American Catholics are awfully good to Africa and the missions. Is it because they are Americans or because they are Catholics?" I told him, "A little bit of both, boy, a little bit of both." And I want to thank you Americans, you Catholics, you relatives and you friends, for the check that I recently received from all of you. You are very good to me, and I am humbly grateful.

Last time I spoke about missionaries. Do you know what the late Pope Pius XII said about missionaries? He said,

> Missionaries have a strange and terrible vocation. Their home-land must become strange to them, and every foreign land must become their home. They are not physical martyrs. They may be if some uprising takes place in the land in which they are work-ing, but not necessarily so. That is not what makes them unique. Neither are they unique because they must leave their home and their family and their friends. Every priest, every brother, every sister does this. They are unique because they must give up and leave behind them their background, their culture, their race, their nation, their country, their homeland. They are in fact social martyrs.[9]

The idea of social martyrdom is hardly noticeable when you first come. Then after a while it begins to sink into you slowly until one fine day you awake to the sober realization that you are indeed a stranger in a strange land and that your homeland has drifted far, far away, not only in distance, but also in the relationship and attitude you have towards it—and it towards you. I sometimes pick up a newspaper or a magazine and read about Americans—those industrious, prosperous, ingenious, uncanny people from far across the sea—and am so intrigued by what I read that I forget that I am one.

The World Series, Rose Bowl games, the Fourth of July become un-real and dreamlike. You know you have reached the point of no return

---

9. Extensive research has not revealed the source of this quotation. One Roman Catholic scholar suggested to me that "the quote might be from a public audience or sermon that would be difficult to track down."

when Thanksgiving passes, not only without turkey, but without even remembering it is Thanksgiving.

And the truth of the matter is that this strange land never becomes your home. You are forever condemned to be a stranger, the outsider, the foreigner. Except for the priesthood which is seen and respected in you, you are still to every African the hated white man, the feared European (which in this case includes also Americans).

But all this has nothing to with happiness which never leaves you, with peace to an extent which you never dreamed possible, and with contentment filled to the brim and running over. I think the happiest group of men I have ever seen are these missionaries I have met, and with whom I work out here.

You hear the most outlandish clowning around on the rare occasions when there is a general get together, such as certain feast days, but of course even the most light-hearted never fails to quiet down and pause a few moments when he passes the grave of Fr. Jake Otto,[10] one like the rest of us who waved and said goodbye, but who lies buried in African soil on the back of the mountain, under the snows of Kilimanjaro. You hear many jokes about *us forgotten colonials*, you hear one after the other say that when his term is up and he is sailing into New York harbor, he is going to look up at the Statue of Liberty, bend way over and say, "Look, Lady, if you ever see me again, give me a good swift kick—right here!" But they come back—they mostly all come back. What is it that brings them back? Is it the exclusiveness of the missionary? Is it the call of the wild? Is it the challenge to build up an infant church? Even in our day, to do the same kind of work the Apostles did—even in the hydrogen bomb age?[11] Whatever it is, you only know you feel like saying, "Lord, it is good for us to be here" [Matt 17:4].

And it is time for this letter to get on its way *there*. Goodbye, you Catholic Americans—God bless you.

Sincerely,
Father Vince

10. This seems to be a reference to Fr. Joseph Otto (d. 1950). His identical twin brother Stanley, also a Spiritan, continued to work in Tanzania until 1969 (Koren, *Memorial*, 487).

11. A hydrogen bomb is one of two kinds of nuclear weapon, the other being the atomic bomb (like those dropped on Japan in 1945).

September 1, 1959

Dear Relatives and Friends

    . . . Before leaving for Europe and Africa, I worked for a year in Harlem, New York.[12] And while working and living there, I became a colored[13] person in thought and sentiment and almost everything except the color of my skin. That may seem a strange thing to say—but I just want you to understand that I came here with no fear of any race, no hatred, no prejudice, as far as I can judge.

    But while waiting in Rome[14] and preparing to come here to Africa, the thought kept coming back to me that I was heading for a continent in ferment. Remembering what had happened in China[15] and the rest of Asia, and the mid-East[16] and India,[17] since the end of the Second World War [in 1945], it was only safe to surmise that Africa would not be far behind. Indeed, even on the Dark Continent,[18] there were signs of it. The Suez, Egypt, Sudan, the trouble in South Africa,[19] and the Mau Mau emergency in Kenya.[20] I thought I was jumping into a boiling pot. And now, after being here for some time, I can only say I still think so. I still have the uneasy feeling that I will live to see the day when the white priest will no longer be wanted or needed in Africa. . . .

    I must go now and will continue later.

    Thanks again, fellow tribesmen.

    Father Vince

    12. After being ordained in 1952, Donovan studied at Fordham University for a year. At the same time, he lived and ministered at St. Mark's Church, Harlem.

    13. The term "colored" was in common use before the introduction of terms like "black," "African American," and "person of color."

    14. See letter of January 2, 1957.

    15. In 1949, China was declared the People's Republic of China and became a Communist state.

    16. The modern state of Israel was founded in 1948.

    17. India had become independent of Britain in 1947.

    18. Henry Morton Stanley was probably the first to use this term to describe Africa, in his 1878 account, *Through the Dark Continent*.

    19. In 1948, the white South African government had introduced a political system of institutionalized racism called Apartheid.

    20. The Mau Mau rebellion against the British colonial administration in Kenya took place during the 1950's, involving mainly members of the Kikuyu tribe.

November 1, 1959

Dear Relatives and Friends

   ... The Europeans have awakened in the Africans a consciousness of the rest of Africa and the rest of the world. And in the end, it may be the Europeans' downfall. Africans are becoming extremely sensitive about discrimination in any form, and incredibly taken up with it. I was not in Africa a week when I was driving a pick-up truck back to the mission where I was staying. A man asked for a lift and I stopped to pick him up. He spoke some English. After he got in the truck with me, the conversation went like this: "*You are a Catholic priest? Where do you come from?*" "America." "*Do you like it in Africa?*" "Yes." "*Why is there color bar*[21] *in America?*" (Silence)

   A Swahili word that is on every African's lips these days is *UHURU*. It means independence, freedom. Ghana is independent. Nigeria will be next year. Tanganyika, within five years. To us it means just that—political independence. To most Africans, it means the going of the white man, the end of work, the end of all laws, the appropriation of all alien property. CRY BELOVED COUNTRY.

   God love you and bless you.
   Father Vince

December 3, 1959

Dear Relatives and Friends,

   ... The present swift and powerful growth of T.A.N.U.[22] right here in Tanganyika is another indication of the same thing. Of course, there is no immediate danger and the government is very alert these days. But to tell you the truth, to look around and see every child who is knee high to

---

   21. At this time, American cities had areas where people of color were officially "barred," including restaurants, bars, churches, washrooms, and even drinking fountains.

   22. The Tanganyika African National Union, the political party which led the fight for independence from British colonial rule.

a bush buck, wielding a *panga*[23] against the high grass, with the precision and dexterity of an executioner, and to remember that the *panga* was the favorite weapon of the Mau Mau, leaves my blood pressure something below normal. And to look at some of the people whom you have gotten to know very well, even some of the Christians, and to realize in your heart of hearts, that if that *bad time* ever came, you wouldn't want to take odds on their not slicing off your head with a *panga* stroke—makes you sleep rather lightly at night.

This has been a rather gruesome letter, hasn't it? I'm sorry. Now, as I wipe the blood off my *panga*, I wish you all a Merry Christmas. God bless you.

Sincerely,
Father Vince

P.S. We have now completed one year of the Father Vince Dollar a Month Club and I am happy to inform you that we have sent Father Vince $476.00 as a result of your generosity. With your continued support we hope to be able to do as well next year.

Thank you very much and may God bless you.
Bill Donovan

January 15, 1960

Dear Relatives and Friends,

A million thanks for all your cards and letters and presents and good wishes for Christmas. It made my Christmas all the more enjoyable. I hope all of yours was a good Christmas. And I wish you now all the blessings of the New Year—this fateful year of 1960.

It will be a fateful year all over the world, and especially so for Tanganyika, the country where I live. This is the year when Tanganyika gets responsible government—not complete freedom yet, but responsible government.[24] It is the next to last step to complete freedom—*uhuru!*

23. A *panga* is a long (18–24 inch) knife, known elsewhere as a machete. The word *panga* is possibly Swahili.

24. There was a period of six months between Tanzania becoming autonomous and its being granted full independence and becoming a Republic.

The story of all this coming about is a fascinating story. It seems all to have happened since I came to Africa. (I had nothing to do with it.) Five years ago, Great Britain was ruling Tanganyika as a Trust Territory[25] in the cold, efficient, and overall fair way that she has been ruling colonies for centuries. Nothing spectacular, except the animals; nothing out of the way, except the scenery; nothing to indicate that she would not go on ruling it the same way for countless years—maybe even centuries. But at that same time, there was an unknown school teacher in a Junior College of the Holy Ghost Fathers,[26] not far from here, who came up with an idea. The name of that unknown School Teacher was Julius Nyerere,[27] and the idea he had was that Tanganyika had a right to be free, just like any other country in the world. And he decided to do something about it. He formed a political party called the *Tanganyika African National Union*, soon afterwards to become popularly known as T.A.N.U., or simply TANU. The goal of that political party was complete independence for Tanganyika, complete political freedom—*uhuru*.

. . . I came out to Africa in the early days of Julius Nyerere. I remember hearing his name mentioned rather casually and offhandedly as a man fighting a lost cause, and TANU mentioned as a little known, half illegal, bunch of dissatisfied troublemakers, fighting for independence in Tanganyika. Independence! Hah, the mere thought of independence in Tanganyika was impossible. "Let's talk about it in another fifty years. These Africans have just come out of the trees. They are not ready for independence." I don't think there were five people in the whole of Tanganyika who realized what was going to happen.

What happened? This year, 1960, a scant three years afterwards, in the month of September, everyone who can read and write in Tanganyika is going to the polls to vote into Congress an overwhelmingly African majority, with only one third of the seats open to Europeans and Asians. And the members of which political party are going to occupy *all* those seats? And who is the undisputed master of all those African

25. Tanganyika came under the control of Great Britain in 1922. In 1946, it became a United Nations Trust Territory, still governed by Britain, but under guidelines which required that the territory be prepared for independence and majority rule.

26. Pugu Secondary School, south-west of Dar es Salaam, a school of the Holy Ghost Fathers. Nyerere was the only African teacher there at that time.

27. Julius Nyerere (1922–1999) went on to become the first president of an independent Tanzania in 1962.

Congressmen, the most important man in Congress, in the country? Why, the ex-school teacher, Julius Nyerere, of course.

Fond greetings to all of you, and three cheers for Uhuru!
FATHER VINCE

February 10, 1960

Dear Relatives and Friends,

Thanks again for the kindness and warmness emanating out of America from you to me in this cold stateside month of February. I thank you all from the bottom of my heart and continue to remember you in my prayers.

Have you seen that fellow countryman of mine, Julius Nyerere, on television in the states, or perhaps in person when he passed through Pittsburgh to receive an honorary Doctor of Laws Degree from Duquesne University?[28] He's a remarkable fellow who has come a long way in a short time. . . .
FATHER VINCE

March 1, 1960

Dear Relatives and Friends,

Greetings from the land of Africa, that land which is like a slumbering giant, that land which is so far away from all of you good and generous people, that land where it is beginning to seem I have lived all my life.

The destiny of this land could be shaped for good in the next few years. And it is in the hands of a few men. I remember the time not so long ago when I got up the nerve to invite one of these men, Julius Nyerere, to visit my little house in Burka. That sounds like a simple matter, but it was not so simple to effect. At that time, "Julius Nyerere" was still a dirty word in the dictionary of the British Colonial Administration. He was being constantly trailed, everywhere he went, by the British CID

28. Duquesne University in Pittsburgh PA was begun by the Spiritans in 1878.

[Criminal Investigation Department], the English equivalent to the American CIA (the ones who sent the U-2 over Russia[29]). I might add at this point that if the American CIA is as comical as the British CID, then I can understand all the mess over the Russian episode. Graham Greene's book, *Our Man in Havana* [1958], about the CID is a bit exaggerated, but there is certainly a basis in reality.

The CID men have always struck me as children playing at a man's game. They are as suspicious of Americans as they are of African nationalists. I remember one of them very sinisterly saying to me, "Remember, Father, render to Caesar the things that are Caesar's" [Mark 12:17], leaving me the very obvious rejoinder of the business about God. I have had a few minor brushes with them. They have spies planted every place you go. Spies in every mission, who listen very carefully to every sermon and public utterance you give and report everything back to headquarters. One of our fathers in the mission of Arusha gave a very nice sermon on Catholic Social Principles[30] regarding labor—management, unions, citizenship etc., and before you knew it, there were several pages in the secret files of the CID on subversive sermons being given at the Catholic Mission, and our superior was called in to explain the matter. The CID could have saved themselves a lot of trouble if they had read some of the Encyclicals of the Popes, or even the Pastoral Letter of the Bishops of Tanganyika of the year before.[31] Ever since I have come to Africa, the Administration has reminded me of a benevolent Russian police state.

At any rate, with that as the background, and knowing that Julius Nyerere was due to make an appearance in the town of Arusha in a few days for a public speech, I went to the TANU Office there and asked the local secretary if he thought it would be possible for me to talk to Julius Nyerere privately when he came to Arusha. He picked up the phone, got Julius, asked him about an appointment, hung up and told me to be at the TANU Office at 2:00 o'clock on the day Julius was supposed to arrive.

29. In 1960, the Soviet Union had recently shot down a U2 bomber and interrogated its pilot, Francis Gary Powers, who confessed that he was on a reconnaissance flight over USSR. (This plane, made famous by the incident, is the origin of the name of the rock group, U2.)

30. Those aspects of Catholic teaching which relate to social ethics, particularly towards the poor. These derive particularly from Pope Leo XIII's 1891 encyclical letter, *Rerum Novarum*.

31. Hillman thinks this letter was written on behalf of the bishops by Donovan himself. It would also have dealt with social ethics.

Well, the day came and, knowing that I was in for a little game with the CID at 2:00 PM, I was inside the TANU Office waiting, with my Land Rover parked outside and across the street. At 2:00 o'clock sharp, a big black American car pulled up outside with the party emblem flying, and several men got out, one of whom I immediately recognized as Julius Nyerere, with an open-necked white shirt, and carrying the ever present hand-carved walking stick. They came into the office straight away, where there was a large group of local party dignitaries waiting to greet him. He threw his hand up over his head in the stiff armed salute (very reminiscent of the Nazi one) with the greeting "Uhuru!" (Freedom) and everyone present did likewise (not me, of course). Then he saw me, came over, shook hands and said, "My name is Julius Nyerere." It struck me at the time that this was rather a humble thing to say, since his face was familiar to everyone in Tanganyika. But I just answered, "I know. Could I speak to you privately?" He said, "Of course, but not here. Could we go to your place?"

So we turned around, walked out the door to the waiting Land Rover and drove off. At five minutes after two, just when the CID was settling down to watch the TANU Office, Julius was there and gone. I went down one street, up another, doubled back, circled around and headed for the main highway and Burka. The CID didn't know what hit them. I have to give them some credit though. A few days later, they came whining to the mission in Arusha (not Burka) saying they had a report stating that some father had seen and talked to Julius Nyerere. Who?—They did not know. When? How? Where? Why?—They did not know, either. I still chuckle about it.

So you see, tending Bingo parties and guiding Altar Societies in America would seem rather dull to me now. God love and bless you all.

Father Vince

April 1, 1960

Dear Relatives and Friends,

Greetings to all of you again from the grateful missionary whom you have helped so much during these many months. Africa still goes on its merry way to freedom and I watch it with avid interest.

The day I brought Julius Nyerere to Burka, there was another father[32] waiting there for us. The two of us wanted to talk to Julius about
several matters concerning our work and his. And it speaks much for
the generosity of the man, that despite the fact that he had much to do in
Arusha that day, and despite the fact that he was one of the busiest men
in Tanganyika at that time, as he is now, he gave us freely of his time and
stayed in my "little house in Burka" for three hours. We talked about a
lot of things—about the future of the Masai and Arusha people, their
prospects under an African government of the future, a government
that would be made up of people like Nyerere himself, infinitely more
advanced than any of our parishioners, among the semi-primitive tribes;
the future of the missions in Tanganyika etc, etc. It would be too much
to go into all of it now. Suffice it to say, that it was all very interesting and
engrossing and valuable for us.

. . . Driving him back to TANU headquarters, I noticed another
slight change in his attitude. He turned to me and said, "Talking now as
a Catholic, Father, how are things going for your missions in this section?" I told him that this was one of the toughest sections for missions,
about fifty years behind the rest of Tanganyika,[33] but that finally, we were
making some real progress. He said he was glad to hear it. I told him that
normally people just have Masses offered for the dead, but that several
poor Africans came to me with a few shillings and asked to have a Mass
offered for Julius Nyerere, that God would bless him in his work. He
seemed genuinely touched. When we reached TANU headquarters, he
turned to me and said, "Thank you for the opportunity of talking to you.
You have helped me very much." With that, he opened the car door and
was gone.

When you read about these African nationalists in Tanganyika and
other countries, don't make the mistake of thinking they are a bunch
of childish fools. I believe they can hold their own with anybody in the
world. Good-night from this part of the world, God bless, and thank you.

Father Vince

32. This was Eugene Hillman, who met with Nyerere many times. Hillman (1924–
2009) went to work in the Kilimanjaro district in 1951. After eight years among the
Maasai, he was made an honorary Maasai and a blood brother by a Maasai chief (Koren,
Memorial, 508). He is author of such books as *Toward an African Christianity*.

33. This is probably a reference to the lack of economic development among herding societies, compared with agricultural ones.

May 1960

Dear Relatives and Friends,

Greetings to all you good people who have been so generous to a struggling missionary in the heart of Tanganyika, one of the last remaining peaceful places in Africa.

Political struggles and upheavals in Africa have been at the top of the world news for some time now, and are the daily conversation of "foreigners" living in Africa. So please excuse me if I digress a bit from these worrisome topics and talk about something else for awhile.

Let me try to describe the picture of American missions out here. Geographically it is something like this. Kilimanjaro is a long, sloping mountain, sloping gradually from the plains right up to the snow peak of Kibo, almost twenty thousand feet high. On its back are countless missions and out-missions going up to about six or seven thousand feet. In the plains below is the town of Moshi, which is also the episcopal seat. These are the longest established missions of the American Holy Ghost Fathers out here.[34] By far most of our men are stationed here. The Church in Kilimanjaro is almost so established that it could soon cease to be a mission territory. As a matter of fact, it now has its own African bishop who is over all the American Holy Ghost Fathers, Bishop Kilasara.[35] The tribe we deal with in Kilimanjaro is the Chagga tribe who live on the back of the mountain. Bishop Kilasara is a Chagga, and the Chagga tribe is one of the most progressive tribes in Africa.

Then to the west of Moshi, beginning about fifty miles or so in that direction, and spreading for several hundred more, is the Masai territory, centered around Arusha, another town built at the foot of another mountain 15,000 feet high, Mount Meru. The tribes here are the Nilo-Hamitic Masai, their cousins the Arusha, and the Meru.

---

34. Spiritans first arrived in Zanzibar in 1862, then moved the focus of their work to the mainland (Bagamoyo—see letters of January through May 1967) in 1868. US Spiritans were at work in the Kilimanjaro District from the 1920s on.

35. Donovan and Kilasara probably got to know each other while studying together in Rome in 1954–55. Bishop Joseph Kilasara (1916–1978) was from the Chagga tribe and was the first African-born Bishop of Moshi from 1960 till 1966 (Koren, *Memorial*, 523), the period during which Arusha became a separate diocese (August 1963). Donovan wrote many of Kilasara's formal speeches.

100 miles to the South and East of Moshi, and stretching in such an odd way that it touches Masai territory at one point is the Pare Mountain section. There is no real town in this section, but a place called "Same." It has a Post Office and two Indian shops, so it is the central point of this section. Here we have the Pare tribe.

So an American Holy Ghoster coming out here knows he will be assigned to Kilimanjaro work, Pare work, or Masai work—one of these three. They are vastly different kinds of work. As I say, most of our men are stationed on Kilimanjaro, with just nine assigned to Pare work and eight assigned to Masai work.[36] The numbers don't give any indication of the amount of work to be done, but rather the newness of the missions involved. I have actually been stationed in all three places, but am at the present time living in Masailand.

The church in the Pare Mountains and here in Masailand is in the infant stage. *We are building that Church.* It would take pages and pages to comment on that. But this one phrase shows what a tremendous challenge and privilege it all is. In its essence, it is exactly the same kind of work the Apostles did.

I was stationed in Kilimanjaro, in the first and main mission of Kilimanjaro for one month to get a start in learning Swahili, the main language of East Africa. That mission is called *Kilema.* There are over twelve thousand Christians belonging to that mission and the main work of the fathers stationed there is with the Christians, since there are so many of them. The reception of the sacraments in a place like that is incredible. For a big feast day, it takes three priests one-half hour to give out Communion.

And Confessions! I learned to hear confessions in Swahili just before Christmas, so I had my first taste then. For four solid days, the people come. You hear confessions from after breakfast until supper, with only a break for lunch—for four days. I was so bone-weary that I hardly knew what I was saying. Add to that, my difficulty with the new language, and the result was disconcerting. The language is a bit tricky, with the person-designations tacked on the front of the word, not on the

36. The likelihood is that these were: Dennis (later bishop) Durning, Fred Trumbull and Jim Burke in Loliondo (work begun in 1957); Gene Hillman and Ed Kelly in Monduli (1959); and Frank McGowan, Raymond Buchler and Bill Jackson in Kijunga (1960?). Jackson served in Endulen from 1970 till 1972; Kelly directed the school at Burka from 1960 till 1963; and Buchler was in charge of the mission at Endulen from 1972 till 1975 (Koren, *Memorial,* 571, 492, 554).

back like in Latin, or with a separate word like in English. Well, I had this one person in there and was asking him an essential question to clear up something vague he had mumbled about a very serious matter. The only trouble was I had mixed up the second person singular with the first person singular and the question sounded like a statement to him. I meant to ask, "Did you commit such and such a serious sin?," but what came out was "*I*" committed such and such a sin. Three times I said it, each time louder than the last time, with my fury building up progressively. And he remained silent. Finally I fairly screamed, "Well, say something!" Then, it dawned on me what I had been saying. The poor devil was there gasping and speechless. You can use your imagination as to what I was screaming for the benefit of the whole church. I wonder what you would have said in that fellow's place. I realized then that I had better leave the box a little while and get a cigarette.

And I had better leave this letter now and get some sleep. Thanks again.

Sincerely,
Father Vince

June 1960

Dear Relatives and Friends,

Thank you again for the gifts you have been sending to me through the dollar-a-month club. It has been helping me more than I can explain.

With so much happening in Africa these days, we missionaries know that the eleventh hour[37] has struck for us, and there is so little time to finish the work we have to do. Especially we in the outskirts of the diocese who are still in the process of trying to build up an infant church and are almost paralyzed with the thought that the last chance in Africa is upon us and we have scarcely begun to work. This thought adds a frantic haste to everything we do. I'm afraid such things as food, rest,

---

37. This phrase occurs frequently in Donovan's writing. It is derived from Christ's parable of the workers in the vineyard (Matt 20:6), where the last group of workers are hired just one hour before the end of the working day—the eleventh hour, or "five o'clock" in modern translations. (See also letter of April 1966.)

recreation, letter-writing and many other things receive scant attention. We become more and more absorbed in the necessity of finishing our work before the approaching-storm hits us. Before it is too late!!! I'm afraid the words of our Lord never had so much meaning for me, as they do now, "Work while it is light. The night cometh when no man can work" [John 9:4].

. . . Every mission in Kilimanjaro has about ten thousand Christians. The mission where I was stationed in the Pare Mountains had about three hundred Christians. Three hundred Christians, but untold thousands of parishioners, if you get the distinction. It is the same with our work here in Masailand. In Kilimanjaro, each mission or parish embraces a few square miles at most, with different churches only two or three miles apart. In this section where I am now stationed, before I came to live here in Burka, I was in a mission whose boundaries embraced 30,000 square miles. The next nearest out-station or church was twenty-five miles away, and the next one after that was 240 miles beyond that. We have gotten more men since then, so we have scattered out a bit. But at that time before we scattered, the mission of Arusha was one of the biggest ones in Africa in extension. Even now, our responsibilities are just this side of impossible. I personally am responsible for preaching the gospel to seventy-thousand Arusha tribesmen, and further up the line, together with another priest, I am responsible for doing the same to fifty-thousand Meru tribesmen. That's 120,000 people on the conscience of Reverend Vincent J. Donovan of Winston Street, Pittsburgh, Pennsylvania.[38] Sometimes, when I sit down to think about it, I wonder if I'm not just dreaming, and that I'll wake up and find myself hearing confessions on Saturday afternoon in some parish in the USA, and turning over in my mind what I'm going to preach about on Sunday morning, to a normal number of normal, non-poisoning,[39] non-independence-obsessed Catholics.

Then I snap out of it, and realize I had better get back to the very real task of trying to make a dent on this veritable sea of humanity that is my parish. Perhaps you understand that it is not easy to get on a personal

38. 246 Winston Street was the Donovan family home in Hazelwood, Pittsburgh. See also February 10, 1964.

39. Donovan had earlier told the story of a young Chagga priest who had been poisoned by a parishioner who was curious about the efficacy of the promise in Mark 16:18.

first-name relationship with all of my parishioners, especially since some of their names are so difficult, that it develops an extra muscle in your tongue if you pronounce them often.

Most of my time is *not* spent around the little mission church, but outside the mission. Most of my work is not with the Christians, but with Pagans and Islams.[40] It is an entirely different atmosphere, and calls for entirely different methods.

I had better close now. Thank you and God bless you.

Sincerely,
Father Vince

July, 1960

Dear Relatives and Friends,

Warm and grateful greetings from the missionary all of you have been helping all these months, so generously. I am writing now from an Africa over which the darkness of night seems to be falling. To say that the events in the Belgian Congo,[41] our near neighbor, have not affected the thinking of the whites and blacks of Tanganyika would be a little less than the truth. There are some signs of panic among the whites, with a cold fear gripping their hearts as they think of the future in regard to their wives and children. But Tanganyika remains peaceful and is likely to do so. Meanwhile, our work must go on.

I mentioned in a previous letter, as regards my work, a parallel with the work of the Apostles. Well, that is not just a figurative parallel. It is amazingly literal. Traveling incredible distances from one establishment to another, trying to capture the thought pattern, the customs, the culture of the African, not to change it, but to fill the flesh and blood of Africa with the soul of Christianity; to walk from village to village, from house to house, to speak of Christ and the good news He died to tell us; to preach literally in the market places; to feel the power of Satan close at hand; to struggle with everything you ever learned, with every talent you have, with all the ingenuity you can muster, to plant the Church, all the time knowing that the outcome will not be up to you, but to God.

40. Until the latter part of the twentieth century, Muslims were often called "Mohammedans" or (less commonly) "Islams."

41. The Congo became independent on June 30 1960, following violent rioting.

It is not easy work. Even when dealing with your Christians, circumstances make your ministry unusual and jolting. The day after I arrived at a mission [Kwizu] in the Pare Mountains to begin my work, a boy came to the mission saying there was a dying man who wanted to see the priest. It had been raining recently, and the car couldn't get out. So I jammed the sick call equipment into my pockets and followed the boy on foot. The way led right up over the back of the mountain, down slopes, and through gulleys. Immediately after we started walking, a terrific storm broke. The path became a muddy stream. It was extremely difficult to move a step up without sliding back. We had to wade through streams that had turned into raging swollen messes. Twice I fell flat on my face, and I was literally soaked to the skin. My shoes were so squishingly saturated that the soles began to fall off. I don't know how many yards I slid through the mud in a sitting position. All the papers and things in my pocket were completely ruined. Several times, I had to sit right down in the mud to rest because I could hardly breathe. Our safari lasted over two and a half hours. I was thoroughly miserable and disgusted. I believe only the thought of the poor fellow who was dying, and in a much worse position than I, kept me going at all. Finally, after some two and a half hours, just as I reached his house, the rain stopped. I ran up to the house and asked where the man was. They told me quite simply that he was dead. Not only dead, but buried, since immediate burial is the custom here. I couldn't even anoint him conditionally. It was the first time in my years as a priest that I felt completely, utterly helpless. I could not say a word. I just looked at the people standing around and turned away without uttering a syllable. I walked over to a nearby rock, dripping, mucky, ragged mess that I was, and sat down in a stupor and thought long thoughts on the God who died for this man, the same God who built the mountains and brought the rains that kept me from reaching this man in time to help him. This is Africa. This is mission land, a place where the sacraments are *not* available to everyone. That is why I am here.

No, it is not easy work. It is hard. It is discouraging, heartbreaking at times. It is thankless. It is lonely. But I wouldn't willingly change it for any other work in the world.

God bless you and thank you.

Sincerely,
Father Vince

August 9, 1960

Dear Relatives and Friends,

Please excuse the delay in getting these letters to you. I can't tell you how much your help has been appreciated these many months. Please do not think my tardiness in writing is any sign of lack of appreciation. My work snows me under at times—so much so that I don't have any time to do anything else but work—and pray, of course, for you people especially.

I once heard that a missionary does not have time to become a specialist in any one thing, because he has so many different kinds of things to do. I have found that to be true to an amazing extent. There are so many things I have had to put my hand and head to out here, from sheer necessity.

Take music. I could always carry a tune so to speak, and sing fairly loud when my mother was pounding out a melody like "Cheer, Cheer for Old Notre Dame" or "Nita, Juanita" on the old piano. But that is where my musical ability began and ended. I knew nothing, absolutely nothing, about musical composition. Now, what would you have done in my place? I was working among the primitive Masai and Arusha tribes. They were completely new to Christianity. They were fiercely tribe conscious and disdainful of everything foreign. Other tribes, like the progressive Chagga tribe, had been raised in Christianity on Alsatian, French and German hymns put to Swahili words. But this would not do for the Masai and the Arusha. They do not like Swahili. They have their own language, the Nilo-Hamitic Masai language. And they do not understand or like European melodies. Their own melodies are like nothing you ever heard or imagined in your wildest nightmares. What to do? I'll tell you what I tried to do.

I had to gather them around, young boys and girls, and men and women, and for hour after hour, day after day, I had to ask them to sing for me all the songs they knew about every possible subject. Then I had to take those melodies and put Masai words to them, words which conveyed the essential teaching of our religion—and presto, we had Masai hymns.[42]

42. Although Maasai hymns were being written at this time by missionaries and Maasai themselves, they have not survived.

As for high masses, where Latin is compulsory, we asked permission to have the high masses in Masai. The permission was not granted, but I was told such permission will be granted at the Ecumenical Council, soon to be held.[43] So, in the meantime, I had the more difficult task of finding Masai melodies for the Latin texts of the mass, such as the Kyrie, Gloria, etc. And, it was difficult. I tried to find Masai songs which represented the attitudes and feelings and thoughts expressed in the various parts of the mass. Things like the Gloria and the Credo were especially difficult, because they change from one thought to an entirely different one, right in the midst of the hymn.

After many weeks and weeks of work in which I became half Masai myself, we were ready. So we scheduled a big mass for Pentecost Sunday, the birthday of the Catholic Church, in the big town mission of Arusha. Masai and Arusha came from miles around, the men dressed in their blanket-like togas, and the women and the girls in their leather skirts and beads. There were people there from other more sophisticated tribes as well, and even some Europeans and Asians (Goans). It was very reminiscent of the first Pentecost, when, as it says in the Acts of the Apostles, "There were people present from every country under heaven" [Acts 2:5]. And the mass began.

And you never heard or saw anything quite like it in your life. The Masai Kyrie and Gloria wafted up to heaven accompanied by the most unearthly groans and grunts, and even a noticeable swaying of the body, as their instinctive urge to express themselves by dancing asserted itself. I was never so moved by anything in my life. At the sermon time, I got up and gave them what was in fact the first Catholic sermon ever preached in the Masai language.[44] Once again, shades of Pentecost, as it says in the Acts of the Apostles, "Each man heard him speak in his own language" [Acts 2:6].

After the Mass, the Masai and Arusha in the blankets and skins came to me with tears in their eyes, to thank me for bringing to them,

---

43. This is the first reference in the letters to Vatican II. The Council did in fact approve the use of vernacular languages in the liturgy. See "The Constitution on the Sacred Liturgy—Sacrosanctum Concilium" (Article 36, December 4, 1963, in Flannery, *Documents*, 13). The *Loliondo Mission Journal*, in which were recorded the daily events of the mission in Loliondo, refers to a mass being held there in the Maasai language on December 26, 1966.

44. This was probably from a prepared text, since the Maasai language is notoriously difficult to learn, and Donovan, according to his peers, was never very fluent in it.

in a way they understood, the message of God and the worship of God. Would you think me strange if I told you that that day there were tears in my eyes, too—if I told you that there is nothing—nothing quite like missionary work?

Sincerely,
Father Vince

September 10, 1960

Dear Relatives and Friends,

Many thanks again for your continued support for this skinny missionary so very far away from home and from all of you in fact—but not in thought and prayer.

You know the missionary working among primitive tribes is faced with the problem of adaptation, as it is called, the problem of taking what is good in any local culture and adapting it to Christianity.[45] We have the most strict directions and warnings from Rome not to destroy what is good in the lives of the people among whom we work.[46] In the best way we know how, we try to tackle that problem. In the best way we know how, we try to search out and use what is good in the local cultures—use it in religious instruction, in spiritual formation, in the liturgy, and in all the aspects of founding and spreading the church.

Unfortunately, this has not always been done everywhere, and the church today is in danger in places where it has not been done. It is action based on deep theological thinking. It is an effort to search out the morally good and true and beautiful in the culture of these people, and

---

45. The term "adaptation" (like the parallel term "accommodation") has been replaced in missiological thinking since the 1960s by the terms "contextualization" or "inculturation." The former terms referred to a more superficial (and often patronizing) approach to local cultures. See Bosch, *Transforming Mission*, 448–49.

46. E.g., "Do not regard it as your task, and do not bring any pressure to bear on the people, to change their manners, customs, and uses. . . . What could be more absurd than to transport France, Spain, Italy or some other European country to China? Do not introduce all that to them, but only the faith, which does not destroy the manners and customs of any people. . . . Do not draw invidious contrasts between the customs of the peoples and those of Europe; do your utmost to adapt yourselves to them." Instructions from the Propaganda to vicars apostolic, 1659. Cited by Neill, *History*, 179.

to use these things in the teaching and understanding and developing of our religion. It is an effort to clothe the soul of Christianity with the flesh and blood of Africa. It is an attempt to find this natural good wherever it exists, and to give it back to Christ to whom it belongs.

The necessity for such a plan of action is becoming more and more apparent as one day succeeds the other on this Dark Continent, suddenly coming to life and to light. Today, European values are in the same danger as Europeans themselves, of being replaced by that which is truly African. Perhaps those very Africans who today try strenuously to imitate the European in everything tomorrow will be the ones most loud in their demands for a reexamination of everything that is not truly African—including religion. If Incarnation, God and the things of God taking on human flesh, has any meaning, it has a meaning here. The religion of the "white man" is on trial today in Africa. I hope it is not found wanting.

I have an idea. To give you some idea of the people among whom we work, and the problem of evangelization with which we are faced, let me begin in this letter to give you some idea of one tribe—the Masai tribe. And then afterwards, I will try to show you how we adapt our teaching to these people.

The Masai are a primitive, semi-nomadic tribe of East Africa. They are a Nilo-Hamitic race—the aristocrats of East Africa, warriors par excellence, and the cowboys of the equatorial steppes. Their history is a proud one and their memories long. Hundreds of years ago, their forefathers came down from the Nile basin in a long trek, searching for land. Their trek was a conquering one, and they succeeded in terrorizing and subduing great stretches of East Africa. They are fierce warriors, with a reputation for toughness and fitness and discipline, and their entire culture is militarily slanted.

They believe in God, whom they call by the name *Engai*, but the same name, *Engai*, is used for rain, which is so necessary for their cattle and their grass. Perhaps for them God and rain are one and the same thing. Evil spirits are also a reality for them.

The Masai are fiercely tribe-conscious—proud of their background and disdainful of everything non-Masai. They are primitive as to luxuries, but they are a supremely happy people. Their clothes made out of skins take the form of a leather dress for women and a combination mantle and loin cloth for men. Their living quarters or kraals are nothing but low, cow-dung houses, surrounded by a circular barrier of thorn branches. They are democratic in government, ruled over by a series of chiefs and guided by witch doctors. The witch doctors are a combination of medicine man and priest, with great and awesome powers. The head medicine man or witch doctor of Masailand is believed to be the son of God.

You see we are not dealing with American Negroes[47] or anything like them. We are dealing with Africans. I'll tell you more about them the next time. God bless you.

Sincerely,
Father Vince

[Donovan was now sent to be Superior and Director of the Senior Seminary at Moshi, "on the back of Mt. Kilimanjaro" (as he describes it on March 3, 1963). The actual location of the school is Kibosho, five or six miles north of Moshi.]

47. This term was not considered demeaning at this time.

3

MOSHI

(1960–1961)

Dear Relatives and Friends,

Congratulations to all of you Pittsburghers on the Pirates' tremendous victory, and to you Democrats on Kennedy's victory.[1] Thanks to all of you for your continuing help to me.

I have tried to describe to you an African tribe, the Masai, in previous letters. Now I would like to try a very daring thing. I would like to try to describe for you the way in which we try to adapt the teaching of Christianity to the mentality of these people. I call it *daring* because you will no doubt find it most unusual, and even jolting. I almost hesitate to do it, because you might be shocked by it, especially if you have tender consciences. You must remember that these Masai are a literal, down to earth, realistic people—close to nature. They are different from us in mentality and background. But I thought you might be interested in how we missionaries *actually, really* speak to our people. And so, if you

---

1. That year, the Pittsburgh Pirates defeated the New York Yankees 4–3 to win the World Series. On November 8 1960, John F. Kennedy defeated Richard M. Nixon, to become 35th President of the USA.

are willing, Gentlemen, hold onto your hats; Ladies, tuck up your skirts a little bit. The going might be a little rough. I now present to you the life of Christ in brief, as I composed it, for use among the Masai.[2]

Once there was a young maiden, a virgin, who was very beautiful and very good. She was so beautiful and so good and so holy, even as an uncircumcised little girl, that God wanted her for Himself. He made her promise that she would never sleep with anyone in her tribe, until the end of her life; and that even if an elder of the tribe chose her to be his wife, they both must understand that she could not sleep even with him. If God permitted a man to take her to wife, it would be only that her off-spring (which would come directly from God) would be a member of that tribe which God loved more than all the other tribes.

And so that girl, who was called Mary, agreed, and she became the espoused one of God Himself. An elder of Mary's tribe, a man called Joseph, was told by God that he should take Mary into his kraal as his wife, but he should never sleep with her, because she was in reality the spouse of God Himself.

And so after some time, God, by His invisible power, without even appearing on earth, placed a child in Mary's womb, and told her that this child was His only Son. Since Joseph and Mary were of the same tribe, the tribe of David, this child would be a complete and perfect member of the tribe of David. David had been a man who lived and died long before Mary was born. He was the greatest warrior and chief who had lived up until now. He was so brave he was called the "Lion."

This child of Mary's would be of David's tribe, and since all the male members of David's tribe were chiefs, this child would be a chief, too, even from his birth. God Himself would give the name to this child, even before He was born. In fact, He would give him two names. His first name would be *Jesus*, which means in his language, the Savior of his people, for he would be the greatest warrior who ever lived, or who ever would live. He, too, would be the "Lion." His second name would be *Christ*, which means the one rubbed with oil by God Himself. Besides

2. Although Donovan retells the story of Jesus for the Maasai in *Christianity Rediscovered* (chapter 5, section "The Man Jesus"), there he omits any account of Jesus' birth, childhood, and youth because, he explains in the section "He Spoke to Them in Parables," "it did not have much to do with the message." In the letter of April 1969, he writes how it took ten years to distill the message to its simplest form. (Subsequent references to *Christianity Rediscovered* will be abbreviated as *CR*.)

being a chief, he would also be the great medicine man, the great priest, even from his birth.

And so after nine months, the boy child, Jesus Christ, Son of God, chief and priest of his people, was born. And the cattle were watching in his kraal as he was born. He was circumcised to become a true member of his tribe. All during the years of his warriorhood, he stayed close to his own kraal, and very few people knew who he really was.

When he reached the age of thirty, the age of *Eunoto*, he became an elder, and he left his mother and his kraal, and went out to begin his real work. He was no longer a warrior, to whom the elders of the tribe do not listen, but he was himself an elder.

I must go now. I will continue my story next time.

Sincerely,
Father Vince

[The next three letters continue the story of Jesus as told to the Maasai. Jesus becomes an elder in the councils of his tribe. He heals people "without using anything, not even a needle." When he rides into Jerusalem, he carries in his hand "a tuft of grass so that his people knew he was coming for peace and not for war." However, "the other medicine men" were jealous of him, and took to their leaders' kraal by night. Then his enemies "drove nails through his hands and through his feet and nailed him alive to a tree," where he died. However, "Christ fooled them again" because "he rose up again by the power of God" so that "the hyenas never touched his body." As a result, "he is alive today, waiting for all of us to come to him." He concludes in his letter of February 1961:]

Every brave man can join the tribe of Christ. Those poor people who have left their own country to go and work in the towns, and who have lost their tribes, can join the tribe of Christ if they are good and brave. And those people who have not lost their tribe, like the Masai, can join the tribe of Christ, and still remain true, complete members of their own tribe. Christ is our head and he needs brave, good warriors for his tribe and his chiefdom. He wants [us] to take up the armor of God, the shield of the faith, the sword of the spirit, the head dress of salvation. As Christ himself said one day, "My chiefdom of Heaven opens to courage, and none but the brave will make it their prize."

That is the story of Christ as I taught it to the Masai, and to the Arusha, their cousins. It was touching to see the natural and childlike manner with which they took to it. We have tried to make the teaching of Christianity more understandable to them by using, as much as possible, their own means of expression in the transmitting of that teaching. I have already explained to you how we did just that in the field of music and the "Masai Mass." And then in the building of their churches, we try to use forms of art that are understandable to them. For instance, the statues of Christ are based on what Masai men might look like, and the statues of the Blessed Virgin are really Masai Madonnas, instead of the Italian Madonnas to which we have become accustomed.[3]

I have visited another diocese where the missionaries work among another tribe, and I found there a round church built after the fashion of an African hut. Inside, on the altar which resembled an African stool or chair on a large scale, there was the tabernacle which was built in the oblong, low-slung shape of a chief's hut.[4]

In my own little church in Burka, the Stations of the Cross are mere silhouettes attached in each case to a background which is nothing but a replica of the Masai war shield. As you can understand, none of this changes the essential teaching of our religion in any way. It just makes it more easily understood by the people concerned, more easily accepted as something not foreign. You might wonder about our concern with the latter aspect of our religion not being considered something foreign. But when you realize that in the Belgian Congo the slogan has been that the missionaries are nothing but emissaries and servants of a foreign government; and the goal of the "Mau Mau" in Kenya has been to chase out the white man *and* Christianity, the white man's religion, then you might understand the reason for our concern.

With thanks and love.
Father Vince

3. Hillman remembers a carver of the Pare tribe at work under a tree in Arusha. There was nothing controversial about portraying an African Jesus or Virgin at this time.

4. This was among the Sukuma people who live on the west and south of Lake Victoria. These experiments in inculturation were encouraged by the bishop, Josef Blomjous (see footnote to letter of October 1963). Photographs of the items Donovan refers to maybe viewed on the website www.philip.greenspun.com/sukuma.

March 1961

Dear Relatives and Friends,

Greetings again from the expatriate American missionary now re-siding on the slopes of Kilimanjaro. From the heart of tropical Africa, I send you my love and gratitude for all you have done for me these many months. I mentioned once before in another letter the various kinds of activities a missionary gets himself mixed up in. Let me describe another activity in which I became enmeshed, an activity which you might think a missionary has little to do with.

The activity which I am about to describe arose I suppose, from two rather nasty experiences I had. One day, riding on my motorcycle up Mount Meru, I saw ahead of me on the path a group of men stand-ing across the path and apparently waiting for me. This is not an odd occurrence; it happens all the time. The only thing odd about it was that as I drew near I noticed that these men did not seem to be friendly. I had to stop the motorcycle, and I did. I greeted them but they did not respond in the normal friendly way of all Africans. As usually happens when a European, especially a priest, stops in any place, children come running out to see him. The children came running out as usual, but the men across the path chased the children away with sticks. Then I *knew* something was wrong.

They explained to me in short order what it was. They did not want me, a Catholic priest, going by this path, or indeed by *any* path on Mount Meru, to see or visit the people of the Arusha Tribe. They were Protestants, these men, and although the Arusha Tribe was a pagan tribe, they did not want to see Catholic priests working among those people. I tried to point out to them that their attitude was hardly a reasonable one in a free country like Tanganyika. Then they grew ugly. They said unbelievably mean and nasty things about the Catholic religion and its priests. Seeing the futility of losing my temper, I tried to speak calmly to them. They became more and more angry. I have never seen hatred so plainly written and burned into the hearts of human beings. In their faces, I could read unbelievable hatred for me. I noticed too the heavy sticks which each of them held in his hand. I was beginning to get a little worried.

Finally one of them said, "Bwana, thirty years ago a white mission-ary came to stay on this mountain. The people told him to get out or they would kill him. He stayed—and they killed him. (I was already acquainted with the story of that missionary.[5]) We are telling you to get out *now*, and not come back. If you come back, and something happens to you, it will not be our fault!" Then they stepped back from the path and let me pass.

A few weeks later, in an entirely different place around the back of Mount Meru, actually in the plains behind it, I was making a visitation of the families of the kids who were in my school of Burka. It was along the main road. A huge red truck, used as a bus, pulled up and two men got out. One was the driver of the bus and another man I did not know— both were Africans. They were also Protestants and they said they were warning me to get out, and never wanted to see me around again.

Two days later, I was riding along that same road on my faithful motorcycle. It was a nice road, wide enough for two cars to pass. A truck was approaching from the opposite direction. Fortunately, I noticed what kind of a truck it was. It was a huge red one. I think I had a premonition of danger. I began to slow down. The huge truck seemed to speed up as it came towards me. Suddenly, it swerved from its lane and came over into my lane, right towards me, at a terrifying speed. I immediately aimed my motorcycle for the side of the road and began putting on the brakes. The motorcycle left the road, and the combination of leaving the road and slamming on the brakes caused the motorcycle to spin around crazily and sent me flying into space. The big red monster roared past me, returned to its own lane and disappeared down the road. I was hurt and shaken up, of course, but more than that, I was sick, sick with the thought of what Christianity had become. Hatred, threats, violence, all in the name of religion—all in the name of Christ. My God!!!

Sincerely,
Father Vince

April 1961

Dear Relatives and Friends,

Greetings, from the jubilant land that is going to receive its full independence and freedom on the 28th of December of this year.

---

5. The only missionaries killed in this area were Ewald Ovir and Karl Segebrock, Lutherans killed by Arusha and Meru warriors on Mount Meru in 1896 (Groop, *With the Gospel*, 40–43).

Tanganyika, alone of all its sister African states, is going its peaceful non-racial way to independence. Pray for us "Tanganyikans," that we reach the goal without mishap.

After the experiences I related in my last letter, I began to think. It is true to say that I never quite recovered from those experiences. They affect me even to this day, not physically, but psychologically. I began not only to think, but to observe and ask questions.

I inquired in places where the Catholic religion was strong and found out that anti-Protestant feeling was very dominant. There were incidents in these places too, not quite as violent as the ones I myself had experienced, but every bit as hateful, directed against Protestants. Catholic Africans hated and feared Protestants, and Protestant Africans hated and feared Catholics, all in the name of Christianity!

We were sick, very sick—all of us. We were, in fact, in the midst of a great war, a holy war; and love and charity and forgiveness were quite left out of it. We were tearing Africa in two in the name of Christ. This holy war has had a little part to play in the misery that is the Belgian Congo and Angola.[6] You will notice that missionaries, both Catholic and Protestant, have been directly affected by the troubles in those places.

And the most alarming thing about it was this. The Africans did not pick up this fear and hatred by themselves. They were taught it by white missionaries! But I do not think the white missionaries even began to realize the fierce, unreasoning forces they were letting loose.

I remember a few years ago, before Tanganyika had started on its definite steps towards independence, feeling was rising high in the country against Europeans. Africans began to feel that they were being purposely held up in their legitimate drive towards independence. Tension reached its peak when it was announced that the governor was going to give an important speech over the radio on a certain date. Everybody was waiting. Africans planned to gather around all available radios in the market places, in the shops, in some of their homes. I remember that time well. In Arusha, days before the big event, trucks and Land Rovers began to roll into the town with more and more K.A.R. [King's African Rifles] troops and police. We in the missions around Arusha were in a particularly vulnerable position. If any trouble started, the people would

6. Both the Congo and Angola were involved in wars of independence, from Belgium and Portugal respectively, at this time. Christians were killed in both conflicts.

certainly make first of all for the missions like my little mission of Burka, where I was living alone.

It would have been bad enough in any case, but close to our missions lived those small groups of articulate, fanatical Protestants (like my friends whom I mentioned in my last letter—the ones I met on my motorcycle) who would gladly have led a howling mob to the mission.

During the time we did not feel much like writing letters home. We were afraid our thoughts might escape into expression in the letters. It is incredible to look back on it now. In the evenings, we gathered quietly in the main mission and discussed what we should do if the worse came to worst. It was a complicated problem—and the solution to it was not simple or direct.

If the people should rise against us because we were Catholic priests, we could not run away, or even defend ourselves. It would be our duty to stay right where we were. This is our vocation. That is our profession. Cardinal Tien[7] of China left China when the Communists took over. He is under a cloud to this day, in the eyes of the Church. Cardinal Stepinac[8] stayed where he was when the Communists took over his country. He died a hero. That is all nice, but suppose the people would come after us just because we were *white*? What would you do?

I know what I must do now—bring this letter to a close.

Sincerely,
Father Vince

May 1961

Dear Relatives and Friends,

Once again, hello from a grateful missionary on the slopes of Kilimanjaro, the one white mountain among the green hills of Africa. Judging from all the Americans suddenly appearing in Africa—the "Crossroads

7. Thomas Cardinal Tien Ken-Sin (1890–1967) was exiled from China by the Communist regime in 1961.

8. Aloysius Cardinal Stepinac (1898–1960) was archbishop of Zagreb at a time when the Croatian government was under the control of the German Nazi party, and worked on behalf of the Jews during the Second World War.

Kids",[9] the Kennedy youth,[10] and several other volunteer organizations—this continent, and especially this country of Tanganyika, seems to be becoming very popular in America.

In the last letter, I mentioned the rather tense feeling that was arising here due to the uncertainty in the air as regards the prospects of Independence. When the governor[11] gave his speech that day about two years ago, he put to rest the fears of his people. After warning them quite severely how any sort of violence would hurt the cause of Independence, he promised in the name of the Queen of England that the first steps would be taken to Independence—in the form of a general election. With that promise, peace came to Tanganyika, and the threat to our mission came to an end.

But the deep seated reason for danger to our missions and to missionary work did not come to an end. That reason was the extremely unchristian feeling that existed between the different Christian groups. So I decided that I had an obligation to do what little I could about the situation. I did not presume to think that I could do anything about the general situation in the country at large, but I thought I could possibly do something about our little section of the country. I sat me down at my old typewriter and tried to put my thoughts onto paper. Once done, I sent that paper to an African English language magazine, *The African Ecclesiastical Review*. They printed my paper as an article, "The Protestant-Catholic Scandal in Africa." That was in July of 1959.

I can honestly say that from that day until now I have not heard the last of that article, nor have I finished with the projects which it started in motion. I have heard from Protestant pastors, from an Anglican bishop, and from priests as far away as South Africa. I received a letter from a priest of another diocese in Tanganyika who said that on the basis of that article he started a Protestant-Catholic Temperance Society which is doing very well. A newspaper in England even picked up the article, summarized it and commented on it for English readers. . . .

9. Canadian Crossroads International was founded in 1958 to further cross-cultural understanding by sending volunteers to work on projects in the global South. (See also letter of December 1969.)

10. The Peace Corps, popularly known as "Kennedy youth," were a federal agency begun under the presidency of John F. Kennedy, "devoted to world peace and friendship."

11. Sir Richard Turnbull was British governor of Tanganyika from 1958 until 1961. On August 18, 1960, the *Journal* reported that he visited Loliondo.

And now, goodbye again for awhile—and thanks.

Sincerely,
Father Vince

June 1961

Dear Relatives and Friends,

Jambo (Hello) from Tanganyika, the country which is progressing so satisfactorily to Independence that the date for final freedom and full independence has been twice moved up from its original date of December 28, 1961, first to December 20th, and finally to December 9th.

Besides the results and repercussions of that article which I wrote in the *African Ecclesiastical Review* (results which I mentioned in my last letter) there were some other developments. Unknown to me, a Lutheran chaplain in Makerere University in Uganda read the article in the library there and showed it some fellow Lutherans. In the meantime, I decided to take the bull by the horns and I got in my little car and drove to the Lutheran mission near Arusha.[12] I went up to the door and knocked.

A young Lutheran wife came to the door and I asked to see her husband.[13] She said he was not at home but was there any message I would like to leave. I said as a matter of fact there was. Would she ask him if he thought some Lutherans pastors would be interested in sitting down some time with a few Catholic priests to discuss different problems concerning religion? She was absolutely startled. She asked, "Are you a Catholic priest?" I told her I was. Then she said that her husband would be back the next day and it would be better if I came around to see him.

The next day I met her husband and he told me that he had read the article in the magazine and he knew for certain that several Lutheran

12. Lutheran missionaries had been at work among the Maasai since 1896. Groop documents suspicion and competition between them and Roman Catholic (particularly Spiritan) missionaries (e.g., 264–69). The *Journal* reported that Lutheran catechists were spreading "traditional lies," adding sarcastically, "Can't remember exactly when Fr. Turnbull poisoned their water source" (April 11, 1965).

13. Groop believes these were David and Eunice Simonson, who later moved to Loliondo and met up with Donovan again (personal communication). See letter of November 19, 1966.

pastors would be very interested in sitting down to a friendly theological discussion. So we arranged a date for such a meeting.

On the day set for the meeting, I started out with two other priests and we drove to the Lutheran mission. There we met four Lutheran pastors waiting for us.[14] The young wife was in the background—and was definitely hostile looking. And one of the pastors was not very friendly looking either. We sat down rather nervously. I yearned to pull out a cigarette, because a cigarette is always a good substitute for any other definite action, and a cover-up for nervousness—but I wasn't certain whether Lutherans smoked or not, and I did not want that hostile looking woman casting any withering glances in my direction. It was rather awkward in the beginning. We exchanged pleasantries in a very formal way and sat on the edges of our chairs. Then one of the pastors reached into his pocket, pulled out a pipe and a tobacco pouch and started filling his pipe. Three pairs of Catholic eyes were glued to his pipe, and in a flash three Catholics priests whisked out packs of cigarettes. Everyone had been in the same dilemma. We all burst out laughing.

In a voice which I scarcely recognized to be my own, I explained why we had come—to see if we couldn't sit down together like human beings and Christians, and, despite differences in doctrine, *very real* differences, which we could make no effort to hide, still discuss those differences and other things like brothers in Christ. They were most enthusiastic.

We started slowly on very general points, worked our way around to the election campaign going on in America (Kennedy vs. Nixon) and ended up in a very earnest and interesting discussion on the Catholic and the Protestant view of the relations between church and state. It was so interesting in fact that we had to be reminded that it was time to end the discussion by having coffee and cake served to us by a slightly less hostile Lutheran wife. We did not break up until we had agreed to continue our meetings once a month, one time in the Lutheran mission and the following time in the Catholic mission. We have been doing this ever since, for almost a year now, and this monthly meeting, this "Catholic-Lutheran Dialogue," has become the highlight of every month for all of us.

---

14. The conversations were held at Usa River, and involved Donovan, Gene Hillman and Ed Kelly. Some of the Lutherans were teachers at nearby Makumira Theological Seminary, which in 1968 produced the first Maasai Lutheran pastors. Hillman has strong recollections of preparing papers for discussion by the group.

Now at every meeting there are present five or six priests and the same number of pastors. The discussions at these meeting have been the most interesting discussions I have ever taken part in in all my life and some of the results have been most heart warming and encouraging.

I must go now. All my love and all my thanks.

Sincerely,
Father Vince

December 10, 1961

Dear Relatives and Friends,

Greetings from an independent Tanganyika! It became independent yesterday. It is thrilling to be present at the birth of a nation. On Friday evening, I waited through the night with thousands of Africans in the town of Moshi before the British Administration Building to watch a ceremony that would be repeated in every town of Tanganyika at the same time, with the greatest pomp, of course, in the capital of Dar es Salaam in the presence of the Prime Minister, Mr. Nyerere, and Prince Philip. In Moshi, a few minutes before midnight the British National Anthem was sung for the last time, and the Union Jack was lowered for the last time, with the British District Commissioner [Francis Townsend] in his shining white suit and white pith helmet standing at rigid attention saluting the descending flag. Then the whole place was thrown into darkness. At the stroke of midnight, the lights came back on again and at the top of the flag pole, the green and black and gold flag of Tanganyika was flying for the first time, and the crowd burst forth singing the new National Anthem—"God Bless Africa! God bless Tanganyika!" Then a tremendous cheer arose and fireworks illuminated the night. And at the same time, from the peak of 19,000 foot Kilimanjaro, giant flares and rockets lit up the snow peaks for all to see. Mr. Nyerere had said previously, "We shall light a torch on the summit of Kilimanjaro for all the world to see. And from it, for all those who until now have known darkness and despair there shall come light; for all those who have known only hatred and injustice there shall come warmth and hope!"

Tanganyika has now taken its place among the free and independent and sovereign nations of the world. And Tanganyika has come to
independence on a wave of peace. Surrounded by such troublesome
spots as Kenya, Uganda, Zanzibar, Ruanda, Burundi, Congo, Portuguese
East Africa, Nyassaland and Rhodesia[15]—Tanganyika has chosen to be
a peaceful country. A country does not become peaceful by accident. It
takes a lot of effort to be peaceful.

It seems dreamlike to have been here while it was all happening.
To have had at your little mission house as a guest and as a companion
over a bottle of beer the man who is now Prime Minister of this country;
to have heard him quote in a major speech in Germany words which
you yourself helped to write for the bishops of Tanganyika,[16] to have
watched at close hand the differing tribes and peoples of Tanganyika
being molded into a nation—all this does not leave you unmoved when
the great moment of Independence finally comes.

And now the time has finally come for me to leave Tanganyika and
return home after being away for over seven years. It will be my first
Christmas at home in twenty years. And do you know something? I'm
frightened! I'm frightened at the thought of coming back to a land and a
city that has changed so much since I left. I'm frightened at the thought
of how I changed since I left. I'm frightened at the thought of coming
back to my family and friends of old who also might have changed much
in seven years' time, people to whom I will certainly be a stranger. I'm
frightened at the thought of meeting nieces and nephews and cousins
and neighbors' children to whom I will be as odd and strange as a visitor
from another planet. If I seem strange and shy and quiet when I meet
you face to face, please try to understand. There is one moment which
I will experience by myself, mercifully away from the eyes of everyone
who knows me. It is the moment when I will first set foot again on
American soil in New York. I want to see and judge for myself if I am
still an American at heart.

And now, all you nice people, I want to thank you again from the
bottom of my heart for your kindness, your generosity, your warm-

15. These last three became known respectively as Mozambique, Malawi, and
Zimbabwe.

16. This may have been a speech written for Bishop Kilasara about the Catholic
Church giving up its schools, a speech later reported in the journal, *Christ to the World*.
However, Hillman says that at this time various bishops were asking Donovan to pre-
pare position papers for them about a number of pre-Vatican II topics.

heartedness towards me. I shall be forever grateful. A blessed Christmas and a Happy New Year to you all from the green hills of Africa.

Love,
Father Vince

[Donovan was on leave in the USA from December 1961 till September 1962. On his way back to Tanganyika, he stopped in Rome and attended Pope John XXIII's last audience before the opening of Vatican II.]

4

USA RIVER

(1962–1966)

Dear Friends:

. . . When I reached Tanganyika, I was told to go to that part described in my address. I will be working with a section of the Masai tribe and the whole Meru tribe. The Meru are a particularly troublesome tribe, with whom we have had no success. There are only thirty-one Catholics in the whole tribe. We do not even have a mission in their country. Usa River is the closest place to it. I am trying to get a plot of ground on which to start a mission right now, in the Meru country. Please remember them and me in your prayers sometime.

As I write to you every month, I will attempt to give you a true picture of Africa in those troubled times and the life of a missionary in Tanganyika.

Love to all,
Father Donovan

February 1963

Dear Relatives and Friends,

. . . A great deal had happened in Africa since I left. Tanganyika has lived under its Independence for a full year now, or almost a full year. The demand for Africanization has been heavy, and the country has been Africanized swiftly. When I left Tanganyika right after it had achieved its independence, only the Prime Minister and most of his cabinet were Africans, but the other administrative posts in the government were still held by Europeans, mostly British, posts like the provincial commissioner (similar to a governor), district commissioner, district officer, educational officers, police captains, etc. Now they are all held by Africans. I live in fact in an African country now. There are only a handful of European policemen and doctors left in Tanganyika now. I find the Europeans left here a little more subdued and depressed, and the Africans a little more realistic in their approach to life in an independent nation. The schools, the life-line of missionary effort, are much more under the control of the government than when I left. Uganda, our neighbor on the Northwest, became independent on the ninth of October. Another section on my black and white map of Africa becomes black. Africa moves another step forward to its place in the sun.

Sincerely,
Father Vince

March 1963

Dear Relatives and Friends,

Thank you all very much for your continuing support of my work here in the missions. What a difference it is now from the time several years ago when I wondered hopelessly how I could ever do what had to be done. Now I am able to do it—thanks to all of you.

When I came back to Africa this time, I did not know what was in store for me. I have to confess that I spent a great deal of time on my return trip just trying to figure out where I would be sent this time. When I left Africa, I left from the senior seminary on the back of Mt. Kilimanjaro, where I held down the improbable job of superior and director. It was interesting work, and I suppose you would have to say important work, since one of our main works out here is to make ourselves super-fluous, replace ourselves with African clergy. I saw three different classes of priests ordained, I saw the ranks of the African clergy in our diocese swell until they equaled our numbers, we of the "foreign clergy." I enjoyed teaching theology and discussing it with young seminarians who belong to the tribes that make up the "nations" which we were sent to evangelize. I found it engrossing trying to absorb their mentality, their outlook on God and human beings, their approach to sacrifice and to vital initiation into a living group, which we call Baptism. I was impressed with their reverence for life and for the ancestors who gave them life. I was thrilled with the deep level of culture which slowly revealed itself to my eyes, a rich heritage which was theirs and which they hid under the surface ap-pearance which they put on for the European.

I felt humbled to realize that down through the centuries God had not abandoned these *nations*, the "Gentiles" as the Scripture calls them.[1] He had been very much with them. In a very mysterious way, he had led them to a knowledge of vital initiation into a living group, to the idea of forgiveness of sins and the need for it, to an idea of the priesthood (in their concept of witch doctor) and sacrifice. I saw that from that time on my work in Africa would never be the same; my mentality would never be the same. I would never again be able to consider myself the great "white savior" coming to lift the Africans for the first time from indescribable darkness. I saw that my task would be simply to build on the groundwork that was already there. All this I learned while I was teaching in the senior seminary. I learned far more there than I ever taught.

In normal circumstances there is nothing that I would have liked more than to stay right there on the back of that mountain doing work that was instructive, challenging and rewarding. But it was not a normal time in Africa. It was the eleventh hour. It was the church's last chance in Africa. I used to walk out on the veranda of that seminary built far up on Mount Kilimanjaro, in the evening hours especially, and look longingly down into the plains far below. They stretched as far as the eye could see, and the eye can see far indeed in the clear, un-smoky air of Africa. My eye used to wander each time to the west of Kilimanjaro, out to Mount Meru, itself 16,000 feet high, and to the immense tract of 30,000 square miles of land that went away from Kilimanjaro and Meru as far

1. The theological notion of "the nations" becomes more important for Donovan as time goes on. This is the first mention of it.

as Lake Victoria and Nyassaland. It was out there the Masai wandered and the Wandrobe,[2] the greatest hunters alive, and the Arusha and the Meru Tribes and the Sonjo, a remnant of a great Bantu civilization[3] that flourished hundreds of years ago in the middle of the Serengeti Desert. It was there, in this eleventh hour in Africa, that my heart was, out there where the "nations" were.

Sincerely,
Father Vince

___

April 1963

Dear Relative and Friends,

I hope all of you consider yourselves as talking and working right alongside me as I go about my missionary work. That is exactly what you are doing. You are here in a very real way. I could do nothing if you were not. I am very appreciative of the fact.

As I tried to explain in my last letter, while the plane was carrying me back to African soil, I was wondering what fate had in store for me. Although I had enjoyed my stay in the senior seminary on Mt. Kilimanjaro, and considered it a singular privilege to work there, I felt like an officer in a training camp at home while a war was going on elsewhere. And there *was* a war going on across the length and breadth of Africa. For a big group of people in our own diocese whose tribal ground covered an unbelievably large land area, the *gospel* was an unknown quantity. They had never heard it. For these people, in a very true sense as far as we were concerned, it was their last chance. There would not be another in our lifetime, in our century, in our period of history. How I longed to go to them!

You can imagine my sense of expectancy as I drove to see the vicar general of the diocese of Moshi[4] to find out what work was waiting for

2. The Ndorobo are hunters, neither pastoralists nor cattle farmers.

3. Bantu is a general term for over four hundred ethnic groups in sub-Saharan Africa.

4. At this time, the Diocese of Moshi was in the process of being subdivided into several smaller dioceses: Tanga, Same, Arusha, Mbulu, Sinida, and Moshi. (See letter of February 1965.) According to Hillman, the new Diocese of Arusha was created in part to give the Spiritans freedom to evangelize the Maasai and other groups. Moshi Diocese ministered mainly to, and was staffed by, members of the Chagga tribe, and was

me. As I sat down in his office, he looked up at me and said, "As you know, the bishop[5] is in Rome for the Ecumenical Council. So it is up to me to give you your appointment. Do you know Usa River?"[6] "Yes," I said, wondering what was coming next. "Well, I want you to go there." "But we have no mission there," I truly said. "No, we don't. But I want you to start one there. There was a plot of ground that belonged to the diocese for years in Usa River. We never used it for anything. Then just to make it less than useless, we put up a school there, a kind of trade school. But the school was a failure from the start. The Usa River is far out in the Masailand section of the diocese, but, as you well know, none of the local tribes ever attended the school. There was never one Masai or Meru or Arusha or Ndorobo or Sonjo boy in the school. Those people never saw the value of a trade school. Whoever started that school made a bad mistake. Just to keep the school going we had to import boys from Kilimanjaro and other far away places. It was doomed before it even got off the ground. Your job is to go there to see that it dies a painless death. But more important—out of the ruins you are to start and build a new mission, a mission for the Meru Tribe. You will be the only one working among the Meru Tribe and the first one officially sent to them. It will be the first mission to the Merus."

I sat back and took a deep breath. The Meru! They stretched out from the south east corner of Mount Meru down into the plains far below. I remembered hearing back in 1958 that in the whole Meru Tribe, there were only eleven Catholics. I asked the vicar general if he knew how many Catholics there were in the tribe now. He said according to the latest statistics, there were now thirty-one. Thirty-one Catholics in a tribe of fifty-thousand! They were one of the most stubborn tribes we had ever come in contact with, rejecting every advance we ever made

not much interested in evangelization. The new dioceses followed governmental jurisdictional lines, which coincided roughly with tribal boundaries. The Vicar General was Fr. Joseph Noppinger (1905–1990), who was also "principal religious superior of the Spiritan district of Kilimanjaro" (Koren, *Memorial*, 326). Donovan worked henceforth in the Diocese of Arusha.

5. On September 8, Dennis Vincent Durning (1923–2002), a Spiritan, was consecrated the first bishop of Arusha by Archbishop Del Mestri, the Apostolic Delegate to East Africa. He led the new diocese, which covered 27,000 square miles, for twenty-six years until 1989, during which time the number of Catholics in the diocese grew from 8,000 to 47,000 and the number of parishes grew from five to twenty-four (Koren, *Memorial*, 500).

6. Usa River is a few miles east of Arusha.

towards them. The vicar general was smiling. Mission to the Meru! Mission to the Meru! My heart began to sing.

Sincerely,
Father Vince

[On June 3, 1963, Pope John XXIII died; on June 21, Pope Paul VI was elected.]

August 1963

Dear Dad,[7]

. . . I read with interest the clipping Bill sent me about our superior general in Pittsburgh. I wish I could be as optimistic as he is about the future of the church in Africa. I agree with a lot of the things he said, but all of us out here were surprised when he said the missionaries in Africa want the Latin instead of the vernacular in the Liturgy.[8] This was truly news to us.

. . . Politically things are happening also. I have the news from a rather inside source that when Kenya becomes independent this year, the plan is to join Tanganyika, Kenya and Uganda, not into a federation as generally supposed, but into one country of East Africa, with one political party, one flag, one national anthem, one President, Jomo Kenyatta, presently of Kenya. Julius Nyerere, our president, may go to the U.N. in New York, and President Obote of Uganda may go to London as ambassador—both of them to fight against Portugal and South Africa.[9] . . .

Happy Birthday again, and all my love,
Vince

7. Parts of this letter which are repeated verbatim in the following letter have been omitted.

8. The Superior General at this time was Marcel Lefebvre (1905–1991), whose disagreement with the reforms of Vatican II led him to break away from the Roman Catholic Church in order (among other things) to retain the Latin Mass.

9. Plans were being made for this union to be headquartered in Arusha (in what is now the Arusha Conference Center), but the plan foundered for political reasons. (Various forms of this proposal continue: for example, in 2001 these countries formed a trade bloc called the East African Community, with a view to immediate economic co-operation and eventual political unity.) Portugal and South Africa are singled out by Donovan as among the few remaining colonial powers in Africa at this period.

September 4, 1963

Dear MMD[10] Members,

Father Donovan's father received a birthday letter from Father Donovan. Since we have received no letters, Mr. Donovan offered the use of this letter so you faithful MMD Members would have some idea why Father Donovan has been unable to write to you.

We quote in part from the letter:

> I feel like someone who has fallen off the face of the earth. I am well. I am happy. I am busy. I guess I am down to fighting-trim again. Like Irene Rich,[11] I weigh no more today than I did when I was sixteen. I weigh 175 again. Gone are the memories of midnight snacks, chocolate cake, chipped ham sandwiches and milk shakes. Looking back on being home seems like a dream that never happened. I am working feverishly again, with days and months passing by almost unnoticed. Sometimes when people tell me what month it is, I am startled. You wonder, as you're working, whether you will have time to finish the work. I'm back almost a year now, but in that year I've had to do work which would normally take almost five years. We are working against the clock, and all the signs are that the clock is running faster and faster, and will soon run out. For the first time in my years in Africa, I have the inescapable feeling that I will not spend the rest of my life in Africa.
>
> All kinds of things are happening here, politically and ecclesiastically. As far as the church goes, there is a feverish haste to Africanize as soon as possible, with African bishops, African priests, African heads of schools and seminaries. The seminary where I used to be, Kibosho, is now completely in the hands of the African priests. Our fathers are being pulled out of the Moshi Diocese, and transferred slowly to the new Arusha Diocese. Our new bishop, Bishop Durning, has not yet returned from America.
>
> We have heard that there have already been nine missionaries (Catholic priests) more or less deported from Tanganyika. We

10. Monthly Missions Donations: Donovan's support community.

11. Irene Rich (1891–1988) was a film star of the silent screen. She adopted the Welch's Reducing (i.e., weight loss) Plan, sponsored by Welch's Grape Juice, and appeared in several Welch's magazine advertisements which boasted that, although Ms Rich was over forty, she weighed no more than when she was sixteen.

have also heard that they may institute a system for foreigners (like us) whereby they have to register every two years, making application to continue working in the country.[12] This way, if they want to get rid of someone, it makes it very easy. They simply refuse permission for renewed stay in the country. This is a very effective system. It is the system they followed in India after independence there.

There is one section in East Africa where missionaries have not yet penetrated. It is the Northern Frontier of Kenya where the Turkana, Karamoja, and Suk Tribes live. They are rather primitive and run around mostly naked. Rome is very interested in sending missionaries there. The Holy Ghost Fathers have been asked to step into the breach and send two men. I should forewarn you that I am on the top of the list to go. I would love to go, of course, but the final decision of our mother house has not yet come in.

Thanks again for your generosity to Father Donovan and as soon as we hear from him, we will get the letter in the mail to you.

MMD Committee

[On September 29, 1963, the second session of the Second Vatican Council opened.]

October 1963

Dear Bill . . .

I have had such a series of disappointments recently that I don't think I can stand any more for the present.

I was all set to go to Turkana, in Kenya, when the bishop (our new Bishop Durning) decided that he did not want me to go. Two others have been appointed—McGinley of this diocese, and Feeley of Moshi Diocese.[13]

12. It appears that this threat never came about, although missionaries did have to register as agents for legal marriages, each being issued with an official government number.

13. Joseph ("Butch") McGinley (1917–1965) had been one of the two first resident missionaries at Loliondo Mission. James ("Jerry") Feeley (b.1924) had been teaching in Moshi for about ten years. Hillman says that they were both poor choices for this new venture in the northern desert of Kenya. They lived and worked out of a small trailer,

My second disappointment was in not going to Rome. The bishop told me he was taking me. Then at the last minute, because of plane reservation difficulties, he said once he got to Rome he would send me a telegram telling me to come on. The telegram never came. I have been working on the super-secret schemata though for the Council, translating them for the bishop, making suggestions, etc., and sending them on to him.[14] I have of course read all of Hans Kung's[15] books and Xavier Rynne's[16] also.

Love to all,
Vince

P.S. I think it is in the October 15th issue of Life magazine, in an article on the Council, that there is a picture of Cardinal Rugambwa,[17] and a quotation attributed to him that comes straight out of my pamphlet, *Unity and Freedom in the New Tanganyika.*[18]

November 16, 1963

Dear Relatives and Friends,

It has been so long since I have been in contact with all of you. I never forget you in my prayers of gratitude, and in my thoughts, but sometimes you seem so far away that I wonder if you were not just people I met in my dreams.

but did not last very long.

14. Hillman says Donovan was at this stage advising the Tanzanian bishops (most of them still ex-patriates) as part of their preparation for Vatican II. In particular, he wrote a paper for Bishop Josef Blomjous of Mwanza, a pioneer of inculturation among the Sukuma people of Western Tanzania.

15. Hans Küng (b. 1928), Catholic priest, theologian and author. Pope John XXIII appointed him an official theological advisor to Vatican II.

16. Xavier Rynne was the pen name of Fr. Francis X. Murphy (1915–2002), a sometimes irreverent eyewitness chronicler of Vatican II. Like Küng, he was a theological advisor to the Council.

17. Laurean Cardinal Rugambwa of Tanzania, the first African Cardinal, elevated by Pope John XXIII in 1960.

18. This described the rights and responsibilities of Catholics in the independent Tanzania. It was printed in December 1960.

I started my work among the Meru Tribe with all the vigor and energy that I had—with the little time we had left. Theirs was another language that I had to begin to learn. There were thirty-one Catholic Merus and I got in touch with them as soon as possible. They could not believe that a priest was going to stay with them and work with them. Some of them, in all their Catholic lives had never been to a mass on Sunday or celebrated Christmas even once the way Catholics do all over the world. As few as they were, they were scattered over a large area. One Sunday mass would not take care of them. So I started saying three Sunday masses, in three different places—one here in Usa River, and the other two in places near their homes.

I saw from the beginning that our plot in Usa River, by itself, would never be sufficient to take care of the scattered Merus. I had to find other plots in among the different places that they lived. I needed helpers. I chose two of the Merus who seemed to be the leaders among the Catholic group. One of them was an extraordinary man. His name was Antoni. During the Second World War, he was one of the "lucky" ones chosen from among his tribe to serve with the British Colonial Forces in the Near East. His travels and adventures carried him as far as Burma.[19] While he was in Burma, he became interested in the Christian religion. He took instructions from a Catholic chaplain, and was baptized before the war ended. After the war, he came back to Africa to take up his life once again among his fellow Merus. He was the only Catholic in the whole tribe. His was an extraordinary and singular position.

In my experience I have heard of no other case similar to his. In any other tribe, when Christianity finally took hold, it was not one man who came forward to accept Christianity. It was always several at one time who braved the wrath of the rest of the tribe—usually at least ten, sometimes very, very many at one time normally being baptized all on the same day.

But here was a strange case indeed. One man alone in all his tribe accepting the Christian religion. As you can imagine, his must have been a hard lot. And from talking to him, I found out that it really was. He knows what persecution means. He knows what being ostracized means. He knows what the long loneliness means. And he has been living this lonely life from the end of the war until last year—seventeen years of it.

---

19. In 1942, the Japanese invaded Burma, which had been under British domination. The British fought back, making use of troops from India, Nepal, and East Africa, and recovered Burma in 1944. This is probably the campaign in which Antoni took part.

All this has had an extraordinary effect on him. He is a very quiet man, very reserved, and very mild. He keeps his thoughts to himself. He has learned the necessity and the usefulness of doing this down through the years. Still water runs deep—and he is very deep. It takes an awful lot to ruffle him or upset him. He is an excellent Christian. He has become a quiet, unobtrusive, effective apostle to his tribe. He has in a very real sense brought the Catholic religion to the tribe. The ways of God are strange indeed. What good was the war in Burma to the world in general? I do not know. But I know the good it brought to the Meru Tribe in Africa. It brought them an apostle.

Love,
Father Vince

[On November 22, 1963, President John F. Kennedy was assassinated in Dallas, Texas.]

[January 1964]

Dear Bill, Rosie and Gang,

Greetings from the country whose capital has the beautiful Arabic name meaning "Haven (or Harbor) of Peace." The waters of the harbor have become a little troubled lately, but things are much better now.

I was in Dar es Salaam last month and I think I sent a card from there to Dad. Dar es Salaam is several hundred miles from Arusha Diocese. I was there for a Catechetical conference, which was extremely interesting. I'll have to tell you about it sometime. The Bishop has asked me to start a Catechetical Institute here in Usa for the training of catechists.[20] It is a very urgent problem here. Ninety percent of the instruction given in Africa (Religious Instruction, I mean) is given by lay Catechists. In many instances these Catechists are ignorant, and they pass on their

20. This reflects a concern of Vatican II: "The number of diocesan and regional schools should be increased where future catechists, while studying Catholic doctrine ... would at the same time model themselves on the lives of Christian men" ("Decree on the Church's Missionary Activity—*Ad Gentes Divinitus*," December 1965, in Flannery, *Documents*, 833). It is no coincidence that Donovan's colleague, Eugene Hillman, was a "peritus" (expert advisor) to Bishop Durning at the Council, and had input into this document.

ignorance to others. The whole structure of our Faith, of our Church, here in Africa rests on these shaky foundations.[21] . . . At any rate I went to the Conference in Dar es Salaam, where priests from all over Tanganyika were present—and I had a few good battles, I tell you. The outcome of it was that last week I received a personal letter from Fr. J. Hofinger[22] of the Philippines, inviting me to a Pan African Catechetical Conference to be held this year later on in Uganda. This time there will be delegates from North, East, West and South Africa—and the conference will be held in English and French. This conference is being held at the request of all the African Bishops at the Ecumenical Council in Rome. Fr. Hofinger explained that it took time to make up the select list of delegates to he invited from all over Africa, but now the choice had been made and he took pleasure in inviting me. I was very thrilled to get a personal invitation from Fr. Hofinger. Do you know him? I think that Sister (what's her name) of the Missionary Helpers of the Sacred Heart, to whom you introduced me at Duquesne, would.

You all must be concerned about Mr. and Mrs. John Doe, that couple who were married not too long ago and have several children, aren't you?[23] I know I was, and still am a little. John is a fine fellow. I think I told you he was my house guest some years ago before he got married. He and his wife have had a terrific fight, and it almost looked as if they were going to break up. I was very worried about him. You couldn't find a nicer husband. I was almost afraid that his wife would go off with another man. There were several men interested in her, one of them a friend of John's. Because he was a friend, John never suspected, but we warned John several times. I think John sees the error of his ways, you can't trust everybody. I think his wife has learned her lesson too. But if you ask the kids about the trouble between their parents they won't tell you anything. They're afraid to, I think. Their parents are very strict about the kids taking tales out of the family and telling outsiders. I guess you can understand that, can't you? It's only natural. And the kids are

21. Donovan refers to the "shaky foundation" of catechetical instruction in the section "Up from Slavery" in chapter 1 of *CR*.

22. Johannes Hofinger (1905–1984) was an Austria Jesuit, and an international leader in religious education and liturgical inculturation.

23. This was a coded reference to the political situation in Tanzania. John Doe stood for Nyerere, his wife for Tanzania, the "friend" for a political rival (perhaps Oscar Kambona, the popular foreign minister), and so on. Donovan tried to be discreet when writing about the country's political affairs.

afraid to disobey on this point because the parent can easily find out if they do. There are so many ways of finding out. At any rate things are fine between them for the time being. You'll pray for John and his wife, won't you—and for the kids?

It's interesting watching local history being made before your very eyes. When I was in Dar es Salaam, I went out one evening with some of the delegates from the conference for dinner at an ocean-side hotel. At the table next to us was Mr. Oscar Kambona, Minister for External Affairs for Tanganyika. With him were leading members of the Afro-Shirazi Political Party of Zanzibar. Next day in the paper they made the news with a very anti-American statement. The following week, Zanzibar became independent. The following month (this month) there was a revolution in Zanzibar and the Afro-Shirazi Party is now in control.

We were glad to hear a very good speech by the President on the radio the other night which ended with the words, "Have no fear. The torch of freedom will still burn brightly on the top of Mt. Kilimanjaro. Uhuru na Amani! Freedom and Peace!"

I am well and happy and thriving. I hope everyone at home is fine. Say hello to everyone, I will be sending some Soundscriber[24] letters again soon. Would you ask the secretary[25] to take special care with #3? Thanks.

Love,
Vince

January 1964

Dear Relatives and Friends,

God bless all of you who have been so good to me these many months. I don't know what I would do without you.

I have been working among the Merus and a section of the Masai in all my waking hours. I think I mentioned that I needed more than the

24. Soundscriber discs were an early form of sound recording system, invented in 1945. Flexible vinyl records were cut, using a stylus cutting head, and playback was on a dedicated player. The discs are a distinctive green color, and come in either four inch or six inch format. (See the Audio History section of the website of Audio Interchange of Waldoboro ME: www.videointerchange.com.) Donovan's brother Bill was a salesman for Soundscribers, and gave him one. He used it to record his articles, not the MMD letters.

25. This was Bill's wife, Rosie.

plot here at Usa if my work among the Merus was going to be effective at all. I traveled with Antoni, the Meru apostle, every day up and down and around the Mountain of Meru, looking for a likely place for a mission plot. We were getting very discouraged, really, when one day we heard of a little plot of ground about ten acres that was up for sale. It had belonged to a European years ago. He bought it from the German government when they ruled and governed Tanganyika. He had abandoned it many years ago, never using it, but keeping the title to it.[26]

I went into the town of Arusha to look up the land deed, and I found out that the land was indeed for sale. Antoni and I went up to look the land over. It was a beautiful piece of land, ten acres set right in the midst of the Meru country, and the whole section teeming with Merus. We walked up and down and around, talking excitedly, planning in our imagination where we could put a chapel, where we could put a dispensary, where we could put a school, etc. We were so excited that we hardly noticed that a huge crowd of Merus had gathered and were watching us with great interest. The Merus are a suspicious people by nature, and the sight of a European stalking over the land as though he owned it roused their suspicions no end. They just stood there talking quietly among themselves and staring at us.

As far as Antoni and I were concerned, this was the answer to a dream. We determined that we would see the vicar general of the diocese as soon as possible and make arrangements to buy this plot.

It was several days later as I was going along the highway by myself in my trusty Land Rover when I noticed Antoni standing alongside the road waving to me like mad. I knew something was wrong, so I stopped immediately. He told me that on the day before he had been called to the *Baraza* or council of the tribe by a council messenger. So he went and found a huge gathering of excited fellow tribesmen waiting with the chief. He was notified without further delay that he was being accused before the *Baraza* and they were going to try his case immediately.

His crime was that he had brought a European (me) right into the Meru country with the evident purpose of buying that land which belonged to the German long ago. In these days of *Uhuru*, this was very bad indeed. The Chief then stood up and made a speech right out of nineteenth-century Africa. It was a blood-chilling speech all right. He told Antoni that if he ever brought that European (me again) back into

---

26. The land had been used as a coffee plantation.

the Meru country, especially into that section called Singisi, where the desired plot was, he personally would order the people to take *pangas* (machete-like knives which were the favorite weapon of the Mau Mau) and *chinja* Antoni and the white man. (*Chinja* is a cheerful word which means hack to death.)

I'm glad I wasn't at the *Baraza*. I would have been at a loss for words to say the least. But Antoni stood up quietly (I mentioned in the last letter that he is a very deep and capable man, not easily upset or frightened) and once again carried the day. I'll tell you how next time.

Love,
Father Vince

Feb 10, 1964

Dear Dad and Aunt Gert,

. . . I am very busy. We have opened up the Catechetical Training School in Usa and this keeps me busy all morning. The Bishop has also left me in charge of all the Masai and Meru work which I was doing before, so that takes up my afternoons and evenings and sometimes nights. But it is very wonderful work and I love it.

At the Ecumenical Council, the bishops of each country were told to set up National Liturgical Committees to study the Decree which the fathers of the Council voted on and announced to the world concerning the Liturgy. In that Decree they simply stated general principles, and they left it up to the Liturgical Committee of each country to apply these principles to the particular country, to make suggestions etc., about changes in the Liturgy. Well, the Bishop of Tanganyika had a meeting last month in Dar es Salaam, and our Bishop notified me that I have been named to be on National Liturgical Committee of Tanganyika, one of six priests. Imagine having a "Protestant Priest" on the National Liturgical Committee!! All I can say is that Rome is going to hear some startling suggestions . . .

I am very well and happy—not up to my fighting weight at home, but still healthy. Please give my regards to all.

Love,
Vince

August 1964

Dear Relatives and Friends,

Please excuse my delay in writing, but a lot has happened in Tanganyika and Zanzibar, or rather the Republic of Tanganyika and Zanzibar since I last wrote. I have been kept extremely busy.

For one thing I have been kept busy among the Meru Tribe, and things have been moving there very well. I was sent here to Usa to work among the Meru Tribe and they have responded very well to any efforts which I have made.

I think I told you of my experience with the Meru fellow who was baptized during the war and has been an invaluable apostle ever since then. He was fearless when the head of the tribe made some extravagant threats about chopping him up with knives if he ever brought those Europeans back to the country looking for land. I was one of those Europeans, of course. But the Meru fellow, Antoni by name, was not only fearless. He was also very clever.

This particular threat was made during one of the tribal council meetings. That is a very official affair. Antoni knew that and he made the most of it. He stood up and he asked the chief very politely, "Would you mind repeating that so that I can understand exactly what you mean?" The chief in some heat fairly screamed, "I said if you bring those European padris back here again to my country, I will tell the people to attack you with *pangas* (machete-like knives)."

Antoni shook his head sadly and said, "I'm afraid I'm not hearing very well this morning. I still do not understand you. Would you mind repeating that just once more?"

The chief was definitely puzzled, but for the third time he repeated the ominous words. Antoni smiled very contentedly and said, "Thank you very much," and sat down. There was a hurried consultation around the chief as his advisors and councilors crowded towards him.

Finally, Antoni stood up and left the meeting, with the satisfaction of seeing a very worried look on the face of the chief. When Antoni told me the story, I did not quite see what he was so happy about. He explained it briefly and said, "That is the last we will ever hear about this affair from my friend, the chief. It finally dawned on him what I was doing by asking him to repeat his threat, but it was too late. I got him to issue his threat publicly against me in front of the whole council and all the people. I am sure his councilors told him that was a bad mistake. Now, anytime I want, I can accuse him to the central government of using threats of violence against us. He would be punished severely if he were ever so accused, and would probably lose his job. He could hardly deny that he made the threat. He made it three times, and in front of the official Council." Antoni was right. We never heard from the chief again on the subject. We continued looking for land, completely unmolested, and found some beautiful land in a section of Mt. Meru called Singisi. It has ten beautiful acres and we made arrangements with the government to buy that land. We had to pay for it, of course, but the bishop helped me and we got enough money together to close the deal.

And once the land was ours we put up a temporary building to serve as a church and a school. It was just a wooden building, kind of long and ungainly looking, but it looked beautiful to me. And it was beautiful to me when I said my first mass in it one sunny Sunday morning, and turned around at the gospel and told the thirty-one Merus sitting there, "In this year of our Lord, the Church has come to Meru."

Sincerely,
Father Vince

September 1964

Dear MMD Members,

Emergent Africa continues to emerge and we go along with the times—sometimes just a little ahead of them, sometimes a little behind them, but always hopeful.

I was always full of hope and full of joy as I worked along with the Merus. You don't always have the opportunity to witness the church growing up among a people right from the ground floor, you might say. I had that opportunity with the Merus. I used to go to Singisi, the new outstation of Usa Mission, every Sunday for one of my Sunday masses, and then go on one other day of the week for mass also. It was a pleasure working with that little group of people. Right before my eyes were the very first people in the tribe who had entered the Church. Everything in Christianity seemed new and shining to them. Preaching to those thirty-one people on Sunday morning wasn't like preaching a sermon in a normal church. It was more like just talking to a big family, or standing among them like a herald or a messenger telling them some startling news—exciting news that always seemed to thrill them. It made me, myself, appreciate the news a little more.

More and more Merus got interested and pretty soon we had some very interesting developments taking place. One pagan Meru, with three wives and several children, came and asked to take instructions. I told him his three wives presented a difficulty. But he saw a way around that. He said he would choose one of the wives, the youngest one, who could still bear him children. He would live with her and her children and he would build two houses in another place for the other two wives with their children. He could not cast them out. He would take care of them as long as he and they lived, together with their children. Just the one would be his wife. He called all three wives together and they all agreed to this arrangement.

Then I went off to see the bishop about this extraordinary case. After some time and much consultation, he gave permission for this arrangement, and the happy man began his instructions. So did his wives.

Some time afterwards, on one happy morning, I baptized him— and his three wives and several of their children who had not yet been baptized. They come to church together, the whole clan, every Sunday morning.[27]

Even though their church was poor, I wanted those Merus to have the best possible things for their services. I wanted, for instance, to have the best church vestments and ornaments that I could get my hands on. Fortunately, I had just the things stored away for just such a use. I had the beautiful vestments made for me and collected for me by Mrs. Lynch[28] while I was home on leave. They are probably the nicest vestments in this whole diocese of Arusha—and I couldn't think of nicer people to use them for than my little flock of Merus. How they appreciated them. I thought of Mrs. Lynch every time I said Mass there. You people follow me right into my work.

The little Meru community has grown some. There are now a hundred and twenty Merus in the church. That might not sound like a lot

27. Over the years, a more tolerant attitude towards polygamy developed among Spiritan missionaries. See, for example, Hillman, *Polygamy Reconsidered*.

28. Mary Rita Lynch, a neighbor of the Donovans and a member of the parish of St. Stephen's.

to you people, but it is so many for us that the little church we originally built is no longer big enough. We just don't try for numbers out here. Our job is not to convert every individual in Africa. Our job as missionaries is just to establish the church among every people, every nation, every tribe, and every tongue [Rev 6:9]. Then we move on. That is what makes us different from the priests at home whose job will never end. Our job will end—and then we will come home.[29]

In the meantime, it was a real joy to me to see the latest Holy Ghost Directory, which lists every work we have all over the world. There, very proudly on page 89, sits the notation, "Catholic Mission, Singisi."

Sincerely,

Father Vince

February 1965

Dear Relatives and Friends,

It has been so very long since I have written and been in contact with all of you that America seems very far away indeed. I think of all of you very often and remember you in my prayers. I hope all of you pray for us sometimes, because we need your prayers! Maybe you would think that since I am writing to you again, there would be certain things that I would write about which are more topical and interesting—but I cannot write about those things. Believe me. Perhaps my brother Bill could explain.[30]

Let me rather talk about the diocese of Arusha and the work here. Our diocese of Arusha is a new diocese, huge in size, small in the number of priests and other missionaries who work here. . . .

A new Diocese has advantages and disadvantages. Its disadvantages are obvious. As far as finances and personnel are concerned, it works under a terrible burden. Its advantages are not so obvious, but they are none-the-less great. In a new diocese like this, we missionaries are given the opportunity to avoid the mistakes made in other and older dioceses.

29. This philosophy that the missionary should work him/herself out of a job was stressed by Fr. Libermann in letters to his missionaries in the 1840s. The idea was not unique to Donovan, nor something he learned from Roland Allen.

30. This is another discreet reference to aspects of the political situation in Tanzania. See letter of January 1964.

That mistakes have been made is undeniable. The Congo was perhaps the greatest missionary country in Africa. The church in the Congo was one of the most highly organized and developed churches outside of Europe and America. When Independence came to the Congo, that great organization crumbled and the church fell apart. It is in ruins in many parts of the Congo today.

What happened there? Many things happened. For one thing, the foundations of that church in many places were not solidly laid. Another thing—the foundations were not always truly African. They were for the most part European, and the finished structure was un- mistakably European. When Independence came, and it came time for the Europeans to give way to the Africans, or to get out, that church was mistaken for something European, and it was attacked as such, along with those who worked for that church.

We here are not much inclined to be martyrs to the color of our skin. If we must suffer for our church, well and good, but let it be for the church as it should be. The church as it should be in Africa is an African church, not an imitation European church.

The Church in Africa must be African—that is the first principle of missiology. It is our job as missionaries to clothe the soul of Christianity with the flesh and blood of Africa. But that is easier said than done. It takes years of research and study and working very close to the people, on their level, not ours.

It takes a tremendous and continuing effort to try to see the African people not as they appear to us, but as they appear to themselves, which is quite another thing.

You people in America are now involved in the great effort to make the liturgy of the church, the mass and the administration of the sacra- ments, understandable and meaningful for everyone taking part in that liturgy.[31] Anyone taking part in this great renewal knows the tremen- dous work entailed in taking these sacred signs and symbols and actions which were put in use centuries ago and trying to make them meaning- ful for the Americans of today.

Well, if you think that is difficult, then just try to imagine how dif- ficult it is to make the church African. So many things we missionaries are tempted to take for granted; so many things we are tempted to accept

31. Liturgical reform had begun in the US before Vatican II, but Vatican II sanc- tioned and accelerated it, to the distress of conservatives like Lefebvre.

as they appear to us through our culture-blinded glasses. It is so easy to make a mistake in these matters.

Folding the hands when praying, for instance, might be a method of praying in Europe or elsewhere, but it is not an African method of praying. So often we have forced them to pray that way. Kneeling down to pray is another attitude we might be tempted to force on the Africans without thinking, not realizing that for them the attitude which shows the greatest respect and adoration is standing. We economical Europeans like to sprinkle two or three drops from the Baptismal font on the forehead of the person being baptized, and consider we have done a proper job. The African on the other hand is scandalized at the stagnant water of the Baptismal font, and cannot see how two or three drops of water from that stagnant pool can signify the wondrous transformation which Baptism is supposed to bring. For them, a stream of living water is necessary.

In your prayers sometimes, remember us in this challenging and fascinating work of ours.

Sincerely,
Father Vince

March 1965

Dear Relatives and Friends,

I want to thank you all again for your generous and continuing support of our work here. You help me so much in our work that I would like to explain just a little more what is involved in this work of ours—at least part of it.

I mentioned the last time the whole transformation in the liturgy which is necessary if we are ever to succeed in making this church of ours African in Africa. If we *don't* make it African, then this church of ours is not really *Catholic*—but merely a European-American affair.

Consider the anointings which we have in our liturgy—in the sacraments of Baptism, Confirmation, Holy Orders, and the Anointing of the Sick. Once again, we use one drop of oil which we quickly rub off. If we try that on the African, he doesn't even know he has been anointed.

An African knows what anointing is all right, but his idea of anointing is a far cry from our economical, antiseptic dabbing on and rubbing off of a drop of oil. The young African girl, when she wants to look her finest, say, for instance, to go to the market place to catch the eye of a possible suitor, shaves her head bald if she happens to be a Masai, or cuts her hair very short if she is a member of another tribe, and rubs her scalp or her closely cropped hair, and her whole head and face and neck with thick layers of cow grease, and lets it stay there until it dries hours later. And while it is still wet, she strides demurely into the market place glistening like a piece of soft coal, catching all eyes. Ask any young African man—she is absolutely irresistible that way. And it does such things for your skin!

A Masai warrior, about to go into battle, sits very gravely and nervously lost in his own thoughts, as an old woman rubs strength and bravery and agility into his trembling frame, with the grease of the sacred cow.

A young mother about to give birth is anointed with cow grease from her head down to her waist, to give her the power and the fruitfulness and the grace necessary for the miracle she is about to perform.

And a dying African is anointed from his head to his toes to instill in his body the force and comfort necessary to sustain the terrible, disrupting shock that is coming upon it, and to accompany it into the darkness.

Yes, Africans know what anointing is, but they hardly recognize it in the abbreviated action which *we* call anointing. To make the liturgy meaningful and understandable to these Africans, we have to restore the symbols involved to their original vigor. For the African, it is not so much that the symbolism has been lost in our liturgy; it is that the very symbols themselves have been lost.

For us in the Western Church, the symbols have all but died. Only the thing symbolized has any meaning and reality for us. But for the African this is not enough. His whole life is lived in symbolism. The words he speaks, the songs he sings, the stories he tells, the dances he joins in, the rhythm he sways to—all are steeped in symbolism. He only asks in our liturgy that the symbols be as real and vital as the things they symbolize.

Consider the songs and hymns the poor African has been forced to learn in church, usually translations of some Alsatian[32] or French hymns

32. Some of these may have come from Alsatian Spiritan Andre Krieger (1875–1967), who made annual safaris through Maasai country in the early years of the twentieth

of the last century. Even-rhythms, neatly rhymed verses, written in our eight-toned scale, a scale which includes two half tones. Fifty million Africans cannot even sing a half tone interval. Their scale is made up of only five full tones. (Try singing five full tones in a row to see how difficult it is to adapt your self to an entirely different concept of music.) Two hundred million Africans prefer a free, uneven rhythm, and abhor rhymes. Their concept of poetry in song is based on presenting to the mind a mystery to feed on which thrills the African mind—not a rhyme which merely amuses it.

Do you see the work we have yet to do?

Sincerely,
Father Vince

April 1965

Dear Relatives and Friends,

Greetings once again from Tanzania. And from the missionary you have helped over the months and years, a repeated sincere thank you.

It has been some years now since an intensive survey was made in East and Central Africa concerning the state of religious instruction given to our people. The result was alarming and depressing. It showed that because of the shortage of priests and nuns and brothers working here, the work of actually teaching religion was falling to lay people. The shortage of priests and other missionaries was intensified because many of the priests and other missionaries who were working in East Africa were doing everything but teaching religion.

They were making long and arduous safaris. They were building churches and schools and hospitals. They were supervising the teaching in the lower schools, and actually teaching secular subjects in the higher schools. They were taking care of bringing supplies to the schools and the hospitals. The sisters were actually working in the hospitals. They were doing a million and one things—but they were not teaching religion. And you know, that is actually why they came to Africa—to teach religion—or "to preach the Gospel", as it says in the Bible.

---

century. He spent a total of sixty-four years in Africa (Koren, *Memorial*, 147).

So if they were not teaching religion, who was? Lay people. That does not sound bad until we look at just what kind of lay people they were. Catechists we called them. Young men and old men having anything from a grade two education up to a grade eight education—but never anyone higher than this.

And what kind of training did they receive before they went out to do this important work? The answer to that question is easy, also: none; absolutely none. They were handed a catechism containing almost five hundred questions to be memorized[33]—and were told to go out and instruct the people. They did just that.

This survey that I mentioned showed that 90 per cent of the instruction that our Christians have received has been imparted by these lay catechists. We have to say it. 90 per cent of the religious instruction our people have in Africa has been given by these catechists—ignorant in many ways of the true meaning of our religion. And they have passed on this ignorance to others. Our whole church in East and Central Africa rests upon this shaky and questionable foundation.

Our whole church in the Congo, Ruanda, Burundi, Malawi, Zambia, Mozambique, Tanzania, Kenya, and Uganda rests on this frightening foundation. Do you wonder that, when that report fell into my hands several years ago, I could not sleep? What are we going to do? I'll tell you next time what we tried to do.

Father Vince

[From Usa River Catechetical Centre. Letter written on receiving the news of the death of his brother Jerome (Jome) at age thirty-six. He and his wife Ellen had only been married a couple of years.]

April 28, 1965, 10:00 AM

Dear Dad,

I was just called out of class to be given the telegram from Father Gallagher.[34] To say I was stunned would just not convey my feelings. I

33. This was probably the Baltimore Catechism, which has 421 questions.
34. Fr. Vernon Gallagher, Provincial Superior of the Spiritans.

feel completely empty. Oh, God! I tried to go back to class afterwards to teach some more, but I found I could not even speak, much less think.

All I can think of is the sadness which has once more settled on the Donovan household. If it is true, and I think it is, that sorrow builds a bridge into the infinite, then surely we must be reaching in that direction with all our might. I don't know why it is that God reaches down so often to touch us in such extraordinary ways. All I know is that He does, and my whole life is based on the firm and unshakeable belief that it is all important for all of us that we react in the way He wills and wants us to react to these inscrutable moves of His—or else everything is in vain. We will become exactly what we make of ourselves after each of these touches of God. These are the most important times of our lives. If it were ever true that God is watching to see what we will do, then surely it is at such times. If we do not react the way He wants us to react, then everything is lost and wasted, and life itself has no more meaning.

If I were a pagan Masai warrior out in Sanya Plains, then I would despair right now. But I am not a pagan warrior. I am a Christian, and also a priest. And I believe with all the power of belief that is in me that our God is not the God of the pagans who created the world and left it to its own devices and miseries. Our God is the Christian God, the God of hearts, the God to whom the broken heart of a father or a brother is more important than all the stars of the Milky Way or of the whole universe. Our God is a God whose face is clouded by human pain and sorrow, and I believe that the face of God is at this moment clouded with the particular pain and sorrow of the Donovans.

I cannot of course come home for the funeral. One does not leave this country so easily. I would like to be there. I would like to share this sorrow with all of you. I know it would be unbearable grief to be there, but it would also give me the strength I need right now. I have been diminished by Jome's death. We all have. It is a thing we share in common. But we also derive strength we need at such times from each other—in common. I feel now as I have never felt before the need of my father and brothers and sister. I get strength from them, as I will never be able to get from the strangers who now surround me.

My heart goes out to you, Dad, more than I can say. I will say a requiem mass for Jome tomorrow, and sing another one on the day of the funeral, and I will remember all of you in those masses.

I am crying now, Dad, and I am not ashamed of it. Christ cried at the grave of His friend Lazarus. Maybe part of the reason He cried was because He had no brother. I did.

Love,
Vince

May 1965

Dear Relatives and Friends,

Thanks once again for all your help. Before continuing my story I would like to ask you people to do me a special favor. Could you please say a prayer for my brother, Jome, who died recently, and for his wife? Thank you so much.

I mentioned the rather dismal situation, as regards religious instruction in East and Central Africa. This can be extremely dangerous for the church, as you can well imagine. I don't think I have to go into any detail of the results of this ignorance of the true meaning of our religion in such places as the Congo, for instance.[35] There it is always the priests and the nuns who are first attacked.

I remember talking to a nun, a refugee from the Congo. She and all the nuns in her convent were attacked. I asked her what she thought about it all. She said her greatest shock came from the fact that she easily recognized those who broke into the convent and attacked the nuns. "They were those who attended church regularly," she said. "They were the ones who used to sing the Sunday High Mass and even the weekday High Mass." Somehow, somewhere along the line, they had forgotten what our religion means—if indeed, they ever knew. . . .

When I first came back from leave in America and was assigned to Usa Mission, I had the occasion to try one hundred catechumens before Baptism. They had been instructed by old time catechists, and they knew by heart the answers to every question in the catechism. They knew by heart what grace was, what mortal sin was, what the ten commandments were—but when I asked each one of them, "Who is Jesus

---

35. On January 1, 1962, twenty Spiritan missionaries had been murdered in the Congo, in what became known as the Kongolo Massacre.

Christ? What did He do?"—not one out of the 100 was able to answer a single word.

I knew then that something had to be done.

Sincerely,
Father Vince

June 1965

Dear Relatives and Friends,

Before I continue with my report, I would like to say how grateful I am to you for your unfailing support.

A church can only be as strong as its foundations, and the foundations of any church are the instructions the people of that church have received—their understanding of their religion. All I can say is that I was convinced that our people had a very meager understanding of our religion.

I got permission from the bishop to experiment. We agreed that something drastic had to be done, so he let me begin on a small scale. The problem was vast. It embraced not only all the Christians who have already been instructed, but also all the catechumens who are under instruction. The catechumens were attending regular lessons, but the Christians receive no instructions. How could we reach all of them? Reinstructing the Christians, and starting off fresh with the catechumens, not letting them into our religion without understanding it?

How did the early church do it? How did the early Christians receive their instructions? They had no parochial schools. They had no schools of any kind. The only instruction they received was when they came to Mass on Sunday morning. That is all the instruction the Catechumens received before they were baptized. All they did was go to Church every Sunday for a long period of time, listen to the sermon of the priest, sing a few hymns, and listen to the readings from the Bible chosen for the day—parts of the Mass. After a certain time had passed of doing simply this, they were ready for Baptism. They were instructed and well instructed in their Religion. As for the Christians, they did the same, and by continually going to Mass, they received continuing instructions.

Why couldn't we do something like that? The first thing to do would be to move the emphasis in instruction from the school to the church, where it really belonged. The next thing would be to examine the Mass and the structures of the Mass to see if it really is a vehicle of instruction as well as of worship.

The third thing to do would be to examine our Religion itself, strip it of all the accidentals that have accrued to it throughout the years and centuries; see if we could get back to a kind of naked Christianity.[36] People have a tendency to cling to accidentals and forget essentials. We wouldn't give our people a chance to cling to accidentals, because we wouldn't teach any. The ensuing study of Christianity has had results not only on the people for whom we have made this study, but also on us. I'm not quite sure you people would recognize the form of Christianity that is being formed in our little section of the church here. It is stripped. It is bare. It is challenging. It is an experience being exposed to it.

Sincerely,
Father Vince

July 1965

Dear Relatives and Friends,

Thank you for the interest and help shown to our people out here in Africa. It is your interest in it that makes our work possible.

We had to find a fitting place to start our experiment of joining the worship of the people with instruction; as a matter of fact, giving them their main instruction through their worship. We found such a place some fifteen miles south of Arusha. It was situated in a settlement of Arusha tribesmen, people akin to the Masai and similar to them in many things. The Arusha are farmers, not cattlemen like the Masai.

They were living in a section which we had never worked in very much. There were a few Christians from a fairly long time ago; a greater number of recently baptized Christians and a big number of catechu-

---

36. This appears to be Donovan's first use of this expression. David Bosch says, however, "There never was a 'pure' message, supracultural and suprahistorical. It [is] impossible to penetrate to a residue of Christian faith that was not, in a sense, already interpretation" (Bosch, *Transforming Mission*, 422).

mens. It was just what we wanted for our experiment. We decided to work with these people for a period of six months with the new method.

We put a teacher with them, not to give formal instructions, but only to prepare the people for the service of the coming Sunday. We took special care with that Sunday service. Until then it had been a pretty sloppy affair. The people did pretty much just as they pleased. Some of them said the rosary during the Mass; others just sat there doing nothing much; still others joined in lustily enough when there was a hymn to be sung. The hymns themselves were a nondescript conglomeration of imitation European melodies fitted to words that did not have very much meaning, and no instructional value. The people sung any hymn they wanted to, at any time during the service. The Priest more or less did the same, preaching on any subject that came to mind. Add to all this, the fact that the whole service was conducted in Latin, and you can imagine the final result left a lot to be desired.

So, in this experimental place, we started weekly Mass. Actually, we had to be rather ruthless. We made people do what *we* wanted—not what they wanted. We *made* them pray together. We banned the rosary during Mass. We threw out practically every hymn they knew and started almost from scratch. We searched for suitable African melodies to carry the simplest words we could find; simplicity was our goal in everything. We wanted to present our religion in the simplest possible form, stripped of everything that was not essential. We reduced it to a form that could be transmitted, not by questions and answers, but by participation in a common worship. We chose the hymns that *had* to be sung, the prayers that *had* to be said, the common action that *had* to be carried out, and the sermon that *had* to be preached by the priest. All these things were directed to one single subject. Our effort was to give the people one thought, *one* lesson, *one* idea, to carry with them, an idea gotten across by every single thing that was done in the church that morning. A different idea each week—gradually building up in their minds and their lives an appreciation of the Christian Religion—step by step.

We ourselves succeeded in seeing the Christian Religion in a new light—a religion that could be summed up in about eight sentences—or eight general thoughts. We became convinced that instruction could indeed be carried out by worship. We were on our way.

Sincerely,
Father Vince

September 1965

Dear Relatives and Friends,

Sometimes I feel so far away from all of you. It is your interest in my work and your help towards my work that makes you seem close again. I am really grateful to you.

The Bishop of the Diocese of Arusha was behind the reform in teaching Religion. After our original experiment with the Arusha tribe, he decided that we should open up a full-time Catechetical Training Centre. He opened the centre at Usa where I live, and asked me to be in charge of it.[37] Then he notified each mission in his diocese, the reform in teaching Religion was to be diocesan-wide and compulsory. He told the Father in charge of each Mission to pick his best catechist, or teacher of Religion, and send him into Usa for a year's training.

And in they came, catechists of every description and every tribe: Masai, Arusha, Meru, Sonjo. Some of them were young fellows, just out of school. Others were married and they came with their wives and children. (This was something we hadn't considered.) One was a young girl—and the training centre was to be a boarding school! We solved that problem by boarding her with a nearby family. But she followed all the classes and ate with the male students.

Actually she was a blessing in disguise. Being the lone female in the school, she kept the others on their toes. Whenever I felt the others not making the effort they could, I called on her. She was quite clever and answered very well every time. The young men were so embarrassed at being shown up by this female that they doubled their efforts.

I had to laugh at how politely and gentlemanly they treated her in the dining hall. They all kept cleaner when she was around.

The question of the wives who came with their husbands was another problem, and one not so easily solved. We could not board them out with different families. We had to keep them right there with their husbands. Which we did.

Their very presence there gave us an idea. Why should they just live there like vegetables? Why couldn't they get some profit out of their staying at Usa with their husbands? As a matter of fact, since they were

37. This is a reference back to the previous year: see letter of February 1964.

married to men who would spend their lives teaching religion professionally, why indeed couldn't they help husbands in their work? Why couldn't they somehow be trained along with them? A husband and wife catechetical team would be extremely valuable, the husband doing the heavy work and the wife teaching little children, first communicants, and young girls who are understandably a bit wary of young men teachers. One idea certainly grows out of another, and you can never tell where you are going to end when you start doing something. Which makes life interesting.

Sincerely,
Father Vince

December 1965

Dear Relatives and Friends,

Many, many thanks for your continuing contributions to our work out here. I feel very humbled by your loyal support.

I have been involved in many kinds of work out here, building, transporting, medical, social, educational, and searching out new sections where the church has never entered, but it was in catechetical work that I truly felt I was closest to the heart of the matter.

Dealing with teachers who spend their whole lives preaching and teaching and explaining the Christian religion, you find yourself touching the raw and vital nerve of our whole missionary endeavor. In this work, you can see the strength and weakness, the promise and the danger of our whole effort.

We missionaries are out here, not to save souls, but to establish the church, among what is probably a minority of each group of people. Everything we do—directly or indirectly—is towards this goal. Well, at the end of the line, this minority of each group—which does enter the church as the foundation of the church in each section—must be instructed in the Christian religion, must know what Christianity is, and what it is all about.

And on whom does the burden of this vital instruction fall? On the catechist, the teacher of religion, who instructs nine out of every ten people baptized in Africa.

This man, this catechist, is the keystone of our work, absolutely essential to its success or failure. How we ever dared to leave him alone to his own devices, I will never know.

The first group of catechists who came into our school for a year of emergency training was understandably hesitant and rather suspicious of the whole project. They were carefully chosen by the Bishop. Most of them were experienced and seasoned catechists; some of them, I believe, feared that this whole new catechetical project was a criticism of them. Little did they know, in reality, it was a criticism of ourselves—the Missionaries.

I found the work very difficult at first, because of this initial hesitancy and suspicion on their part. But gradually this obstacle broke down, and they became friendly and willing and openly cooperative. It was at this point, that our most valuable work began—valuable for them and for me—the representative of the Missionaries involved in this vital work.

Slowly I began to draw out of them just what they understood by the Christian religion, and what they therefore taught to others. It was an interesting, revealing and sometimes shocking experience.

Through this work I think I have had the opportunity to come closer than most missionaries to sounding out the basic religious insights of the African mentality, at least in this country.

With the Bishop's encouragement, I set out to use these basic religious concepts in the reforming of our catechists. As far as the Christian religion was concerned, it called for a wiping out of practically everything they knew about our religion—and starting again—almost from scratch.

Sincerely,
Father Vince

March 1966

Dear Relatives and Friends,

I am so grateful for the help you have been giving me that I cannot express my thanks sufficiently.

When you teach Africans religion you must be extremely careful; they already have their own ideas about many of the things you want to teach them. They may or may not see the difference between their idea and the somewhat new idea you are trying to get across. Even the idea of God. We naturally have to use the word for God which already exists in their language. But they have practically already made up their minds what this word means—and they are a bit reluctant to add to that idea.

For most of the tribes out here, God is a pretty fierce person who created the world at some time in the past and has let it go its merry own way ever since. He doesn't care a whole lot about it. He is kind of a god "way up and out there," who is not much interested in puny, individual human beings. As a result, they are more than a bit afraid of him, and hardly ever pray to him. They would much rather pray to their ancestors or someone who would be a bit more understanding than God. Thinking that he would not be interested in the personal problems of an individual, they don't mention them to him.

About the only time they would pray to God is when a public catastrophe would hit the whole tribe. The Christian idea of God is quite startling to them, and has to be handled carefully. A priest, or someone else teaching them about God, and not knowing their pagan ideas about God, could make a lot of mistakes. You might (and do) end up with many Catholic Africans who would never think of praying to God, but would *only* pray to the Blessed Virgin or the saints, who have taken the place of their ancestors.

They have their own pagan ideas about sin, which is nothing but a breaking of a law, or a violation of a taboo. The whole thing is quite easily rectified by a simple paying of a fine—a goat or a cow. When they hear us talking about sin (in their language) and penance and confession—unless we are very careful, they think they understand the thing immediately. As a result, we have some of the most fantastic legalistic approaches to sin you could ever imagine—and some of the most formalistic and, I might add, useless confessions you ever heard of. . . .

Teaching religion here is no child's game. It is fraught with dangers and pitfalls.

May the God of our forefathers bless you all, and keep you free from the harm of the banshees.

Love,
Father Vince

April 1966

Dear Relatives and Friends,

Thanks ever so much for being so kind to me and so loyal and so helpful during these many months and years. I have learned what it means to be grateful.

One is surprised, time and time again, in teaching religion to the Africans. You never know what reaction is lurking in their minds. Once I was discussing the Eighth Beatitude of the Sermon on the Mount with some catechists. They told me they had trouble with a few of them and would like to discuss them. They actually asked my permission not to have to teach the eighth beatitude, "Blessed are those who suffer persecution for justice's sake." They didn't like it personally. They said the people would never understand it, that it would frighten them out of the church, and that it would actually encourage our enemies to attack us physically. This might sound like a childish reaction, but you must remember the amazing literalness with which the Africans sometimes interpret scripture. This is not surprising seeing that the African lives in a land that is amazingly biblical. He is often born in a "stable" with animals sharing his abode; he knows the sheep by name and his cows, and they know his voice. The shepherd is a symbol of a great leader. The desert of Moses and John the Baptist and Christ is a reality to them; a cup of cold water is no small charity in a land where water is so scarce that the Masai often do not drink water, but leave it for their cattle so both can live. The evil spirit roaming about like a lion haunts their days and nights.

African time is exactly like biblical time—completely different from American time. Seven o'clock in the morning is the first hour of the day to the African, one o'clock, as it was for Christ; the hour when Christ died is not three o'clock, but nine o'clock, just three hours before the day ends, as it is for the African. When the Africans hear the parable of the man who went out to hire laborers for his vineyard as late as the eleventh hour, they are as startled as Christ's listeners must have been. That is what the Africans call five o'clock in the evening. The story must make much more sense to an African than to an American, who probably doesn't know what the eleventh hour is.

Add to this all the African knows about the Congo and the Sudan, and you might understand his reluctance in accepting the eighth beatitude.

I calmed the particular catechist in question by pointing out that the Uganda martyrs[38] didn't leave the church because of persecution, and added that I couldn't give them permission they requested because the Eighth Beatitude was a mysteriously essential part of our religion.

I couldn't help wishing wistfully at the time though that the Gospel would have as direct and startling an impact on Americans as it does on Africans.

Sincerely,
Father Vince

May 1966[39]

Dear Relatives and Friends,

I mentioned the trouble our catechists had with one of the Eight Beatitudes—the one about being persecuted. The trouble they had with some of the other beatitudes was even more serious—and perhaps insoluble.

Take the one, "Blessed are the merciful—for they shall obtain mercy." They told me this goes against everything they have ever learned in their various tribal backgrounds. And as they spoke to me, it was not the thoughts of their tribal backgrounds that they were giving me, but their solid convictions as Christians—and more, teachers of Christianity, as they understood it—or rather, misunderstood it.

To them, mercy was no virtue, but a weakness. They told me that a man who was wronged by another was not a man unless he worked out his own revenge—even if it took all of his life to do so—or beyond his lifetime. One Christian catechist told me that if a man does not work out his revenge in his lifetime, he will have to come back in some other form, perhaps in animal form, most likely in the form of a black snake—to do

38. The Uganda Martyrs were a group of forty-five Roman Catholics and Anglicans put to death by the *kabaka* (ruler) of Buganda (now part of Uganda) between 1885 and 1887. The twenty-two martyrs who were Catholics were canonized by Pope Paul VI in 1964. Bishop Durning named half of the parishes in the new Arusha diocese after one or another of the martyrs, using their indigenous names.

39. May 1966 is also the date on the letter Donovan sent to his bishop, asking permission to visit and teach the gospel in the Maasai *bomas*, at the beginning of chapter 2 of *CR*.

so. I have reached the point of not being able to be shocked or startled at anything anymore. But I couldn't help thinking how unfit I have become for chatting with the Sodality women of St. Bridget's in Connecticut about their difficulties in arranging a cake sale.

This revenge is not an empty word on an African's lips but a reality in his life. I have seen it worked out in its most horrible forms. The slow and agonizing poisons obtained from a witch doctor, a young man hacking his brothers to pieces with a machete-like knife because they cheated him out of his land; a man dousing a woman who wronged him with a tin of gasoline when she wasn't looking, and making a living (or rather dying) torch out of her; a man coming to the mission to offer a mass for a man he was going to kill that night. It was only after the man left that the priest who took the offering thought there must be some mistake. How could you offer a mass of the dead for a person who was still living? There was no mistake—the person in question died that night. And finally, the most terrible revenge of all—the major vendetta of Hamlet, that incredible perversion of paganism and Christianity combined— killing a man when you are practically certain he is in his sins, with no time for repentance.[40] I have known them to send an African prostitute to an enemy and at the moment he is finished with her—to kill him—to make sure that he not only dies, but descends to the pits of Hell.

These people still live for the most part in the Old Testament. I had the experience of discovering with my catechists that chapter twenty-one of Exodus is nothing but everything they have ever learned from their mother's knee; they themselves were amazed to discover it. Read it sometime. It is the section about "eye for an eye, a tooth for a tooth." Read it and you will see an amazingly exact picture of African tribal, pagan life.

I tried hard to convince my catechists that we are living in the New Testament, the Testament of the Sermon on the Mount. I don't know if I succeeded.

Please pray for the missionaries who have wronged Africans in the Congo, the Sudan, Rhodesia, Angola, Mozambique—and Tanzania. Thank you for your help and interest.

Sincerely,
Father Vince

40. William Shakespeare, *Hamlet*, Act III, Scene III.

June 1966

Dear Relatives and Friends,

As I completed my three years at Usa River and my two years at the Catechetical Centre, and moved on to my new appointment, I couldn't help thinking of all you people and how much you had helped me in my work in Usa, and how grateful I was to all of you.

I boarded the bus of Ram Singh, an Indian Sikh,[41] who has the only transport between Arusha and Loliondo, my new destination. Ram Singh, a big powerful character in his late fifties or early sixties, with flowing gray beard and white turban wrapped around his head, is a person who is hard to forget. He is a real pioneer in travel and transport in this section of Tanzania. For thirty years, twice a week, going and returning, he has made the trip to Loliondo come rain or shine. The road between Arusha and Loliondo is perhaps the worst road in all of Tanzania. It is the worst road, called a main highway, that I have seen anywhere in the world in all my life. It is 250 miles long, but it takes a small car, like a Jeep or a Land Rover, eleven or twelve hours to make the journey. It takes Ram Singh's big seven and a half ton Thames truck sixteen hours to make the trip, if all goes well.

Thirty years ago he started making the trip with donkeys. It took him several months. Then, he graduated to mule carts. Finally, he arrived at the stage of huge lorries or trucks such as he has now. There are times when it rains, when even Ram Singh cannot get through—but he tries. He has been stuck on the highway for weeks at a time, moving fifty yards, a hundred yards, or a mile a day. He is the one who brings the post, our letters, back and forth for us. He is our lifeline, and one of our few contacts with the "outside world." By the way, that is why my address is Loliondo via Arusha. The big post office is in Arusha, the nearest town. The one room in Loliondo which serves as post office, radio station, and administration office, is a bit off the main line, and can't really be called a post office. They don't even sell stamps. We get them from Arusha. I got a letter recently from someone in the States who said,

41. Many Sikhs had been brought from India to East Africa in the 1890s by the British to work on the railways. In Arusha all the blacksmiths were Sikh. Many of them ran general stores out in the bush, and their weekly truckloads of provisions, mail and personnel provided a lifeline to remote places like Loliondo and Ngorongoro.

"Good heavens, if you live in such a place that the postman has to be told which way to go 'via', then you really *are* out in the bush." It's not really as bad as it sounds.

Ram Singh's bus is really a big truck, with three compartments besides the driver's seat. One right behind the driver's seat, with wooden benches for about twelve passengers, then a big section for supplies, and finally in the back another very narrow compartment, as wide as someone's lap, for five more passengers.

Into that back compartment went four manacled prisoners for the tiny prison in Loliondo, together with a guard. In the other passenger's compartment went twelve people, five of whom were an African mother and four pre-school age children. I shuddered, thinking of what the Safari was going to do to that mother.

As the guest of honor, I was invited into the front seat, together with an African policeman. I climbed in with sandwiches which a very kind person had thoughtfully prepared for me. We left at eleven o'clock in the morning. We arrived in Loliondo at 3:00 A.M.—the next morning, or wee hours of the night.

It was a Safari into the wildest, most rugged, most beautiful and interesting country I had ever seen.

Sincerely,
Father Vince.

5

LOLIONDO

(1966–1968)

Dear Relatives and Friends,

Many thanks again for all the wonderful help you are giving me.

As I continued on my drive to my new mission of Loliondo, I wondered if my parishioners were going to consist mainly of animals. . . .

Night found us in the middle of the Serengeti, and we stopped, and all of us got out of the big truck to stretch our legs and me to eat my sandwiches and drink some hot tea. It was unbelievable how cold the desert was at night. The clouds had cleared and it seemed as if the night was jealous of the spectacle of animals which the day had given us. The night put on an even more splendid spectacle. There were no mountains, no skyscrapers, not even any trees to block the vision of the sky.

I had all I could do to stop from saying, "Ooooh!" as I stepped out of the truck and looked up. You could see where the sky "touched the ground" at both horizons, and then vaulted up over the earth in a giant dome. You could almost see the world was round.

The stars out here always seem much clearer and closer because there are no lights to distort the vision, and no factories and no steel mills to cloud it. But the vision of the stars that night was the most magnificent I've ever seen in my life. I lay down on the ground and just looked up in awe. There was the Big Dipper upside down, and the Milky Way, and the Southern Cross tilted at a slight angle—and a million others.

I felt so strange, a white man in the midst of an African desert, just two degrees away from the Equator, surrounded by animals, lying there underneath the Southern Cross. A thought that strikes me about once a year struck me then. What was I doing so far away from home?

I sat up suddenly and was just about to start heading home when the driver blew his horn and called us all back to the truck. We continued our journey at about ten miles an hour and reached Loliondo at 3:00 AM. It was too late to find the mission, so I took out my sleeping bag and slept in the Indian *dukah* (shop) for what remained of the night. I think I dreamed of wildebeests.

Sincerely,
Father Vince

September 1966

Dear Relatives and Friends,

Many thanks from a guy who finds himself back again in the midst of the most basic and primitive missionary work.

At the northern end of the Serengeti Desert, you come to the highlands of Loliondo. Forty-five miles of unbelievable road through the hills lead you to the mission of Loliondo. When you arrive there and look around, you forget that there ever was a Serengeti Desert. There is a group of hills, tree and grass-covered hills, rounded and lush, forming the Loliondo Valley. The hills are about 8000 feet high, and on the side of one of them, at about 7300 feet, is Loliondo Mission. . . .[1]

1. As early as 1931, the Lutherans had discovered that, "Having natural water flows throughout the year, Loliondo was more or less permanently populated, not only by Maasai but also by other ethnic groups, such as Kikuyu. Since 1931, Loliondo was the seat for the assistant district officer and, as such, was something of a centre in the wilderness. These factors made Loliondo an attractive place for a mission" (Groop, *With the*

Loliondo means "the visible hill" in Masai. Loliondo Hill is the highest peak in this valley, well over 8000 feet. It must have been visible to the Masai from far away as they neared the end of their journey. The whole valley and the whole section takes its name from that peak today. They came to stay here. Every mountain peak, every valley, every stream, every field here has a Masai name today. It seems to be their hobby—giving names to things.

These are the toughest and hardiest of the Masai, much closer to the traditions of their ancestors. The warriors in this section live alone in their own kraals or circular enclosure of huts. No one else is allowed in there. They are real military fortifications, with a flag or banner flying proudly over them.

They are as completely oblivious of the twentieth century as can be imagined. They go on stealing cattle, fighting over girls, fighting lions and leopards, fighting wars with all the neighboring tribes, gleefully attacking anyone who ventures through their territory, and dancing their primitive hearts out under the noon-day sky. For them, the whole rest of the world are *ilmeg*, farmers and fools. They pay about as much attention to the proud and sensitive central government of Tanzania as if it didn't exist.

You may remember when I was home on leave I collected money for a hospital for the Masai. Since Loliondo was the most remote, cut off, and isolated section of Masailand, it was here that I decided to build it.[2] It stands here today as part of the Mission of Loliondo. It serves these wild sons of the plains.

Gospel, 160). The Catholic mission at Loliondo had been begun by Gene Hillman, who had been visiting the area since 1951. In August 1956, he built a fieldstone church with attached rooms for resident priests. The first priests were Butch McGinley and Jim Burke (who began *The Loliondo Mission Journal*), then, at different times, Dennis Durning, Fred Trumbull, and Tom Tunney. Gerry Kohler and (Austrian) Herb Watschinger came in 1964, then Donovan in 1966. Medical sisters first arrived in 1960, and, around 1967, a convent with a chapel was built for their use. The complex grew to include a hospital at nearby Wasso. The Mission served an area of 5,000 square miles.

2. Responsibility for the founding of the hospital at Wasso, eight miles from Loliondo, is variously attributed. In 1964, Fr. Gallagher refers to it as "the new hospital Bishop Durning has started at Wasso" (Gallagher, *Six Weeks*, 10). The Web site of the Catholic Archdiocese of Arusha Medical Board says, "The catholic priest and physician, the late Dr. Herbert Watschinger, founded Wasso Hospital as a mission hospital in 1964" (www .ambhospitals.org). Watschinger himself says he was asked in 1960 to build a hospital in Loliondo. Kohler says Fred Trumble, "a great builder," had started the hospital.

They take some getting used to. They call me *Sapuk,* which means big or tall. There is no use arguing with them. The way their names stick, I'll probably be *Sapuk* for the next 300 years.

Sincerely,
Father Vince

October 1966

Dear Relatives and Friends,

My brother has been keeping me informed about how much all of you have been helping me. I can't tell you how much I appreciate your interest and help.

I still remember vividly, when I was home on leave, the times when I made appeals for a hospital for the Masai—on television with Alice Weston (Luncheon At the One's[3]) on the radio and at several benefits. I was very anxious when I got back to get started on the hospital right away. But the difficulties were tremendous. I chose Loliondo because it was the most remote, out of the way spot in all of Masailand. It was ideal in that it would cater to the needs of the most forgotten Masai. But it was nightmarish as regards the actual building problems involved. I have already described to you the state of the roads between Arusha, where the stores and shops are, and Loliondo, where the hospital was to be built.

The central Masai Council,[4] located about 200 miles away from Loliondo had to get in on the act also deciding where the plot should be located, whether there was enough water and a hundred other things which they love to throw into every discussion. It took months and months and months before we could even think of beginning to build.

An American brother, Brother Francis,[5] was put in charge of the building, but he had to just sit and wait in Arusha, until the Masai fin-

3. *Luncheon at the Ones* was a "ladies' chat show" on *Channel 11* (the "ones"), then the NBC television affiliate in Pittsburgh. Alice Weston was the host.

4. The Maasai District Council was the government administration serving all of Maasailand. Its offices were in Monduli.

5. Brother Francis was originally William Sullivan (born in State Island NYC, 1918). He learned his "bush skills" with President F. D. Roosevelt's Civilian Conservation Corps during the Great Depression, and joined the Spiritans in East Africa in the 1950s. As well as constructing buildings for the Order, he did some "boma teaching" under

ished all their pow-wows. But when he finally got the go-ahead signal to begin building, I think he wished he were back in Arusha waiting. I don't think you can begin to imagine the difficulties in moving tons and tons of cement and other building materials up Ngorongoro Mountain, down its back, across the Serengeti Desert and along the famous muddy roads of Loliondo. Brother Francis told me there were many times when he would gladly have strangled me in my sleep for choosing Loliondo as the spot to build. When a seven ton lorry [truck], loaded with cement, gets bogged down in the mud, there is only one way to get it out. You must unload the seven tons of cement, jack the lorry out of the mud, move ahead a little, but not too far—reload the cement and go on to the next mud hole.

And then there was the actual building itself. If you remember, a Pittsburgh architect[6] very generously donated the plans for the hospital. They were magnificent—but unfortunately they were not quite realistic enough for Africa. The main lines of the plans were followed—but tremendous alterations had to be made, while the building was going on. I flew out in a small plane to see how it was getting on. It was pretty much of a mess at that time and plans were being altered on the spot. The building was finally finished, but I never saw it again—until I was stationed there this year.

When I drove up to it in a Land Rover and saw the long, sprawling, buildings, each section a delightfully different light color, nestling under the many trees on the river bank, with a beautiful lawn and unbelievable variety of flowers planted from one end to the other—I could not believe my eyes. To say I was touched was an understatement. To say I was grateful to Brother Francis would not quite adequately express my feelings.

There is now an Austrian Doctor[7] in charge of the hospital, and two Austrians, who are sisters (one of them a midwife), assisting him. Because of the many safaris we take here to far flung places, we all have

---

Donovan. In 1967, the *Journal* reported one of many vehicle breakdowns in the bush and comments, "Bro. Francis to the rescue as per usual, and all returned safely tonight." He died, still in Tanzania, in 2009.

6. There appears to be no record of who this was.

7. As a medical student, Dr. Herbert Watschinger had been drafted into Hitler's army and fought on the Russian Front at the end of World War II. At the end of the War, he went to seminary and was ordained in the Diocese of Linz. He was recruited by Sister Guida, who was home leave in Austria, to come and work in Loliondo. He was involved in the founding of the hospital at Wasso and later the one at Endulen (where Fr. Ned Marchessault serves). He wrote a book about his experiences, entitled *Don't Give up Hope: A Life in Service of the Maasai.*

to learn medicine. I'm being trained in diagnosing sickness, giving injections, administering medicine and first-aid—and a few other things. . . .

> Sincerely,
> Father Vince

[The following letter to Donovan's family is in response to news of his father's death. It is a little cryptic, but the background seems to be that he was flown by the Flying Doctor from Loliondo to Nairobi in order to telephone his family, and then flown back the next day.]

November 19, 1966

Dear Gib, Bill, Matt, Nora, and Aunt Gert,

Greetings from the worst correspondent known in African annals. Sometimes it is not very pleasant being the worst correspondent— especially at a time like this. To be out of contact for so long, and then have news like this come along is really shattering. I feel so very bad about it that I cannot begin to tell you. Neither can I tell you all the things I wish I had done . . .

I'm sorry that it was so much trouble for you to get in contact with me. I'm a bit off the beaten track. I got the news when I was on my way to, of all things, a political rally. Big political leaders coming to visit Loliondo for the first time since independence. Even though Europeans are not honored guests at these affairs, I felt I had better go, put in an appearance, and hear what was being said. I was just getting ready to sit down to watch the proceedings when a Land Rover, with the Protestant Minister in it, drove up. He waved to me and called me over. Then he told me the news and I was stunned. He took me to his house where he has a radio hookup with Arusha. I got in touch with the bishop and he told me to get in contact with you as soon as I could. The Protestant Pastor, Mr. Simonson,[8] offered to leave with me right then and drive into Arusha all

---

8. Dave Simonson was the Lutheran missionary, based in Loliondo, who gave Donovan a box of books, including three titles by Roland Allen, who is not mentioned in the letters but whose influence is explicit in *CR*, chapter 3, the section "St. Paul and Mission." Simonson had been sent to Loliondo after criticizing his bishop for tribal favoritism (Groop, *With the Gospel*, 306). The *Journal* for August 19, 1965, noted, "The new Lutheran pastor, Mr. Simonson, arrived by plane today."

through the night. That is a desperate trip, and although I appreciated his offer, I didn't want to take him up on it. I went back to the mission house, where we have a radio hookup with the flying doctor in Nairobi. I explained my difficulty and they said they would send a plane for me the following morning. They did and I flew to Nairobi. I checked in at a hotel and I felt sorry for you waiting so long in the early hours of the morning. It was afternoon in Nairobi. I was just sitting around the hotel room looking out the window afterwards when the pilot who brought me to Nairobi suddenly appeared at the hotel, and said I shouldn't be sitting around alone and that he would like me to meet his family. He took me to his beautiful home in Nairobi where his wife had made a special meal, and his kids entertained me. They couldn't have been nicer, and they were absolute strangers.

The very next morning I was brought back to Loliondo by plane. So I spent one day in civilization, got the call through, and was back in the mission yesterday. Those flying doctor people are really nice.

I was glad to hear that Fathers Gallagher and Trumbull had planned to concelebrate for the funeral. Was Joe Healy there? How is Father Trumbull making out? He was in Loliondo for seven years. He finally became so frustrated with the work of a mission priest, and so interested in medicine that he asked permission to study medicine. He's got a long hard road ahead of him. I hope he makes it. If determination and motivation count for anything, he will.[9]

I've appreciated the letters I have received from you, Bill and Joani and Nora. It hardly seems that four, going on five years, have passed since I last saw all of you. You know, Jome's death and Dad's will not seem real to me until I come home and find them not there.

I can't tell you how sorry I feel for all of you because of Dad's death. I am of course saying masses for him and for all of you.

I trust that all of your respective families are doing well. Please say hello to all of them for me.

Love,
Vince

9. Trumbull was influenced by his positive experience of missionary doctors in East Africa (such as Watschinger) and of the Flying Doctors out of Nairobi. He told Kohler that religious talk had become "dust in his mouth." He returned to the US, qualified as a medical doctor, and later married his childhood sweetheart, a hospital administrator in Connecticut, who had waited for him.

November 1966

Dear Relatives and Friends,

I had hoped I would see my father once more, next year when I came home, but I somehow sensed in the airport when I was leaving for Africa that I never would. His death saddens me and leaves me feeling kind of lost. Please remember him in your prayers, a man who has been lonely and sad, I think, for some twenty-four years, since my mother died.

There is another tribe with whom we deal, equally as fascinating as the Masai. They are the Sonjo. Their country is just over the hills from Loliondo, but impassable by car. So you have to go there over forty miles of steadily deteriorating road. You're riding through the wilderness, take this little used road, and finally you find yourself on the edge of a cliff looking down into an amazing, green, lush, tropical valley. This is the valley of the Sonjos, one of the most primitive and backward tribes in East Africa.

You have to hand it to their ancestors or forefathers who found this paradise in the midst of the wilderness. It is a fertile valley watered by the rivers that begin above Loliondo—but outside of that, it is completely, and I mean completely, cut off from the outside world. Its only link with the outside world is that battered road, which no one in his right mind (except a missionary) would ever travel over. Can you imagine a people so cut off from the outside world that their only contact with it is the visit of a lone missionary or of a few Masai who wander into the valley? That is the state of the Sonjo tribe.[10]

The location of their valley of paradise in the midst of a desert is the least surprising thing about the Sonjo. You drive slowly down the steep escarpment that leads into the valley, and you find that their villages, all five of them, are built, not on the valley floor, but on the steep walls of the valley. Each village is a fortress with a thick barricade running around it, with a single huge fortified gate serving as the entrance. It is for all the world like you would have pictured an African settlement, or

10. In spite of this comment, the *Journal* reported on January 17, 1967, that: "The [Sonjo] religion of Shambage [Khambegeu] is sweeping Masailand. Not only do they come to Sonjo for the Mase feasts . . . but 'services' to Shambage are being conducted by the Masai themselves these days—mainly to pray for rain in the famine time."

African village, if you had never been to Africa! It must have been the way most Africans lived seventy or a hundred years ago.

It is the most unforgettable experience to go to Sonjo. You never lose the air of unreality, of walking as if in a dream. The valley is steaming hot despite its fine watering places. A stillness and quietness hangs over the valley, the stillness of centuries. This is a place that time has passed by. You are reminded not only of long ago, but almost of prehistoric times, like the Garden of Eden—after the fall.

And the people. They are gentle, friendly—and mysterious. They have fine, even features, more like the Masai than the Bantus, but still unmistakably unique. Their women wear the most tantalizing garment yet devised by African fashion designers. When they walk through the villages they cover themselves with a long cloth which reaches from shoulder to knees. But when working in the fields on the floor of the valley, from 7:00 in the morning until 6:30 in the evening, or when dancing in the village square on moonlit nights, they wear nothing else except a little skirt about six inches long from waist to hem, made out of leather and cut into very thin strips so that for all the world it looks like a miniature hula skirt or grass skirt. Married women don't cut it into strips but wear it like a leather apron.

The young men, or warriors, dress just like the Masai warriors and carry the same artillery as the Masai—sword and spear.

The pagan religion among the Sonjo is almost as developed and organized as our own, with priests, sacrifices, feast days, temples (the only pagan temples I know of in East Africa) and elaborate rites. Their religion is based on a belief of a god called Khambegeu, who became a man, lived in the Sonjo valley, preached, worked miracles, suffered, died, and rose again, and will come again at the end of the world to save those Sonjos marked with his mark. If you are amazed by the resemblance to Christianity, so are we.[11] But we are certain of one thing. This religion preceded the coming of the white man and Christianity to Africa. If there is a real connection with Christianity, that connection must have taken place in the early ages of the Church.

At any rate, for these people the Sonjo Valley is the place where God walked and lived on earth, literally the Holy Land. We are strictly

11. For a fuller account of Sonjo mythologies and religion, and their relationship to Christianity, see Vähäkangas. He believes that less than 10 percent of the Sonjo today are baptized.

forbidden to enter or even go near their temples. This presents an entirely different kind of problem for us—a highly organized, developed and openly hostile pagan religion.

It is my problem, since I am the one who goes there.[12] I go to Sonjo every weekend and stay about half a week each time. Eventually I may live there permanently. We have a little house beneath the largest village. It is a strange sensation living there, the only white man in the valley, the only white man among a whole tribe.[13] I'll have to tell you some time what it feels like to be one of a minority (the only one as a matter of fact). The primitive, child-like innocence of these people never ceases to fascinate me. I see it when I talk to them. I see it when I watch them dancing in the moonlight. I saw it one evening at 6:30 when I was bathing in the river. Quite suddenly, right next to me, there were several Sonjo maidens asking if they could borrow my soap!

Thanking you once again for your generous support.

Sincerely,
Father Vince

[In Donovan's letter of January 1967, he describes a visit to the coast, where he went to visit Bagamoyo, the first Spiritan mission opened on the African mainland. This letter forms the basis of the section, "Bwaga Moyo" in chapter 1 of CR. For a scholarly assessment of this phase of the Spiritans' work, see Kollmann, Evangelization.*]*

March 1967

Dear Relatives and Friends,

Thank you for your continuing support. Without your generosity I don't know what I would do . . .

---

12. Since his arrival in 1965, Kohler had also been visiting the Sonjo for days at a time, sometimes walking the whole way there from Loliondo and back. On his last visit in mid-July 1968, just before Donovan arrived, "he finished presenting the Kerygma . . . and bade farewell to everyone" (*Journal*).

13. Although this was true, Lutheran pastors and evangelists of the Chagga, Meru, and Pare tribes had been at work among the Sonjo since the 1940s (personal communication from Vähäkangas). According to Kim Groop, there were 150 Sonjo Lutherans in 1960, and 251 in 1963 (Groop, *With the Gospel*, 287).

With the slaves gone, and the schools gone—what is a missionary going to do? I was reading a report recently, given in Washington, DC, about the state of the missions. The one who made the report traveled extensively and interviewed missionaries from all over Africa. His conclusion was that since Independence, the missionaries in Africa had lost their nerve, their sense of direction and purpose.[14]

I have witnessed this confusion. Some say what we must do now is get into the organizing of hospitals and dispensaries, or the organization of some other social works. This sounds convincing on the surface, but it really just does not go deeply enough into the problem. To say, "Let us get into the organization of hospital systems" is just the same as saying, "Let us get into the organization of school systems." That has been the cry of the missionary for this whole twentieth century. And that truly is just the same as saying, "Let us get into the organization of slave buying," which was the cry of the nineteenth century. We saw how that turned out.

Let us not get into any organization at all! We missionaries did not come to Africa to start a school system or a hospital system any more than we came to start a slave buying system. We came to found the African church—and then get out. . . .

[The buying of land to provide for former slaves] started a precedent that is hard to break. Most young missionaries coming out to Africa believe that the surest way to show that they are zealous and working hard is to somehow acquire land in the midst of the people for an eventual out-station or mission. Acquiring land seems to be our primary preoccupation. It is a hangover from the slave days. It gives rise to the "mission compound" concept, one of the most paralyzing concepts a missionary has to deal with. If you stop to think of it, St. Paul in all his travels never looked for land anywhere, or tried to acquire it. He didn't think it was necessary for the job he had to do. His work was essentially something else entirely. And he didn't do so badly at it.

Sincerely,
Father Vince

---

14. Cf. the section "Up from Slavery" in chapter 1 of *CR*.

April 1967

Dear Relatives and Friends,

. . . There are so many traces of the old slave buying days of the missions. I can't go into all of them, but I would like to mention some of them. One of them is, of course, the missionaries' excessive attention to and care of children . . . When the second phase of African missionary work began, school work, it is obvious which section of the population once again gets the main attention of the missionary—the children. Wherever you go in East Africa you see that children take up most of a missionary's time. We have become a child-centered organization.[15]

Stop to think of it. The Pope, of course, is the head of all missionary endeavor. We march to his orders. Then there is the Congregation of the Propagation of the Faith, with headquarters in Rome, and with a Cardinal at its head. In every major city in the Western World there is an office of the Propagation of the Faith collecting money for this huge task. Then the Maryknoll Fathers and Sisters, and the White Fathers and a hundred others! This whole gigantic machinery put in motion, the whole missionary church in action, a worldwide organization in a state of campaign and assault—on and towards what? Primarily, towards the children of this world! I hardly think that this is an effort and a posture worthy of the universal Church of Christ.

Our concentration on schools has brought with it many undesirable effects. We have neglected the teaching of religion to adults. We have neglected the training of African priests to take our place. We have neglected the development of the African Liturgy. We have begun to regard the successful running of our schools as the measure of success achieved in our whole missionary effort.

We have let the African people think of us as a land-grabbing, child-centered, school-running institution—instead of what we are supposed to be. What else could they think? We have brought an institutional Christianity to Africa.

Christianity is not an institution. It is a way of life. But no matter how strenuously we might tell the Africans that, they can hardly believe us, and you cannot blame them. At every step we put an institution between them and us, or between us and this Christian way of life that we talk about. We say we come to preach the gospel of Christ and the

15. Donovan returns to this theme in his letters of September and December 1968.

Christian way of life—and we buy land, or we buy a farm and hire men to run it, or we put up a school building and an educational system, or we put up a hospital, or we put up a mission house, or we put up a church building—before they even know what Christianity is. Or they think they know what it is—those buildings, those institutions. We say we come to set up the church of Christ in Africa, that is the African Church of Christ—but we set up a million things before we even attempt to set up that African Church. And everything we set up instead of it hinders us to some degree from establishing what we came to establish.

I am more and more convinced that every single building we put up, every institution we begin out here, buildings and institutions which will, of course, require the continued presence of white men to run and supervise and maintain them puts off the day when the African Church can come into existence on its own. Even the house in which I am now sitting and writing, which no African could ever maintain, puts off the day when I can leave and let the African Masai priest take over. This is a personal agony which I could never adequately convey to you—this conviction and conclusion at which I have arrived. It is the most painful conclusion of my missionary life. We want to spend our lives here, in this beautiful country—this big game country—among these most interesting people. We want them around us, dependent on us, giving us a sense of security and comfort. We have no intention of ever leaving here—not for the next hundred years anyway.

What have we come to establish: The Holy Ghost Fathers? a school system? a hospital system? a system of social services?—or the African Church?

What would you do if you were a missionary who suddenly realized just how badly it was that we had lost our sense of direction?

Sincerely,
Father Vince

May 1967

Dear Relatives and Friends,

Remembering the failure of the apostolate to the slaves, and concerned about the misdirection of the school apostolate in Africa, when

I came to Loliondo, I began to wonder and worry about what to do with the Masai. They were practically untouched by Christianity.

Work among the Masai in Tanzania was begun thirteen years ago, by the Catholic Mission.[16] There are hundreds of Catholic Masai. But most of them are schoolboys, and all of them are scattered over thousands and thousands of square miles, without any vital relation to each other or to the church of which they are a part. Many of them on leaving school, after Standard Four or Standard Eight, return to an environment that is so foreign to the Christian life that they are simply swallowed up in paganism, retaining not much more than their Christian names.[17]

I remember recently meeting a Masai warrior, all decked out in his battle gear, who told me his name was John. I asked him if he was a Christian and he said he was. I asked him then why he became a Christian and he said, "Because I went to school." But the last he saw of Christianity was the last day he spent in school. He thought it was no more necessary to continue on with the practice of Christianity than it could have been to continue on with the study of Geography after he left school. Religion and Geography were both school subjects.

I began to wonder if it would be possible to leave aside schools and education, leave aside hospitals and medicine, leave aside all social works and go directly to the Masai and preach the gospel directly to them.[18] I began to wonder not only if it could be possible, but also if it wouldn't be far better. And I was not interested in children—but in adults.

---

16. Around 1951, Gene Hillman was assigned to Arusha parish, which included the town itself, the surrounding areas, the colonial plantations, and all of Maasailand—a total of 24,000 square miles. His superior was Fr. Egbert Durkin (1912–1987), an English Spiritan, who had arrived in 1944, had taken charge of the Arusha mission in 1951, and was later to become Provincial Superior in the UK (Koren, *Memorial*, 425). Together, Durkin and Hillman traveled the length and breadth of their "parish." Durkin supported Hillman's interest in going to the cattle markets to meet the leading people among the Maasai. Hillman pioneered Catholic schools in the area, and baptized numerous students.

17. Cf. the section "Ndangoya" in chapter 2 of *CR*.

18. His letter to Bishop Durning on this issue (*CR*, chapter 2) is dated May 1966. Hillman comments: "The bishop was approachable . . . and he would encourage a person, 'Go try it!'" Kohler adds: "Loliondo [is] where Durning cut his teeth, and so he had a soft spot for Loliondo to begin with."

Donovan setting up his safari tent near a Maasai *boma*, c. 1970.

Donovan standing on the Sale plains, looking towards Oldonyo L'Engai.

I remember reading a major article in *Newsweek* several years ago concerning missionary work all over the world. It contended that social work, schools, hospitals, etc., was the *only* way missionary activity could be carried out today. The article quoted several missionaries, Catholics among them, as saying that the direct preaching of the gospel in the manner of St. Paul was an impossibility today in the mission fields.

I wonder if such an opinion does not stem from the mentality that the pagan peoples of this earth are a kind of lost people—that they are not quite bright enough, or open enough, or good enough to accept Christianity directly, if it is presented to them, but must somehow be *lured* into Christianity.

I have heard this opinion expressed often enough about that uniquely pagan tribe in Tanzania, the Masai: "It is impossible to preach the gospel directly to the Masai."

Well, the Masai would be a good test. They are probably the most difficult pagans in all of East Africa. If the direct approach worked among the Masai, it should work anywhere.

With this thought as companion I went with a catechist[19] to a carefully selected Masai kraal, called on several carefully selected Masai elders, and said to them directly, "You know us. You have become accustomed to seeing us working in schools and hospitals. You have heard us talking about the grazing of cattle and many other things. Today we come to you not to talk about schools or hospitals or cattle or anything like that. Today we come to talk to you only about God and religion. We want to know if you would be interested in learning about the Christian religion, and perhaps after learning about it, actually becoming Christians?"

Their answer was straight and simple and startling. They said, "Yes, we would be very interested. Why have you waited so long to come to ask us?"[20]

I hardly had time to recover from the shock of their answer before going to another kraal to ask the same question. From there I went on to another kraal and another and another. And in each place the reaction was identical.

"Why have you not come to us before?"

Why not indeed? That answer of theirs, in question form, has been the beginning for me of the most interesting, important and disturbing work in which I have ever become involved. I would love to tell you about it and will continue next month.

19. Paul Soiyaan, who had attended one of Hillman's schools. He had followed his brother in converting from Lutheranism to Catholicism.

20. Cf. the section "Ndangoya" in chapter 2 of *CR*.

Thanks again for your continuing support. It has been a tremendous help to me.

Sincerely,
Father Vince

September 1967

Dear Relatives and Friends,

Hello again from a guy who got lost for awhile, not like the poor Peace Corps Volunteer who underrated the chilling challenge of Masailand and has disappeared,[21] but just lost in the complexity and loneliness of my work. I have not forgotten any of you, though, and I am extremely grateful to all of you.

The loneliness, I refer to, is not exactly a physical loneliness. It is rather a loneliness of isolation in missionary policy and activity. I have continued the work of going directly to the Masai, and it is the most gratifying work I have ever done, but it has proved to be a shattering education. There has been a basic missiology or mission strategy and the policy leaves much to be desired. Much worse, I found I could no longer agree with it all. As a matter of fact, I disagree with it in everything from A to Z. This is a frightening position to be in. It turns the whole missionary world upside down.

In an article in the *National Catholic Reporter*,[22] I tried to describe some of the results of my work, but I did not go into all the reasons, motivation and convictions underlying the work. It would have been impossible in an article. I think it would be impossible for me to explain it to you now, in any complete way. It is very complex and complicated. But I would like to begin to talk with you about some of the things involved. I hope you don't mind.

One problem is the question of individual conversion versus group or community conversion. In the western tradition, one is urged to stand on his own two feet, and not to depend on anyone else. This is the

21. Peace Corps Volunteer Mark Raymaker disappeared (with his rifle) in Maasailand in 1967. The Peace Corps database reports that he was presumed eaten by lions.

22. "The Church in East Africa—100 Futile Years," *The National Catholic Reporter,* May 24, 1967.

western way—especially the American way. This is not the African way. This might seem a small point, but I am convinced that in choosing the western way rather than the African way, we have steered the missionary apostolate down a wrong path. Our whole missionary effort is geared to the individual. Yet the African way is the community way. I may be alone in my conviction, but I believe that if we had followed the African way, after these hundred years of work in Africa, the missionary task here would be finished. And I believe that if we continue to follow the European way, we will never finish our missionary work in Africa.

ABOVE: Donovan performing the first communal baptism of Maasai in Loliondo town, c. 1967. Anna (?) Parokwa was sponsor for women. Photograph by Herbert Watschinger.

RIGHT: Donovan baptizing a Maasai elder at Ng'arua in the Loliondo area, c. 1967. Thomas Parokwa was the sponsor for men.

This individual approach has influenced our teaching of Religion, or Catechetics, our conversions through the schools, our liturgy and conferring of the sacraments, our training of candidates for the priesthood in the seminaries, our very idea of the work and meaning of the priest, our church and mission buildings.

A priest in America might approach an individual, influence him, interest him in religion, ask him to come to the rectory for instruction, and convert him—all in the brilliant Fulton Sheen[23] method of individual conversion. We have tried to carry that method to Africa. We visit a particular man, and ask him if he would like to come to the mission for instruction. Even worse, we don't even visit him. We hope the mission itself will attract individuals to come to ask for instruction. Even if he or they do come, even if many individuals come, we have approached them only as individuals. And while we might expect individuals to walk a mile, or two miles or five miles every day to come to the mission, we could never expect a community to come. Structure of a community, with its division of labor and so forth, forbids this. Our apostolate is geared to individuals. This comes, I think, from our American background. Our apostolate should be geared to communities.

We have worked at great length with children in the schools, perhaps with great numbers of them, but this is still on the level of individuals. A classroom, in no way, represents an African community. The structure of an African community is not based on numbers, but on a hierarchy—the ruling elders, other elders, and the rest of the community in unison with them. We must approach them on this level.

The approach to children in the school is directly opposite to the community approach. The direct approach to youth, an approach perhaps based on our American worship of youth, is disastrous. Either the young people refuse to enter the church, as the Masai youth have, because to enter without the elders means to buck the whole tribal system, or we succeed in getting some young people, and in so doing automatically put them outside the tribal structure.

If we approach individual elders, we find they normally refuse, because they cannot make decisions in this way. Even if they agreed, we

23. Fulton John Sheen (1895–1979) was an American archbishop of the Roman Catholic Church. He was Bishop of Rochester and American television's first preacher of note, hosting *Life is Worth Living* between 1951 and 1957. He later hosted "The Bishop Sheen Program" in syndication, with a virtually identical format from 1961 to 1968.

might well find that all further progress in the area is blocked, because we did not go to the ruling elders first. And if we go to a ruling elder on his own as an individual, we find that he also must refuse. He is not a dictator or autocrat. He can only agree in unison with other elders who help him to rule. All this goes against the American grain, but it is the African way, which we have consistently ignored. Christianity must come to those people in their way, not ours.

All this is theory. But when I put it into practice, I found it to be true. In every section of Loliondo Mission, I have gone to the ruling elders and told them there is something important I wanted to talk about with them. Inevitably they told me to wait until they could call other elders, or to come back when they had all the elders assembled. Then when they were all assembled, they sat in a semi-circle facing me, and the ruling elder would ask, "Now, what do you want?" I said each time that I wanted to talk with them about God. After hearing this they would talk among themselves for awhile and at the end the ruling elder would infallibly say to me, "Who can refuse to talk about God?"[24]

The next step, I have found, is Christianity.

There seems to be no limit to this. It is only the scant number of hours in the day and the few days in the week which keeps this entire section from becoming Christian.

Love,

Father Vince

October 1967

Dear Relatives and Friends,

Hello again from a guy who is just yearning to see all of you with everything that is in him, but is delayed just a little while by the necessity of finishing off some very important things.

The last time, I explained our way of working with the Masai as a community. Perhaps some of you think that this method makes impossible the dealing with people on a personal level. Just the contrary. It is only in a community that an African personality can develop and blossom. And we have seen some remarkable instances of this blossom-

24. Cf. the section "Ndangoya" in chapter 2 of CR.

ing of extraordinary personalities, especially among the Masai women. Christianity adds that gentle something to an already existing community that makes it possible for a woman to come into her own, in a way that is not possible in an existing pagan community. I have seen the look of gratitude in the eyes of several Masai women, for whom Christianity has indeed been the "Good news."

I just wish I could convey to you the happiness and even excitement I feel about the way the work among the Masai is going. Doors are being opened which perhaps have never been opened before. I don't know if I could explain to you, briefly, what I mean.

When religion comes to a pagan tribe, several possibilities can occur. Individual items can change. Several features in the old way of life can change and be replaced by some things from the new. People could stop wearing fetishes or charms and start wearing medals. People could start genuflecting or making the sign of the cross instead of their old way of praying. But changes like this are very superficial and don't mean anything. But this is what has happened in almost every case with the Christianization of African tribes. The abandoning of African clothes for western clothes on the day of Baptism is another example of this superficial change. What often happens in such a case is that Christianity is only a shell, and the deep needs of these people continue to be satisfied in a pagan way, not in a Christian way. Before Christianity came, paganism was for these people a structure that held up all of their life, fulfilled all the functions of their lives, satisfied all the needs. There was no gap between religion and life. Christianity came and left a vacuum in their lives, which vacuum became, in effect, a reservoir preserving the old pagan religion. For the real deep needs of their lives, they turn not to Christianity, but to paganism. Paganism takes care of those needs; Christianity does not.

Paganism looks to initiation rites and childbirth and fertility and lack of it. It looks to the grazing of cattle and planting of crops; it looks to famine and floods and wars. It looks to the reverence due to ancestors; it looks to marriage as a meaningful step in the life of the tribe. The Christianity that has come to Africa looks to none of these things.

The Chagga tribe of Kilimanjaro is the best example I can think of to demonstrate this. They are probably the most Christianized tribe of Tanzania. Western in education, western in dress, western in the Christian names they bear, the churches they worship in, and the hymns they sing, they are nevertheless a very troubled people, as far as religion goes. They still feel a desperate need to honor and placate their ancestors. The Christianity brought to them forbids this. They continue to do it, to take part in sacrifices of sheep and goats offered to their ancestors, sometimes right after Mass, back in their own homes. They feel guilty about it and confess it in confession. They still have a tribal marriage ceremony, carried on parallel to the religious ceremony held in the Christian Church. They still have circumcisions which are frowned on by the church, miss Sunday mass for months in the period surrounding the ceremony, and then confess it all afterwards in the sacrament of Penance. In 1960, when so many people thought the world was coming to an end, they flocked in the evenings to the ancient pagan groves and sacred trees (which have never been cut down), carrying rosaries in their hands. The greatest crises always seem to push them back to the paganism which everyone thought they had abandoned. So, externally the African customs change to European ones which they think are Christian, and inside the old paganism continues—a reservoir of paganism which one day might well once again fill the vacuum which Christianity has left in their lives.

We have tried with these new Masai Christians to bring only the bare essentials of Christianity, stripped of everything that is European. But we have insisted, from the beginning, that these bare essentials of Christianity are enough to carry the whole Masai life, enough to fulfill all the functions of the Masai life, enough to satisfy all the needs of the Masai life.

Together with the Masai women, we will bless the cows as they go off in the early morning. We will pray with the mother who is about to give birth, while she is being anointed for this solemn and important event. We will pray with the woman especially who is sterile and cannot give birth, in a fertility feast. We will pray over their sick, and we will fight with all the powers that Christianity puts at our disposal to ward off the evil spirits that seem to hover over their lives. Their marriage ceremony takes several days out in the Masai villages. Why should we bring them in to a church for a ceremony of rings and veils and joined hands, which has meaning only in the churches and marriage offices of Europe and America? Instead, we will go out and live with them in the Masai kraals and perform the sacrament of Matrimony there, even if it takes several days to do so.

I am delaying my trip home because a Masai elder, a new Christian, came to me and asked me to join with him in a big feast day. He is having a circumcision ceremony in which a child of his, a youth, will go through the initiation rites and become an adult member of the Masai tribe. He said to me with nervousness and fear in his voice (fear at the thought of being refused), "There is nothing I would like more, nothing would make me more happy, than to have you come and make this a Christian ceremony." Circumcision is the most important day in a Masai's life.

Just the thought of it—for the first time in Masai history, a Christian priest, going with the select elders, to give the final indoctrination to the youth! And after the elders have imparted the values which they consider most important, and the bits of history which they consider most memorable, the priest, for the first time, will impart that little bit of light of Christianity which has transformed many tribes before this. And he will be there for the ceremonies the night before, and on the day itself, in the midst of the ceremonies, bringing Christianity with him into a ceremony and a tribal structure that might well go back a thousand years into the past. It is the first time that I know of that an African circumcision ceremony will have been Christianized. I think the Masai elder senses the significance and importance of the event. And I think I do, too. Many Masai guests come from far away for circumcision. There are going to be an awful lot of surprised pagans on that day.

Next week, I will baptize my last group of Masai before heading for home, right next to Oldonyo L'Engai, the volcano in Masailand. I just came back from there after making final preparations. I can still see some of those elders, in the evening hour, looking up at Oldonyo L'Engai (the Mountain of God), the home of that cruel, arbitrary god of theirs who played with men like so many puppets. I wonder what thoughts were going through their heads on the eve of their Baptism. I can still see the leading elders in the places where we have already baptized, standing up during our Mass and giving sermons to the Masai, explaining Christianity to the Masai, and what it means in the Masai life.[25]

---

25. The *Journal* for January 1967 noted that "At the Masai mass in Ngarua, Kiriko [called Keriko in *CR* chapter 4—the section entitled "The nations"] gave the talk today. And resumed without assistance the entire doctrine [with] which the people had been presented: from Adam and sin to Christ and redemption and the orporor [age brotherhood] of the Church."

Donovan and Kohler (left) concelebrating the first Mass with baptized Maasai in the Loliondo area, c. 1967.

Donovan baptizing an uncircumcised Maasai boy in the Loliondo area, assisted by Maasai catechist Thomas Parokwa (Kohler is in the background).

I can still see the Masai woman, who having heard our final instruction before Baptism, asked, "Is that what you mean by Christianity, and is it possible that it is true?" and then put her head down on her knees and sobbed like a baby.

I can see them all now, as I prepare to go home and leave them, and I wonder if I could convey to you how much I love these people. Even more, I wonder if I could convey to you my hope, even my conviction, that a light, faint and dim and wavering now—but a real light—has come to the people of the Masai Steppes in East Africa.

And I wonder if I could convey to you just how happy I will be to see all of you again in this month of October.

Love,
Father Vince

[Donovan was on leave in the USA from October 1967 till May 1968. He returned only to find that he was being transferred.]

July 1968

Dear Relatives and Friends

. . . When I got to Arusha, our Diocesan Center, I found that the bishop [Durning] had already gone out to the Loliondo area of Masailand and was waiting for me there. The only word he left was that he had a job for me "somewhere in Masailand" and would explain it to me when I come. So I took off as soon as I could, in the four-wheel- drive Toyota, on the long safari to Loliondo. It was only 250 miles away, but it would take as long as the flight from London to Nairobi. It was night when I reached the Serengeti Desert, and the stars in their millions covered the desert like a ceiling, and I was once again alone underneath the Southern Cross, where I have spent so many nights of my life. I was home.

Love,
Father Vince

September 1968

Dear Relatives and Friends,

It is said that gratitude is nothing but love running out to meet love—love on the part of those being kind to him. That would be the best description of my feeling towards you. If someone were to ask me to describe my feeling towards all of you people who have been so good to me, I would have to answer simply, "It is love."

When I got to my destination of Loliondo, the bishop was waiting for me with a peculiar smile on his face. He said, "You had better sit down." He asked me about my leave at home, how everybody was—but I could see he was anxious to get to the point.

He said: "I know how interested you are in the Masai communities which you have brought into Christianity. But you always claimed that the work of a first-line missionary was simply to bring the people into Christianity and then leave them, with an African priest taking over. Well, there's not much we can do about that until Rome lets us do that. We are right now training Masai deacons, however.[26] We'll see what happens. You said you wanted to go into another area of Masailand, not this Northern area, and begin again with some other Masai—perhaps together with Fr. Hillman.

"Well, I have put another priest[27] in charge of the Masai Christian communities while you were away. He is taking care of the communities you brought into Christianity until we get a Masai priest. In the meantime, several more communities have come into Christianity. Instead of sending you to another completely different area of Masailand, there is a job uncompleted in this very Northern area of Masailand. The *Sonjo*."

---

26. This program was later vetoed by the national bishops' conference. One correspondent told me that other bishops tried for twenty years to get Durning to resign.

27. Sr Julia Kubisto (see letter of October 1972) says this was Fr Anton (Toon) de Smet (1923–1970), who had survived the Kongolo massacre in 1962. In 1970, he replaced Fr. Marchessault (who was going on leave) at Loliondo, but died eight months later. Donovan then took over the town work and the Maasai work, while remaining committed to the Sonjo work.

Bishop Dennis Durning, first Bishop of Arusha, confirming Ndangoya, the Maasai chief described in *CR*, c. 1967 or 1968. Clemence Enjui is the sponsor. Donovan is on the right.

Donovan and Thomas Parokwa at a *boma* liturgical rite.

The Sonjo![28] The Sonjo are a tribe more primitive than the Masai, mysterious in their origins, more mysterious even in their continued existence in the very middle of Masailand, living for centuries in the very midst of the Masai—enemies of the Masai—somehow managing not only to exist but to thrive. They have to this day remained almost completely impervious to any outside influence. More than that, they resist outside influence. They are the despair of the new Tanzanian government with its five year plans,[29] its goals of nation building and the like. They are conservative, difficult, and suspicious of outsiders. Because of their hostility to outside influence, they can be an extremely difficult people with which to work.

Doctor Gray, an American anthropologist who studied the Sonjo in the fifties and wrote a book about them,[30] was supposed to come back and do further studies about them. He wrote in a letter that the reason he has not yet come back is "the subconscious dread of the Sonjo."

And here was the bishop asking me to go and live and work among the Sonjo. It was a familiar enough story. We had opened a mission among the Sonjo at the same time as among the Masai—almost sixteen years ago. We had opened several schools among them, at a primary level, and a dispensary for medicine. We had worked among them, baptizing the school children during most of those sixteen years, and now we stood at a point very late in the day indeed without a single adult Christian. All of them, on reaching adulthood or on leaving school, had gone back to their pagan religion. When I first came to Northern Masailand several years ago, I took part in this work, going to the Sonjo country for weekends to say Mass for the school children, giving out

28. The Sonjo, a tribe numbering over 30,000, have lived for centuries as an isolated enclave in the midst of Maasai territory. (Vähäkangas points out that their word for Maasai is the same as their word for "enemy.") Donovan worked with them from 1968 until he left Tanzania in 1973, and a number of the stories told in CR are about his work among the Sonjo rather than the Maasai.

29. Tanzania, like many socialist countries, sought to achieve economic growth through a series of five-year plans.

30. Gray, The Sonjo of Tanganyika. The Journal reported his departure after a further six months research in February 1965, but added, "since he pays [his subjects] to sit and chat it is doubtful, at least, that he is getting much straight habari [news]."

medicine to the sick, and wondering in my heart at the uselessness of it all—a children's religion[31] with no real future.[32]

The bishop continued, "Of all the works we have right now, this one is the most discouraging of all. If there is any way to reach the Sonjo, I think your way would be the only way. Go there for one or two years.[33] If you can do something, we will all be happy. If at the end of that time, you tell me honestly that you believe nothing can be done, I will accept your judgment and we will close the mission to the Sonjo."

The bishop said that since I would be surrounded by Masailand, I could go from time to time to see the Masai Christian communities and confer with the missionary who is taking care of them. But in the valley of the Sonjo, I would live entirely alone. There are no Indian shops there, no Post Office, no police, no government outpost, no government officials, and only one terrible road around the mountains and into the valley. I would not have to take the job if I didn't want to.

Of course, this is what I had been dreaming of, what I had been saying we not only can do but must do—evangelize one tribe after the other, and move on, never settling down, never letting the word *mission* be changed from the active, moving, dynamic thing that it is supposed to be into a static, settled down, comfortable, turned-in, institutional, end-of-the-line type thing that it usually becomes. I knew myself I didn't want to move on, *just yet*. I guess too, I wanted to settle down for just a little while among the Masai Christian communities. I had forgotten the words of Pope Pius XII, "A missionary is cut off front his homeland,

31. This was how the Sonjo characterized Christianity, because of the emphasis on schools. See letter of December 1968. (Donovan had also expressed concern about the Spiritans' preoccupation with children in the letter of April 1967.)

32. Fr. Gallagher, the Provincial, on his tour in early 1964 had visited the mission school among the Sonjo with Fr. Trumbull. He comments that "the Fathers have started what may someday be a station." "Several of the warriors . . . though not Catholic . . . greeted us with a courteous 'Praised be Jesus Christ.'" One purpose of the visit was "the customary reason; to induce the elders to send children to school." The following day, Fr. Trumbull conducted a Mass at Digo-Digo, and, although there was only one Catholic family among the Sonjo, "three Chagga teachers led by the Chagga catechist started the Gregorian Introit. At its end, the school children split our ears with a vigorous rendition of the Kyrie, Sanctus, and Agnus Dei in the Sonjo language and set to Sonjo melodies" (Gallagher, *Six Weeks*, 16–20). The translations were probably done by a catechist called Melkiori Theodore.

33. In the end, Donovan spent his last five years in Africa (1968–1973) with the Sonjo.

his family, his background, his roots, and his friends. He is condemned forever to be a foreigner, to walk forever as a stranger, among strange people, in a strange land."[34] I took the job—*and* a stiff drink the bishop offered me.

Love,
Father Vince

Donovan greeting a Maasai girl near a *boma*, c. 1967

34. See letter of August 10, 1959.

6

THE SONJO

(1968–1973)

Dear Relatives and Friends,

Hello again and thanks again from Africa to all of you who must be eating, drinking, and sleeping elections and campaign speeches.[1] I follow the excitement from afar each night on the radio.

Many of you were interested, while I was home, in knowing the actual living expenses of a missionary. Well, I am more interested in it myself now that I am looking forward some day to having lay people come out here to work with me. During the month of August, I kept exact and scrupulous account of every cent (or shilling) that I spent. I would like to put it down for you so that you can see for yourself. Remember, this is a new system of missionary work that is being followed here. You might call it the non-institutional approach—an attempt to bring nothing but Christianity to a people. Anyway, here is how it went for the month of August 1968:

1. On November 5 1968, Republican Richard Nixon narrowly won the presidential election over Democrat Hubert Humphrey.

Food 20.25 (including cigarettes)

Gasoline 20.12

Supplies 16.24 (for safari)

Personal .70 (haircut)

Office 15.71 (stamps, books, etc.)

Total $73.02

Of course, I am only in the beginning of my work here in Sonjo, and have not begun the full extent of my rounds, which will swell as the months go by. The petrol (gasoline) bill will rise as time goes on—and supplies. But even if it does rise, I don't think it will go past the $150 mark. I think that is the figure I gave at home when someone asked me what it costs to support a missionary for a month in Africa. Of course, that does not include the price of the car itself, which is a necessity. And after a few years, when the car literally falls apart from the terrible battering it takes from the roads out here, all the money you have saved up goes into the buying of a new one. This total doesn't include, either, the price of a tent or a place to live. But that is an expense that is called for only once every tour.

I still have my tent from the last time, because the priest who took my place in Masailand felt very uncomfortable in a tent, and he is experimenting with having a pre-fab, portable house built, which can be put up or taken down in a day or two, and in which he will live while he works in a certain area.[2] I will have to find out what his house costs.

At any rate, the total I put down represents the actual living expense and working expense of a missionary in this new, non-institutional approach to bringing Christianity to a people. Sometime I will have to send you a comparable report of a mission's monthly expenses working in the old system. I think you would be astounded. I know that the mission of Loliondo, when I first arrived there, was spending $35,000 a year.

Figure that there were two men there at the time. Each one of the men had to raise the astounding figure of over $17,000 a year by his own resources, without ever leaving Africa or the mission—in other words by writing letters alone.[3] I knew one man who wrote an average of thirty

2. Marchessault had the "prefab house" built by Br. Francis (see letter of October 1966). It consisted of three rooms, bolted together, and could easily be dismantled if necessary. He located this at Soit Sambu, where there was a dispensary and where lots of Maasai were in the general area.

3. Fr. Francis Greff (b.1920) took care of thirty homeless boys in his house in Mbosho, even after he was robbed and shot in 1991 (Koren, *Memorial*, 480).

letters a night to try to keep up with expenses—but he cracked up. That old system has broken many a man. If finances were the only thing involved in the old system, there was need for an agonizing reappraisal of missionary methods. But finances were not the only thing involved. There was the whole questionable approach to Christianity involved. Dear God, I wish we had seen it sooner. I wish I were younger, and we had more time left.

I have just heard that 500 miles away in Southern Masailand, there are eighteen Masai villages ready to accept Christianity and to be received into the church, the brotherhood. And in central Masailand, depending on how one man decides, a whole section is ready.[4]

Fathers Hillman and Jackson, both of this diocese, have just recently returned from a trip to Ethiopia.[5] They said that there are at least four whole provinces of Ethiopia without a single Catholic missionary, with tribes as primitive as the Masai and Sonjo of Tanzania. What does one do? One can only dream—and get down to the work in hand.

My work in hand is so very different from the Masai work that I did for two years. The physical terrain to begin with is so different. From the highlands of Loliondo, there is a drop of three thousand feet to the valley of the Sonjo. The valley is maybe fifty or sixty miles long—green and hot. Down here I have to worry about an enemy that I had almost forgotten about—the mosquito. This is malaria country and snake country. When you curve your way around the mountains and get your first look at the Sonjo valley from above, you can't help but be startled. After getting used to the brown, scorched grass and landscape of Masailand, the green that meets your eyes in the valley of the Sonjo takes your breath away. And as you descend into the valley, you can begin to feel the heat. Lush tropical country, almost like the Africa that Tarzan[6] runs around in. It is what I always thought Africa looked like, before I came to Africa. There are rivers and streams and springs. And high up on the valley walls, so uniquely situated, that at first you don't notice them—the villages of the people. Each village a walled-in, barricaded fortress, with the entrance

4. In all likelihood, this was due to the work of Frs. Ralph Poirier and Ned Marchessault out of Kijungu Mission in South Maasailand, and of Frs. Hillman and Everhard (Eef) Nass (b.1937) and others in Simanjiro in Central Maasailand.

5. In 1972, Frs. Eef Nass, Ed Kelly, and Bill Jackson went to Ethiopia to pioneer evangelization of the Burana people.

6. *Tarzan of the Apes* was the creation of Edgar Rice Burroughs in 1912, and inspired numerous sequels and movies. Tarzan lived in the jungles of

to each village being a fort-like, stockade-type gate, designed for defense against the Masai and all other enemies.

I drove down into the center of the valley, stopped the car and got out into the heat. I wiped my forehead and looked up at the villages and the gates. Somehow, I had to storm those villages and those gates, and I didn't have the faintest idea in the world of how to begin.

Love,
Father Vince

November 1968

Dear Relatives and Friends,

Warm greetings of love and gratitude from Africa, which finally got on the Olympic map. The people of the Kipsigis tribe who stream across the border from Kenya to set up the African shops all around the Loliondo area are proud of their fellow tribesmen, Keino and Kiprugut and Temu,[7] whose names they suddenly started hearing in the midst of the world news.

I listened with interest every night to the Olympic news on my little radio, and then went back each morning to work with a people who have scarcely heard of the outside world, much less the Olympics—the Sonjo.

It is strange writing to you about my work among the Sonjo. When I began to write to you some time ago to explain my similar work among the Masai Tribe, that work had already begun, and was already reaching the point where the first groups of people were coming into Christianity, [so] I could write from the secure vantage point of seeing the work succeeding even before I began to write. It is quite different with the Sonjo. You are sharing with me the very beginning of the work. As I write these words, I have no idea how this work will turn out. You may well be the readers, as the months go on, of a progressive description of the failure of a missionary work. It will be a comfort to me to know that all of you are present with me at every step of this missionary journey. When we

7. At the 1968 Summer Olympics in Mexico City, Kipchoge Keino won the gold medal in the men's 1,500 meters and the silver medal in the men's 5,000 meters; Wilson Kiprugut won the silver medal in the men's 800 meters; Naftali Temu won the gold medal in the men's 10,000 meters. All were Kipsigis, a subgroup of the Kalenjin tribe, from Kenya.

come to the end of it, in a year or so, I think you will know why we will have succeeded or failed, without further explanation on my part. It might also give you the unvarnished view of the inner workings of a missionary's task, a thing I find so difficult to explain to people who have never been on the missions. It might also show you, along the way, the heartbreaks and disappointments involved in missionary work, which are as common and numerous as the joys and satisfactions in it.

Sometimes people who stumble across me out in the bush, people like the flying doctors, white hunters and their clients, are startled. White women especially will ask me how I can be content to exist so far from the mainstream of human life. If they only knew! In my work I am constantly dealing with the deepest workings of human life, at a level which these tourists perhaps never have an opportunity of touching in their own lives. When I worked out here as a school man and medicine man, I could sense that I was touching only the surface of these peoples' lives, but now with these things put aside, I can feel that I am probing deeper and deeper into the things that really have an importance for these people—what they think of life and death, of the world around them, of the powers that confront them, what they think of man and woman and children, of the relationships between people—and the incredibly clever systems they have worked out to cope with the mysterious span of life that is given them. What you find out about them is not always pretty and uplifting, but it is always fascinating, and absolutely necessary to know before you begin to work with them.

Sometimes, as I'm working among the Sonjo, I wish I were an anthropologist or a linguist or an historian or a musician.

I think I mentioned that the Sonjo country was a valley about forty or fifty miles long, roughly the area from Pittsburgh to Butler. On the sides of the valley, the Sonjo build their barricaded villages. That day I drove into the valley in the sweltering heat to begin work, I felt like a general going in, without any army, to commence the operation of occupying the valley. The whole thing would remind one of a military campaign in a way. I was going to have to know the strength and weakness of each one, and the opposition I was likely to meet. I was going to have to try to establish a beachhead, and if and when I did, I would get out and let others take over the work. I even had my maps of the area, with each village marked on the map. One of the big problems was going to be logistics. There were no shops in the entire valley, and I would have to have supplies if I was going to live there. My line of communications with the outside was bad—a single, torturous forty-four mile road around the mountains and into the valley.[8] And I would have to have a headquarters.

Fortunately, halfway up the valley, almost right smack in the middle of the valley, the mission had built, years ago, a little brick house with a tin roof for an African teacher or dresser. It was no longer occupied, but it would be perfect for keeping my main stock of supplies in the valley. What I needed for immediate use I could take with me along with my car and tent as I roamed up and down the valley. I was ready to begin my work among the Sonjo!

The first thing I noticed about these people was the extreme cautiousness which they use in dealing with outsiders. Craftiness might be a better word. All the government maps of the area list the names of each one of their villages, and the Sonjo will use these names in referring to the villages when they speak to outsiders—but they have their own names for the villages which they use when talking among themselves. This is extremely odd. What is even more odd is that the very name of the tribe—Sonjo—is also a name used only by outsiders and for outsiders. Among themselves, they refer to themselves as the *Batemi*. I don't know of any other tribe that goes to such extraordinary lengths to shield itself from the outside world that it would actually have a tribal name for foreign consumption only. Each Sonjo, male and female, is marked with a huge scar on his or her chest, or on the back between the shoulder blades. This scar is celled the *Ntemi*. So the Sonjo are really the people of the *Ntemi* scar—or the *Batemi*. The scar is very visible, but if you look a Sonjo right in the eye and ask him about the meaning of the scar, without batting his eye, he will deny that it even exists.

I think I am up against the most mysterious tribe in East Africa.

Love,
Father Vince

8. Donovan grew impatient of this trip, and developed a more direct route over the mountain. The *Journal* for November–December 1968 described the opening of the road as "the biggest event in Sonjo. . . . Now Vince is weekly using this road, which is only 15 miles instead of 42 on the old one. You can make it in less than two hours." In May 1969, the *Journal* reported that Fr. Watschinger's Toyota, carrying two Austrian nurses and seven children returning from hospital, "on the bad hill near Sonjo . . . turned over three times. Fortunately no one was badly hurt." As a photographer, Watschinger's first reaction was to photograph the upturned car.

December 1968

Dear Relatives and Friends,

I want to tell you how much I marvel that all of you, with all the work and worries and preoccupations you have, would still care enough to worry about me and remember me. I kind of need the feeling that you are with me these days. I really wouldn't want to be alone just now among the Sonjos.

Sonjo villages are much bigger than Masai villages—each Sonjo village having hundreds of houses—all enclosed within the village wall and gates. There are about twelve or thirteen of these villages existing today. At least nine were destroyed completely by the Masai during the Sonjos' incessant warfare of survival with those warlike Hamite neighbors of theirs. These villages were always built on the side of mountains, with layers and layers of houses built right up the mountain. In each village there is a big field which serves as the village square—and is the main place set aside for dancing in the village. There is always a huge and ancient tree in every village square. This tree, as well as similar trees found throughout the valley, is sacred. Situated near every village are several springs—also considered sacred, and completely out of bounds for any outsider. The penalty for trespassing is death by poisoned arrows—in the use of which the Sonjos are highly skillful. I know of no non-Sonjo who has ever seen the springs. Even in the tribe itself, only those considered sexually non-active are allowed near the springs—young girls and old men.

In every village, there is a temple; in some villages, two temples. And in one village, considered the most sacred, three temples. Entrance to the temples is strictly forbidden to outsiders, of course, under the same penalty—death. In the village with the three temples, fully one third of the entire village is considered sacred precincts, and completely restricted. Outside several of the villages are little wayside shrines, and you see people, especially women, often praying there. I might add that not only is it strictly forbidden to take any pictures of these temples or shrines, but also it is forbidden for an outsider to take an undue interest in them—for instance, to stop and stare at them, as he is passing by.

There are the remains of guard houses just inside each fortified gate, a little bit off to the side. These are also sacred. You can hardly turn around in the Sonjo valley without bumping into something sacred. Living around here is like walking on egg shells. All this, of course, has nothing to do with Christianity. It has to do with the pagan religion of the Sonjo.

The Sonjo are a God-intoxicated people. I have never seen their like in Africa. They have a whole series of feast days. I have been here about four months, and have witnessed the celebration of feasts on the average of one every two weeks. And their really big feast is yet to come

They have a priesthood, too. Every village has twelve priests (twelve, mind you) except the village of the three temples which has sixteen priests. They have a religious capital, like Vatican City, the village with the three temples and vast restricted area. This valley is really the holy land to these people, and I am obviously a trespasser.

I have asked some Sonjo elders what they thought of the Christian religion. This is what they answered, "The Christian religion is the religion of the school, the religion of children—the second way. These children will follow the second way while they are in school, but when they grow up they will return to the first way—our way."

I think the whole sad state of affairs is best symbolized by the forlorn mission buildings, such as they are: the few schools, the dispensary, the little mud brick house all far outside the village walls down in the valley—far away from the villages, far away from the life and heartbeat and mainstream of Sonjo existence. That is as close as the Sonjo have ever allowed them to be. No non-Sonjo has ever lived in the villages.

Whenever I look at those mission buildings, all I can see is the symbol of that second way, the symbol of sixteen years of bitter, frustrating mission failure.

"Go out and preach the gospel to every nation" [Mark 16:15; Matt 28:19].

Even to *this* nation, Lord?

Love,
Father Vince

January 1969

Dear Relatives and Friends,

The MMD Committee sent to me the total amount of money you people have been responsible for collecting and contributing to my work since I came back to Africa. I was astounded at the amount, and I was overwhelmed at your generosity. I can't tell you the feeling I have when I think of you people, relatives and friends, Protestants and Catholics, who have been so sincerely outgoing in your concern for my work. With all the turmoil in the church and in the world today, all in all the dangers on every side, I am quietly convinced that whatever hope there is for the future of the church lies with people like you who are reaching out beyond yourselves.

You know, when I listen to the radio these days and hear news about men leaping off the earth and going around the moon,[9] and then look around me at the life of the Sonjo people, I wonder if we are talking about the same planet Earth. I remember a few days before Christmas, looking up at the night sky and seeing a satellite passing towards the Southern Cross and wondering if it was the three astronauts on their voyage to the moon; and then, a few days later on Christmas Eve while they were circling the moon, I walked through a Sonjo village and talked to the people and watched them dancing. What an incredible disparity and distance between members of the same human race!

The very first days that I went to live among the Sonjo, six months ago, I watched the people of one village dancing at their Mbarimbari, or harvest feast, and even after all my years in Africa, I was at least faintly surprised. The harvest feast, unlike some of their religious feasts, is a time of unmitigated rejoicing. The religious feasts have a more somber and sober atmosphere about them. At this harvest feast, they were completely gay and unrestricted. The young men danced without a stitch of clothes on them, their bodies painted with white stripes, possibly in imitation of the zebra, of which they are very fond. The girls and young women didn't really have much more in the line of clothes, just a leather mini-skirt about five inches long that rests on the hips and is slit into many strips like a hula skirt. The Sonjo have a rhythm, gracefulness and beauty, and variety in their dancing that the Masai, for instance, could

9. Apollo 8 circled the moon on December 24, 1968. The first moon landing was on June 20, 1969.

never imitate. In fact, they would rank among the finest dancers that I have seen in Africa.

Time and time again, I have been struck by the uniqueness and strangeness of the Sonjo. They are very hard to classify and categorize. When they are not self-consciously trying to deal with outsiders, they have an innocence and primitiveness about them that makes one instinctively want to place them in another age and time, another place—as though they had inadvertently wandered into our world as the remnants of a lost paradise.

Their origins and stock are mysterious, lost in history, not nearly so well determined as the Masai. Their religious mythology is astounding, and some of their religious beliefs, as far as the research I have been able to do can determine, are absolutely unique among the thousands of tribes on the African continent. Their beliefs are neither Bantu nor Nilotic, nor Hamitic, nor Nilo-hamitic, nor Arabic, nor of the category of beliefs associated with the Bushmen. They are simply Sonjo. And as far as their beliefs are concerned, they are completely sincere and open and willing to talk with you about them at any length and depth. These beliefs are contained in their mythology—and the endless stories they never tire of telling of the past that they can remember. Every man, woman, and child in the Sonjo tribe, clings to these beliefs with all the simplicity and sincerity that you could expect of anyone.

It was because of the openness and obvious sincerity of their attitude toward this basic body of beliefs, an openness apparent to any outsider, that I was so astounded and shocked when I came to the matter of their religious ritual. Surrounding their religious ritual, or their way of celebrating their religious ceremonies, there was another set of beliefs, which, as far as I could ascertain, were quite different from their main body of beliefs and actually in conflict with and in open contradiction of their ritualistic beliefs, and a hostility surrounding them that was very difficult to penetrate. The heart of these ritualistic celebrations is the feast which the Sonjo call Mase. The feast of Mase takes place during a period of about eight days, but it is preceded by a time of preparations that last a month. It takes place in one village at a time, and does not begin in one village until it is completed at the previous village. Actually the feast of Mase began to be celebrated in the Sonjo valley in the first village in the month of September and it is only now reaching the last village, where it will begin to be celebrated next week. This information was not volunteered to me. It never is. It is kept strictly secret, the element of surprise as to the timing of the actual beginning of the feast being an essential part of the whole affair. I can only guess at the timing from having watched the pattern followed in other villages.[10]

A Sonjo, who was trying to be friendly, said to me one day, "Padri, learn all you can and want about the stories of the Sonjo. Everyone will be glad to tell you all you want to hear. But don't ever try to enter into or interfere with, or find out about the meaning of Mase."

Here is the dark side of the moon.[11] From my first dealings with Mase, I have found everything about it shabby and shoddy, deceitful, treacherous, dishonest and somehow unworthy of the Sonjo. Here, to me, was an indication that if these people were indeed the struggling remnants of a primitive paradise, it was of a paradise that was forever lost.

I was told this much at least. During the feast of Mase, God would come to visit the particular village of the Sonjo that was holding the feast. And when he came, I would hear him. My first experience of his visit came not long after I reached Sonjo. I was camped about a mile beneath the village down in the valley. It must have been about two or three in the morning, or the middle of the night, when I heard it—a high, loud, piercing, wailing, plaintive sound in the darkness. It was repeated again and again. I went outside to listen to it. It was an eerie sound in the night. Then it was answered by the shrieks of joyful women up in the village and the shouts of warriors ready to dance. The god of the Sonjos had come at that "ungodly" hour, and they were going out to meet him. If their god had come, I wonder if he knew about me, the only European living there, standing down in the dark valley looking up at the hills. I wonder what he thought about me. I wonder if he was thinking that I was a danger to him or that he was a danger to me.

Love,
Father Vince

---

10. Two of the first Sonjo catechists, who told the missionaries too much about Mase, were killed by poison (Watschinger, *Don't Give up Hope*, 114).

11. Pink Floyd's album of this name was not released till 1972. However, with growing interest in lunar exploration (the first US spacecraft had landed on the moon in 1968), the phrase had come into fairly common use.

February 1969

Dear Relatives and Friends,

I have here before me now a list of all your names. And as I look at it, it fills me with a kind of nostalgia. And the gratitude I feel is not a general gratitude, but a very specific and personal gratitude, different for what each name means to me. And I feel very humble.

To begin the evangelization of the Sonjo people requires a little bit of calm thought. They are situated in eight or nine main villages. Perhaps it would be enough to try to evangelize one village and then hope that it would spread? Or try all nine, and hope that you would succeed in one? I have, as a helper, a catechist that I trained several years ago when I was running the Catechetical Training Center in Usa River, near Arusha. I have only myself to blame if he is not effective. His name is Michael.

We have done an awful lot of reading and studying together. There is not a great deal written on the type of work that we are doing. Most missionary manuals and magazines and articles have to do with a kind of work we really don't want to get involved in—aid to underdeveloped countries. There are volumes written on mission schools and hospitals and socio-economic programs. There is a scarcity of written material on the subject we are interested in—simply preaching the gospel, with no added attractions. In fact, we have found only one book on the subject, *The Acts of the Apostles*. It is an eye-opener. . . .

[Here follows an account of St. Paul's missionary journeys, which became the basis of the section "St. Paul and Mission" in chapter 3 of CR.]

The Sonjo people are a people suffering from a good deal of underdevelopment, and a state of womanhood that would undoubtedly shock most of you, plus a few other things thrown in. It is not an easy thing to decide what to do. Christian missionaries have been among them for sixteen years, dispensing charity on an enormous scale, but their underdevelopment has not changed an iota, nor has their state of womanhood. It is a difficult decision to make, to coolly plan that you will do nothing directly about their underdevelopment, or their womanhood, or their other problems. To make matters worse, every outsider who has ever been among them has spoiled them by perpetual handouts. They have come to expect this of outsiders, and they have become the most beggarly tribe in Tanzania.

Michael and I shuddered at the thought of what lay ahead for us. Would we dare come to the Sonjos with nothing to offer except the gospel? . . . The Gospel had better be enough for the Sonjo people. God help me, I have nothing else to offer them.

Sincerely,
Father Vince

April 1969

Dear Relatives and Friends,

Since the last time I wrote I have heard of the sorrow that has come into the lives of several of you.[12] I am much more affected by this news than you might suppose. I share your sorrows as you share my work. I am very sorry.

I decided to make a start among the Sonjos in the two biggest villages, Ebwe and Soyetu, and two smaller villages. This requires a knowledge of the people beyond ordinary familiarity or friendliness with them—something very close to an anthropological knowledge of the people. I just have to make use of the scientific knowledge available about these people, and to hope that the information acquired on my own can help to fill in the gaps of knowledge so very necessary for the first step.

What I am referring to is the group structure of these people, who must be approached as a group. Besides my own theological conviction that Christianity makes no sense outside of a community, I am faced with another hard reality. It would be useless, if not impossible, to try to bring Christianity to these people as individuals.

I am trying to bring change to these people—not a change in their customs, or their way of living or even their morals. A change in belief could well be the biggest change of all. Social anthropologists tell us very clearly that change—like the acceptance of the Christian message on a meaningful level—does not take place in one individual at a time. Groups adopt changes as groups, or not at all. I remember a student at Pitt University telling me that in reality I was an agent for group and

12. The son of Francis "Bud" Breniser, one of Donovan's MMD committee, had committed suicide.

social change. His description was very accurate. We missionaries are not merchants of individual salvation.

The problem is not as simple as it looks. You might be tempted to say that all the people in a village are a group or a community. But they are not. A Masai kraal of fifty people might well be a community. A Sonjo village of two thousand people is not. And that is about the size of Ebwe. Within that one village there are different and distinct communities. And it is not just a question of neighborhood. A man belongs to a community if that group of people vitally affects him in the most important actions of his life, and he affects them. If he is approached to become a Christian, he must think of the effect his decision will have on that group of people vitally connected with him—his community. I could pick a certain man in the village and know that his becoming a Christian would not affect the entire village, but it would most definitely affect a certain group of people in the village, people I could almost put my hand on. It is that group of people we must search for and find. They are essential to our work. They are the keystone of our work. Without finding them and working with them, there is no possibility of succeeding. This is perhaps the most significant difference between what I used to do and what I am trying to do today, this searching out of a real community to work with. What was impossible with an individual becomes amazingly possible with a community. I often thought of this fact when I was home on leave when I looked around at the strange and fractured communities of America.

But, whether in Africa or America, I do not think it is fair to a person to approach him or her on behalf of Christianity outside of and apart from his or her community.

If you should succeed in "converting" an individual apart from his community, what you have succeeded in doing is separating him from his community, making him forever an outcast, an outsider to the structure of the tribal community. And this thing that made him an outsider—Christianity—will be abhorrent to the community. You have probably cut off forever the possibility of bringing Christianity to that community. As for him, poor man (or imagine if he is a child), he has two bleak choices: either to struggle and fight against the structure of the tribal community as an outcast, or to give up the Christianity in which he might well even believe. Historically, he has most often chosen the latter course.

I would have to pursue this matter of the real communities in the Sonjo villages. To start with, I would have to approach the symbols of authority in the different communities. I asked Michael, my catechist, to see if he could arrange a meeting with the main chief of the village of Ebwe, and with his assistants, the sub-chiefs—at their convenience—so that I could explain what I was doing in their country. With all the chiefs involved, I was bound to touch every community in the village. They agreed, and several days later, under an extremely hot tropical sun, at high noon, to be precise, I went with Michael to one of the fig groves in the village, where they rest at midday. They were waiting for me. I sat down on the ground among these modern descendants of the Kushites, sons of the ancient kingdom of Kush in the Sudan, present day adherents of the secret ritual of Mase and worshippers of the god-man, Khambegeu, who had lived in and walked through these very villages years ago. I told them why I had come or, to be more exact, why I had been sent.

I told them that it was well known that the Sonjo were men of great piety and religion. That is why I had come to them. I had not come to denounce or to rail against that religion, or to ask them to cast away the things that were familiar to them or to deny the knowledge of God which they had. I had come to add to it, and perhaps to bring new meaning to it. I just wanted them to listen to what I had to say.

I had decided that on that afternoon I would tell them the whole story in brief, from the beginning to the end—from the evil that first appeared in man long ago at his very beginnings, an evil that made fair to destroy the beautiful world God gave us, to the hopelessness of the centuries, to the promise of a way out of the darkness, to the hope that has actually dawned on the world bringing a new meaning to the world and everything in it, and finally to the end chapter of a new earth and a new heaven all summed up in the mystery of the person called Jesus Christ.

It took a few hours. I was not trying to convert these men. I was only trying to get their permission to tell these things to any of their people who would care to listen. I told them that I would go into greater detail on every point I mentioned, but that they had already heard the Christian message in its entirety. I wanted them to know ahead of time everything I would tell their people. It was not even necessary that these very men would follow the instructions in more detail which I would give to any interested people. But it was vitally necessary that these men would allow and want their respective communities to hear these things.

Otherwise, any individuals who did afterwards follow the instructions would be heading for the old dilemma of the outcast.

They asked a few interesting questions about evil, about the presence of God, and about death. Then they spoke together for awhile and the main chief, Saliase, told me what they had decided. This procedure in itself was a far cry from the ordinary American notion of African chiefs. Here was no autocratic dictator, deciding for everyone on his own what would be done in his section of the tribe, but a man consulting with his peers and acting as their spokesman for a decision towards which they had all contributed.

Saliase said what I had told them was not bad, and was even interesting, and it would be good for people who wanted to listen to hear what I had to say. He himself and several of the others would like to be present whenever I came for instructions. But he was making no promises beyond that. When I had finished all my instructions, they would decide what they would like to do—and only then.

I could ask no more of these sons of the ancient kingdom of Kush, a kingdom that predated Christ by a thousand years.[13] I told them that we would make further arrangements for weekly instructions. And then I left.

I don't know what they were thinking as I walked away, but I know what I was thinking. This was no chance or accidental meeting, or just a normal afternoon in my life. Nor was it just a casual conversation under a hot African sun, with words and thoughts tumbling out, unprepared and unrehearsed. Those men might not have known it, but I had prepared my speech very well indeed. Years and years of honest effort at trying to distill the meaning of the Christian message and to arrive at the essence of Christianity had gone into the preparation of that speech. In truth, I had been preparing for more than ten years for that meeting under the fig trees of Sonjo. As I walked down the mountain back to my tent, I felt relieved, contented, and very exhausted.

Love,
Father Vince

---

13. The Kushite kingdom existed from about 3,000 BCE till the fourth century CE, between what are now Egypt and Sudan. The Maasai and the Sonjo are believed to be descended from the Kushites.

July 1969

Dear Relatives and Friends,

In the midst of my work, I am so grateful when I remember all of you, and know that I am not alone as I often seem to be, but that you are with me in a very real way.

As I go day after day from one village to the next, in a never ending circle, through the four Sonjo villages which I am evangelizing, I am struck by the reality of these African communities. Each community seems to have a different character, a different personality, a different face—differences which you would normally associate only with individuals. And I am affected by these communities also in a way which I never expected.

You can prepare what you are going to teach them in the privacy of your own thoughts, in the long hours of the night—but it is only when you are in the midst of one of these living pagan communities that thoughts you never had before come crowding in on you, only when you are facing them as a group that meaning and significance which you truly never saw before dawn on you.

I had been to one village for several meetings. The instructions had been set up in that village just as in the first village. I had been encouraging the people of this village—men, women, and warriors—to talk and tell me what they thought about the world and life and death and God. One cannot but be deeply moved listening to people of another culture, a culture more ancient than one's own, speaking their deepest thoughts about such things. And I was moved. Here was a way of looking at the world, and a whole world picture entirely different from anything I had known.

Then they moved into more familiar territory.[14] They spoke of the God who loved the Sonjo fiercely, jealously, and exclusively. His power was known throughout the lush green valley of the Sonjo; his protection saved them from the marauding Masai; his goodness was seen in the water and crops and rain he gave them. But his salvation was for them alone. Only the Sonjo would be saved.

They were not shy about telling me this. I finally spoke up and told them that they reminded me of another great people that lived long ago and live until the present day. They are famous the world over for having

14. Cf. chapter 4 of *CR*, the section, "The Unknown God."

preserved in the world the knowledge of the one true God. But it was not always easy for them. They often tried to restrict that God to their tribe and to their land, and so made him less of a God than he really was. One day in the early days of their tribe, he called a man named Abraham, and said to him: "Abraham, come away from this land of yours. Leave your people and your tribe and your land, and come to the land which I will show you. And all nations will be blessed in you if you do this" [Gen 12:1–3].

The God of the tribe of Abraham had become a God who was no longer free. He was trapped in that land, among that tribe. He had to be freed from that nation, that tribe, that land, in order to become the High God. When Abraham followed him out of his own land, there began on this earth the history of the one, true, living, High God.

I continued talking with the people who were listening very closely now:

> Everyone knows how devout you Sonjo are, the faith you have, the beautiful worship of God. You have known God. But I wonder if perhaps you have not become like the people of the tribe of Abraham. Perhaps God has become trapped in this Sonjo country, among this tribe. Perhaps God is no longer free here. What will the Masai do to protect themselves against this God of the Sonjo? and the Kikuyu? They will have to have their own gods. Perhaps the story of Abraham speaks also to you. Perhaps you Sonjo also must leave your nation and your tribe and your land, at least in your thoughts, and learn of the High God, the God of all tribes, the God of the world. Perhaps your God is not free. Do not try to hold him here or you will never know him. Free your God to become the High God. You have known this God and worshipped him, but he is greater than you have known. He is the God not only of the Sonjo, but also my God, and the God of the Masai and the Kikuyu, and the God of every tribe and nation in the world.

There was silence. I did not know if, perhaps, I had not gone too far. Then someone asked a question. Whether the question he asked was asked in sarcasm or not I do not know. I only know that it startled me. He asked, "This story of Abraham—does it speak only to the Sonjo? Or does it speak also to you? Have you found the High God? Have you known him?"

I was going to give a glib answer, when, all of a sudden, I thought of Joan of Arc.[15] I don't know why I thought of her, but suddenly I remembered that since the time of Joan of Arc, if not before, the French have conceived of God (*le bon Dieu*—what would the Sonjo think of him?) as being rather exclusively and intimately associated with their quest for glory. The Americans have some kind of a certainty that "Almighty God" will always bless their side in all their wars. Hitler never failed to call on the help of *Gott der Almachtige* in all his speeches, in all his adventures. School children were ordered to pray to God for him.

I sat there stunned looking at the Sonjo people. They called their God, "Khambegeu." Well, that is no more strange-sounding than our gods. The God invoked by Pius XI to bless the troops of Mussolini about to embark on the plunder of Ethiopia,[16] and the God invoked by Cardinal Spellman to bless the "Soldiers of Christ" in Vietnam,[17] and the God of French glory, and the German God of Hitler, were no more the High God of Scripture than is "Diana of the Ephesians" [Acts 19:20–41] or "Khambegeu" of the Sonjo of East Africa.

To each one of these cultures must ever be presented again the proclamation of the message, symbolized in the call of Abraham—to leave their land and their nation, to learn of the High God, the God of the world. All nations are to be blessed in Abraham.

I spoke again, and I marveled at how small my voice sounded. I said something which I had no intention of saying when I had come into the village. I heard myself saying, "No! We have *not* found that High God, not even those of us who have been sent to tell you about him. We have not known him. But we believe that he exists, and we have a certainty about that belief. I have come to ask you to join me. Let us search for him together. One day we may find him. The story of Abraham speaks to all of us."

That night, with the lamp burning long hours on my little table, I sat with the Bible opened before me, reading over the speeches of Paul to

15. Joan of Arc (?1412–1431) led the French army while still a teenager. She was executed as a witch by the English, but canonized by the Roman Catholic Church in 1920.

16. Benito Mussolini (1883–1945), Italian dictator, invaded Ethiopia in 1935. Pope Pius XI called him "a man sent by Providence."

17. Cardinal Spellman of New York (see footnote to letter of August 1, 1959) was a supporter of the war in Vietnam, in opposition to the attitude of the Vatican.

the different pagans that he evangelized. They came alive for me as never before. I almost had to smile as I came across one of them:

"Men of Athens, I compliment you on your piety and your sense of religion which is everywhere well known. I wandered among your monuments, and I found among them an altar which bore the inscription, 'To the Unknown God.' It is of him that I have come to speak" [Acts 17:22–23].

I knew that wherever I might yet go, and among whatever people I might be sent to speak, the first part of the bare, essential Christian message would have to be about this widely unknown God, the living, High God.

All my love,
Father Vince

September 1969

Dear Relatives and Friends,

I thank you for your continued interest in and support for my work here, despite your own concerns and worries in your work and lives. Remembering you people helps me to keep my balance when my own work almost sweeps me away.

The Feast of Mase was in full swing. The high point of the religious year of the pagan Sonjo Tribe had arrived. They had prepared for it with at least a month of advent before it actually began.

And then it began about two or three in the morning with a loud, wailing sound awaking the whole village. This sound was the voice of Khambegeu, the God of the Sonjo, coming to visit his people. For a full week following this sudden arrival of their God, the Sonjo would be engrossed in their secret ritual of Mase.

This is one time when outsiders are not particularly welcome. One has to stand and watch as unobtrusively as possible. From early morning, processions wind in and out of and around the village. Everyone is singing, and everyone is dressed in skin garments and hides. European type clothes are not allowed. Warriors are particularly hostile at this time, with the skins pulled up over the lower half of their faces, and sullen eyes glaring out straight ahead. Women are in a pitch of religious fervor. Children are quiet and awed. And every once in a while, you hear that ubiquitous voice of God; now here, in the lower part of the village, and then there, in the upper level. The music and dancing is slow and somber. There are two temples in the village around which much of the action swirls. (The Sonjo are the only tribe I know in East Africa which has pagan temples existing until today.) The main square of the village has a sacred enclosure where secret actions are carried out. During the feast, eligible young men enter the warrior-hood through the death-oath of Mase. Cows and goats—the voluntary offerings of the people, especially women—are sacrificed in great numbers, and they are mysteriously devoured by Khambegeu at night.

There is a group of priests in the village—twelve of them—in charge of the whole feast. Prayers are offered to Khambegeu through these priests, and then they, having spent some time in the temple speaking with Khambegeu, emerge to pass on his messages to the people.

It is all quite formidable, even when you find out from a nervous informant in the secrecy of the night that everything is not exactly as it appears to be—that the voice of Khambegeu is a *kudu* horn blown by trained warriors, guarded every moment of the blowing by fellow warriors with poisoned arrows at the ready. You never can tell which one of those warriors, with his face half-covered, has the horn hidden under his skin garments. Warriors and men are the only ones in on this secret and must guard it with their lives. No woman is ever told the secret. For the rest of the year the horn is kept in the temple. The priests, under the watchful eye of the main chief, keep the people in control through this system. All the sacrifices are devoured at night by the elders—and a hungry God is blamed. No one can talk to God except the priests. The people, especially the women, can talk only to the priests.

Keeping on the fringes of the crowd, I took it all in, with mixed feelings. I felt a sense of respect for what I saw, because I could only agree with St. Paul that all nations can seek and find God, and that each nation goes its own way with the evidence of God available in the good things he gives each nation [Acts 17:27; 14:17].

But I also felt sad and slightly sick.[18] Every single thing I saw, I recognized, not from my acquaintance with other pagan religions, but from my acquaintance with our Christian religion.

---

18. Much of the remainder of this letter is incorporated into the section, "Eucharistic Community with a Mission," in chapter 8 of *CR*.

The temples kept up at the people's expense and labor; the priesthood, the class apart, the privileged ones, the ones who make themselves the most important in the religious community, the ones *who alone* can talk to God; the ordinary people, especially the women, completely at the mercy of the priest—no reaching the throne of God except through him; the discrimination against women; the offerings for the sacrifice, the manipulation of sacred signs; the air of unfathomable mystery about it all.

There is scarcely a pagan trick that we Christians have overlooked or missed.

But surely all this is the very reason why the Christian religion came into being. This is why the early Christians cried out in anguish that their religion was different from the pagan religions, why the early Christian writer felt it necessary to say, "But we have no temples, no altars, no sacrifices, no priesthood."[19]

Was it for nothing that Christ entered once and for all into the Holy of Holies and offered the one and only Christian sacrifice? During all his life, he never once performed what we call a "priestly" action. He was not a member of the Jewish priesthood. In that one supreme moment in his life when he *did* offer sacrifice—himself—he gathered into himself, once and for all, the whole meaning of priesthood and sacrifice, and obliterated forever the need of a priestly caste. His entirely original contribution was, for the first time in the history of religion, to enable an entire people to be priest. Is this not the one big difference between Christianity and all the other religions on the face of the earth?

St. Peter, at a later time, described this new situation: "But you are a chosen race, a royal priesthood, a consecrated nation, a people set apart to sing the praises of God who called you out of darkness into his wonderful light. Once you were not a people at all, and now you are the people of God" (1 Pet 2:9, 10).

We believe, don't we, that we need no contemporaneous mediators, no privileged caste to lead us to God? Is it not so that we believe that we, the *laos* [people (Greek)] of God, the laity, can reach even to the throne of the living God, by the power given to us as a Christian community by Christ? Is not this what the *Good News* is all about?

19. This is probably a paraphrase of Tertullian: "Temples and tombs, we detest both equally; we know neither kind of altar, we adore neither kind of image, we offer no sacrifice, we celebrate no funeral rites" ("On Spectacles," chapter 13). This information was supplied to me by my colleague, Dr. Alan Hayes, who points out that "an early Christian writer wouldn't have denied priesthood"—this part is Donovan's gloss.

Anything less than this would not be worth taking to the pagan Sonjo people. Nothing less than this would be worthy of them.

Throughout the world, we are fighting for the rights of the priesthood. It is an important battle. But it is to be hoped that, whether we be in Washington or Nairobi, we never lose sight of what we are fighting for—the rights of the Christian priesthood, and not of a pagan one.

All my love,
Father Vince

December 1969

Dear Relatives and Friends,

Greetings from a guy who is very grateful that you people of the country of the Moon Age still take a real interest in the work in a country that hasn't quite reached that stage.

As one goes about working among a pagan people like the Sonjo, one becomes increasingly aware that a high degree of professionalism is needed to work with them effectively. Perhaps that is a surprising notion to you, that such a thing as a professional missionary is needed and desired—as professional, as a matter of fact, as a doctor or a lawyer or an anthropologist. But it really is true. A practicing doctor or surgeon deals with one person at a time, and tries to cure him. An anthropologist, while studying groups of people, generally intends to do nothing about those people except to understand them. A missionary is a kind of mixture of the two. He deals with large groups of people and fully intends to affect them. Unprofessionalism in his case can be disastrous on a large scale. If his work is filled with less precise details than that of a doctor or lawyer, it is no less challenging for that reason, and no less filled with anguish and self-doubt.

I suppose every missionary desires to be professional—or at least to be less unprofessional.

There are two facets to this missionary task which are particularly demanding. The first is the concern with the message itself, with which we have been entrusted. Just what is the Christian message? The second is with the people to whom we must take this message. Who and what are these people? Both of these aspects are vitally important, and they intersect one another. To give you some idea of what I mean, maybe I can use, as an example, a group of people more familiar to you. Recently I had to travel to Nairobi for retreat, and on the public bus I ran into a tribe as exotic as any Sonjo or Masai I have ever dealt with. They were "Crossroaders,"[20] a group of American college students out for a few months to Africa, to help in community development projects. During the course of a long seven-hour journey, I got to talk with most of them. They were warm, open, friendly and attractive. They reminded me of the college students I had met while in America on leave. And whether they came from New York or Missouri or California, they were strikingly the same in their appreciation of things human and earthy, their approach to life, their scale of cultural values—much more alike than I think they would care to admit. But that is what makes a tribe a tribe, a common acceptance of values. We talked about many things, religious and non-religious, and at the end of the safari I was prompted to ask them, "Are you atheists or agnostics or what?" They laughed, and one very sharp-looking and sharp-minded girl said, "When we were in high school we asked ourselves that question, but now we don't bother. It's not important enough to think about."

That answer kind of shook me. Here was a group of people, who by their own reckoning, were not very anxious to be defined as theists, much less Christian, or rather, really didn't worry about what they were. As I looked at them in wonder, I realized that here was a tribe whose language I did not speak, and to whose tribal customs and values I was a stranger.

I suppose a doctor, even when off duty, sometimes diagnoses people subconsciously. An off-duty missionary is tempted to look at any interesting group of people he comes across and to wonder if the gospel could possibly have any meaning to them.

I have a great deal of respect for pagans. I have been working among pagans for most of the adult years of my life. I know them when I see them. The word "pagan," though often thrown about very loosely, is not a derogatory term. *Paganus* means "pertaining to the rural areas, the villages, the countryside." It has the further meaning of civilian in contradistinction to a soldier. Considering the happenings at the Woodstock Aquarian Rock Festival[21] in Bethel, N.Y., similar happenings at other

20. See also letter of May 1961.

21. Woodstock was a three-day rock concert in August 1969, attended by approximately half a million people, which has since come to exemplify the youth counterculture of the 1960s.

festivals, the hippie farms in California, and the instinctive aversion to war, inherent in all these happenings, maybe *pagan* is not a completely inaccurate description of some of young Americans—they (the peaceful ones) of the religion of the countryside.

Adaptation[22] is the problem for any professional missionary. The gospel must be preached to the audience in front of him, to *this* audience—whether it be made up of stately Masai herdsmen, secretive Sonjo elders or the ingenuous young people of America.

We must reach them as they are and where they are. It is no use sitting in our stale, celibate cells and dreaming up a straw theology to use against straw men. Whether we are considering Masai tribesmen in their system of utterly free love, or Sonjo people with their very fluid idea of marriage, or the young people of Bethel bathing naked together in the river, we must make contact with that real pagan world. . . .

What does it mean to preach the Christian gospel to such a world? Freeing ourselves from all prejudgments, and letting the New Testament witness speak for itself, can we discover in what the apostolic preaching consisted? It is fairly clear that it was not a sexual assault on a pagan world. A reading of Peter's and Paul's approach to a non-Christian world is revealing. It would go something like this:

The God of love created the beautiful world and everything beautiful in it. God loves this world and wants man to be happy. The human race is one. The loving kindness of God has appeared to every nation, as it goes its own way. All can find God. All are called to share in the kingdom. All who do right are acceptable to God. Men are to be led from their gods to the one High God. The promise of the kingdom is for all.

If you study this approach very closely, you will see that something is missing. Sin is missing. There is no mention of original sin or any other kind of sin.[23]

And if you work among pagans long enough, you begin to become conscious of the hopelessness you engender in them by building your teaching on the foundation stone of Adam and Eve and their sin. Peter and Paul did not do this. And you are haunted by the look in the eyes of these good pagan people, if you go on insisting that their ancestors and their peers (who haven't heard this word that you bring) were and are steeped

22. See footnote to letter of September 10, 1960.

23. The following three paragraphs are part of chapter 4 of *CR*, the section "Sin, Salvation and Culture Blindness."

in sin. What are you trying to accomplish? Despair? Where is the good news you are supposed to be bringing them? The Sonjo and the Masai consider their ancestors beautiful, and the young people of America consider their peers so. It is no part of the Christian message to tell them that they are not. And if you look honestly and openly at pagans—as almost every missionary can testify—they are beautiful people.

St. Paul and St. Peter said as much: "The loving kindness of God has appeared to all men . . . God lets each nation, each tribe, each culture go its own way. . . . He is evident to them in the happiness He gives them" [Acts 14:16–17; 17:26].

There is no use arguing that it isn't true happiness they have, or that they aren't really happy—because they are, at least in that momentary escape from their loneliness and hopelessness, while bathing in the river at Bethel, or striding across the Masai plains, or dancing the beautiful dances of the Sonjo. St. Paul says that this happiness is a sign of God among them, of Christ among them. He was there before we ever got there. It is simply up to us to bring him out so they recognize him. Sin will come in later, after Christ, after getting to know Christ, in relation to Christ, but the sin portrayed by the first preachers of the Christian gospel is forgiven sin, something entirely different—the *felix culpa*.[24] This is not a mere difference in words. This is where Christianity parts company from Judaism and from Hinduism and from paganism. Sin is a conquered thing. This is a redeemed world. One wonders if one should dare talk to pagans about sin—until they know Christ, or apart from Christ.

The whole approach of Peter and Paul was open and positive. There was nothing negative in it, not even towards the pagan gods. We have the testimony of an impartial witness that Paul did not commit sacrilege against the local goddess.[25] Paul did not excoriate any pagan god. And neither should we, whether that god be Khambegeu of the Sonjo, or Engai of the Masai, or pot and hard rock.

All this is not a weakened and apologetic preamble to the gospel message. It is as Christian as the apostles. It is a necessary preamble if we ever expect these pagan cultures to be ready and willing to make the contribution that they can make to Christianity, which they must

24. "Happy fault" (Latin): sin is seen as "fortunate" because it leads to redemption, which is a more blessed state than would otherwise have been possible.

25. The city clerk in Ephesus points out to an enraged crowd that Paul had not blasphemed their goddess Diana (Acts 19:37).

make if the Church is to be really catholic—that revelation of God, that chapter in the history of salvation which they alone can tell us. It is a necessary preamble also to the startling revelation and demands of the Christian gospel. Those altruistic and social demands will be crucifying to the Sonjo, whom anthropologists classify as essentially narcissistic.[26] One wonders also what effect these demands would have on a generation of rather thoroughly in-turned young Americans.

And so, bit by bit, the revelation *from* the Sonjo goes on.[27] And slowly the message for the Sonjo builds up, and ever so carefully we pass it on to them, realizing, with true anguish, that the more unprofessional we are in this whole process, the more they will suffer for it through all their lives.

All my love,
Father Vince

Dec. 30, 1969

Dear Bill, Rosie and Gang,

Thanks for the Christmas cards and gift of *Time* magazine. I got your letter this week, Bill, with its explanations of driver's license, M.M.D. letters and several other things. I'm sorry I didn't get off a letter for Christmas. I hope it is not too late to wish all of you a happy New Year. I came back from the Dar es Salaam meeting[28] with just three days left before Christmas. I was too disgusted to do anything.

I wasn't disgusted at the meeting, just at the time it took, and not only in December, but during the whole year of 1969 with meetings, papers, studies, critiques, and politics. Many is the time during the course of the year when I wanted to throw in the towel as far as my participation was concerned, but we felt that it was all somehow important and

26. This is not actually a term in anthropology. The sentence which follows suggests that Donovan is using the term to describe the self-contained nature of Sonjo culture.

27. This appears to be the origin of *CR*'s original subtitle, "An Epistle from the Masai." The emphasis is original.

28. The Seminar Study Year was a program to consider the church in Tanzania in the light of Vatican II. It began with diocesan discussions (led in Arusha by Donovan and Fr. Ed Kelly), and culminated in national meetings in Dar es Salaam.

necessary. The idea was a study of the church in all of Tanzania in the light of Vatican II, from the perspective of the first hundred years of missionary work here, looking into the future. It was sponsored by the Tanzania Episcopal Conference. We in Arusha felt we had better take part in the whole thing, because we are pretty far out on a limb in many things, because we feel we have something to offer the church in the whole country on other things, and because we stand a much better chance of getting Rome to listen if some of the ideas are filtered through the episcopal conference of an entire nation.

How much we succeeded in all our goals, I don't know. We had to take part in a lot of things in which we weren't interested, so that we could be in on some things in which we were very interested. The case of the married priest or the village priest is one of the latter. You asked about Keriko, the old man among the Masai.[29] You just can't ordain a married man who doesn't know how to read and write in one Diocese in the world without putting yourself in a state of Schism, and thereby becoming some kind of sect. You have to somehow get the Church to agree to it. As a matter of fact, one of his functions would be to act as a sign of unity within his community and with the outside Church. As a leader of a sect, this important function as a sign of unity would be fairly well blotted out. We have more than Keriko now among the Masai and two even among the Sonjo as possible future priests. We have to keep very secret what we are doing with these people or we might spoil the chance of getting the Episcopal Conference to present our case to Rome. Meanwhile we are preparing them and giving them more and more functions in their communities. I hesitate to talk about it in any letter which might become public. I would never forgive myself if advance if premature publicity would spoil the chance of the thing becoming a reality.

And our hopes are growing. A year ago, when this Seminar Study Year (as it is called) began, the hostility from the local clergy of other Dioceses and from Bishops towards the idea of married priests was incredible, we almost thought insurmountable. After a year of meetings, discussions etc., the change in mentality is just as remarkable

I think everyone agrees that *something* must he done and although everyone is not yet prepared to go as far as we want to go, they are at least willing at last to discuss the problem.

29. Although there is no mention of Keriko in the letters apart from this, Donovan had talked about him during his leave immediately before this.

The value of the Seminar Study Year was that it was a meeting of the entire Church of a whole country—bishops, priests, sisters, brothers, and lay people—all meetings as equals. Bishops were there not to preside, but merely as delegates just like everyone else. Every person there had a vote and no one had a veto power. It was an incredible thing to see. No bishop ever presided at a particular meeting or at a general session. Different people were elected chairmen for different sessions. I was chairman for one session. An African lay woman was chairman for another. Aunt Sarah might even know the woman—Bernadette Kunambi.[30] Her husband studied at Duquesne and knew Mayor Barr. It was the first meeting of its kind in Africa—and perhaps in the world. It would do your heart good to see the kind of lay people there are in Tanzania, and what power they have. Bishops were there in civilian clothes. You could not tell a bishop from a father of a family. The final sessions were covered by Dutch Television, and there were representatives from many countries as observers.

Opinions and thoughts from Arusha always caused much commotion, and were inevitably received with much suspicion and fear, but a lot of them got through, I think, many more than I thought possible last June. Some of them didn't. Arusha, for instance, was the only voice raised to ask for a policy of realistic disengagement on the part of missionaries. It would seem that all the other missionaries in the country want to stay here for another hundred years. They fought our suggestion with a fanaticism that took your breath away. I think the problem will be taken out of our hands in a few years. Bishop Durning attended the June session. Kelly and I represented Arusha in this final session. . . .

All my love,
Vince

January 1970

Dear Relatives and Friends,

As the year 1969 passed into history, I thought of all you people who had helped me so much during that year, especially of those of you

---

30. Bernadette Kunambi (b. 1934) held such posts as YWCA National General Secretary and Chair of the Tanganyika Council of Women, and was a Member of Parliament ("Kunambi, Bernadette," in Kurtz, *Historical Dictionary*, 99).

who help me put out this MMD letter, and I just hope that some of the dreams that everyone of you dreams for 1970 come true. I wish I had it in my power to make them come true.

I parked my Land Rover outside the old fortified gate, and walked up into the Sonjo village for my weekly instruction leading to Baptism.[31] Yesterday I saw a particular man in the village and told him I would be coming. I know he will gather the people to see me. I've been watching that man for some time. He is not what you would call brilliant, but he has the talent and the ability to call these people—this community— together, and to hold them together. My teaching would be impossible without him. He is not the brightest one in the community, nor the most important, but he seems to be the only one who can hold the community together. Whenever I think of this community, I think of him.

During the meetings this particular man doesn't talk much, al-though he does keep order in the meetings. Other people often seem to grasp the teaching better than he does. As the months of teaching go by, different people apart from him appear more capable of carrying out the different functions called for by the nature of our meetings. Sometimes we open the meeting with a spontaneous prayer, or close it with one, and there is a certain person beginning to emerge as the *pray-er*. If we sing instead of praying, someone else again leads the singing. Some of the best questions are asked by a handful of people, men and women. Others again seem much better at explaining what they have heard—or, should I say, at preaching? And there are two different people who seem to have the power to stir this community up, to move it, to make it think. I suppose you might call them prophets. Even before Baptism I can see a Christian community forming, and it is not exactly the pattern of a Christian community to which I have been accustomed.

That man who calls the community together and holds them together—at the end of the instructions he won't be the one in the com-munity who knows the most theology. He won't be the preacher or the evangelist of the community. He won't be the prophet. He won't be nec-essarily the most important member in the community, or the one to make the most important contribution of which the community might someday be capable.

---

31. The following four paragraphs appear in the section, "Eucharistic Community with a Mission" in chapter 8 of *CR*.

But he would be the focal point of the whole community, the one who would enable the community to act, whether in worship or in service. He would be the animator of the individual members of the community, enabling them to make their various contributions. He would be the necessary sign of the power that is in all of them. He would be the sign of the unity that exists among them. He would be their link with the outside, the sign of their union with the outside, universal Church. He would be their priest.

And what of the ordination of that man? We have made an awful lot out of ordination, but what does it really come down to? Isn't it just the outside Church, in the person of the bishop, saying in a sentence or two, "Yes, you are the sign of the reality of that Christian community, the sign of the power that is in them. We recognize you as such. Because of you, that community is not a sect, but is a true part of the universal Church of Christ, is a true experience of Christianity." Is there really much more to it than that?

Long ago in Africa, I began to see that no Christian community could exist without a priest. It is only now that I'm beginning to see that no priest can exist without a community. Can there be a priest without a community? To answer that question by pointing to the invisible mark that forever remains on the soul of a priest is about as meaningful as talking about the invisible mark of Baptism on the soul of the non-believing, non-practicing Christian.

So many priests I know who were contemporaries of mine in the seminary are now teaching in high schools and colleges and universities, and seem very happy in their work. But I wonder what their ordination means. What does the priesthood have to do with their teaching, and vice versa? The man who runs the Vatican Library—isn't he called a priest, and even a bishop? What meaning does that have? Where is the community of which he is priest and bishop? Karl Rahner,[32] the great theologian-priest! I wonder why he felt it necessary to be priest in order to make his great theological contribution to the Church. And good Father Greeley,[33] smiling out at us from the pages of so many Catholic papers: surely his greatest contribution to the American Church has little to do with the

32. Karl Rahner (1904–1984) was a German Jesuit theologian whose theology helped shape Vatican II.

33. Andrew Greeley (b.1928) is presently Professor of Sociology at the University of Arizona and is a popular columnist in newspapers and periodicals.

fact that he is called priest. Couldn't all these people have made their unique contributions to the Church without being priest? . . .

What is a priest? Is he an expert or authority in a specialized area, or a specialist of the world within, as some would have it? Or is he simply a man taken from among men, to stand for them, to signify and focus for them the meaning of the life of the people of God in community? Haven't we twisted and distorted the meaning of priest? Perhaps you're thinking, "Aha! There is that missionary putting everyone else down and claiming that only missionaries are priests." Well, not exactly. As a matter of fact, it was the consideration of my own position which started me thinking.

For a full year I was evangelizing pagan Masai.[34] There was no Christian community at all. At the beginning of that year I faithfully got in my Mass early every morning in the privacy and secrecy of my tent—all for myself. Put yourself in my place. Would you have gone on for a full year saying Mass for yourself, with no Christians and no Christian community in existence? During that year when I realized I was not a priest, I yearned for the end of the year, for the Baptism that would bring a new Christian community into existence, so that I could be a priest again, so that I could be their priest. It was only when that Christian community did come into existence that I realized numbly that I would *never* be the priest to that community. They would have to have their own focal point, their own animator, their own sign of unity. They would have to have a priest of their own.

I began to see that this pattern could be repeated over and over again in a missionary's life. I am rather slow. It was only then I knew that a missionary did not have to be a priest at all.

In the aftermath of Vatican II, we have been striving mightily to charge the priesthood with new meaning and significance. But I sometimes feel that all we have been doing is simply trying to change the circumstances in which the old priesthood functions—more challenging, exciting, fulfilling circumstances—but still the same old priesthood, the same old status, the same old number one position in the new circumstances. What I think we are afraid to do is to look at the problem in such a way that we might end up changing the meaning of the priesthood, or at least what it has come to mean down through the centuries.

A change like this could bring in a lot of differences. For one thing, the importance of priests in the midst of their communities would no

---

34. This section is quoted in *CR*, chapter 8, "Eucharistic Community with a Mission."

longer be measured by their position alone, or by the fact that they occupy such a position, but rather by the way they fulfill the meaning of
that position, by carrying out their function in the community—just as it
is measured for every other Christian. If, besides fulfilling that function,
they could, because of personal charisma, serve as prophet or teacher in
the community as well, they would indeed be valuable Christians.

Everything we believed about the priest in the past is true. It is just
that all that dignity, all that power is equally as true of the Christian
community as it is of him. It is not so much that priests must decrease,
as that Christians must increase [John 3:30].

That shouldn't be any reason for priests to be disheartened and
discouraged and confused. The Sonjo wouldn't understand what the
confusion was all about.

All my love,
Father Vince

February 1970

Dear Relatives and Friends,

You have been very kind and generous to me and I am very grateful. I wish some of you could suddenly appear here ready to go on one
of my safaris with me, and I could say thank you in person. Loliondo
sometimes seems so very far away, especially when one wants to express
a very personal feeling of gratitude.

The valley of the Sonjo is an isolated place.[35] It is a country surrounded on all sides by the land of the Masai, a people who are not exactly notorious for their contact with the outside world. One would think
that, in such isolation, discussions and decisions about religion would
be pretty insular and provincial, having little relevance to the rest of the
world. Yet, sometimes, sitting there in the Sonjo valley, under the magnificent fig trees, I can sense that what these people are pondering, many
have pondered before them. They are touching the raw nerve of a sore
that is festering throughout the world. They are reflecting on the invitation proffered them to bring all the cultural and spiritual riches of their

---

35. Cf. *CR*, chapter 4, the section "The Nations."

tribe into a worldwide brotherhood, which means at the same time, of course, opening themselves up to every other tribe and race on the face of the earth. What they are wrestling with is a decision and a dilemma, in miniature, that the whole world is facing. A tiny drop of history right before your eyes.

Before I came to Sonjo, or even to Africa, I used to wonder, whenever I came across it, at the insistence the Bible, especially the New Testament, placed on the nations, on the drive towards the *nations*. I used to wonder if this was not perhaps an obsession of classical times that had little meaning for today, for us. It is only since I came to Africa, that I have seen how deadly wrong I was.

The burning hatred, hostility and prejudice of one race or tribe towards another is the force that has already torn apart the Congo and Nigeria; the force that is building up to an explosion in South Africa and Rhodesia; is boiling over in the mid-East between Arab and Jew, in the far East between China and Russia, and in America between black and white.[36] It is the same force that Paul and Peter had to fight against so desperately. The whole Bible squared off against this elementary evil.

The neglect to see this in the New Testament is to miss indeed the main thrust of the gospel message—the universalism of the Good News. So many people today are asking if missionaries are important or even necessary. I would have to answer, "Yes, they are, perhaps more for this reason than for anything else." Every artificial attempt, from the time of the Tower of Babel up to the United Nations to "make a great people, a people which is one" has failed. I believe that only Christianity has the inherent capability to accomplish this, the inner strength necessary to match the primeval force of racism and tribalism.

For this reason, more than any other, do the final words of our Lord make any sense at all to me, "Go out to the ends of the earth and preach the gospel to every nation" [Mark 16:15; Matt 28:19].

We tend to think of nations as the artificial and political divisions made by statesmen and politicians, which we can so easily see drawn

---

36. There was violence in the Congo for some years before and after independence. There had been civil war in Nigeria over the breakaway province of Biafra in the late 60s. Apartheid still ruled South Africa. Rhodesia (later Zimbabwe)'s white government declared itself independent of British colonial rule in 1965. The Six-Day War had been fought between Arabs and Israelis in 1967. In 1968 and 1969, the Soviet Union and China came close to war. In 1968, Martin Luther King, leader of the civil rights movement in the USA, had been assassinated.

with straight lines on maps—such as the incredible divisions made by someone in the British Foreign Office, which resulted in tribes of Africa being cut in two, and remaining so even until today.[37] I don't think the Bible had this type of nation in mind; indeed, did not even know of it. Kenya or Tanzania would not be nations in the biblical sense. Neither would the United States.

The word for *nation* that is used in the language in which the New Testament is written is *ethnos*. An *ethnic group* would come closer to the meaning of the biblical *nation* than the modern political state. A biblical nation might well be a group of American Indians, or the Masai, or the Sonjo, or the American blacks. It is to *these* nations that the gospel must be preached, according to the command of Christ [Mark 13:10; Matt 24:14]. It is they who must become disciples, must be brought into the brotherhood.

The Jews, the first ones to hear this command of Christ, did not take to it very kindly. The first crisis in the Church arose because some big-named people badly misunderstood this command.[38] The next ones in charge of the Christian message, and the command of Christ, were the people of the Roman Empire. They couldn't conceive of the message being entrusted, or the brotherhood extended, to the barbarians.[39] Then the barbarians—our ancestors, the white Europeans (and Americans)—having come into possession of the message, became the most arrogant and dangerous possessors of all. Their tenure has lasted longest of all. They have, in fact, refused for all practical purposes to pass on this message to those outside—to the blacks and browns and reds and yellows of the world. Because to pass on this message means, in effect, to extend the brotherhood to those outside, to accept those outside into the brotherhood, as brothers. Whereas the Jews and the Romans eventually got around to doing just this, under the press of history, the barbarians have never really brought themselves to do it—until now. It is a stark fact that until now the non-white world has not become Christian, has not

37. Although this is most pertinently true of the Maasai, who straddle Tanzania and Kenya, it is true of other colonial national boundaries too.

38. Donovan probably has in mind the controversy over the admission of uncircumcised Gentiles to the church, e.g., Acts 15.

39. This may be a reference to the fact that in the fourth and fifth centuries, the Arians made more converts among the barbarians than did the Orthodox. In this period, many bishops were from the privileged Roman classes.

been accepted into the brotherhood. That is the meaning of the statistic that four-fifths of the world has never heard the gospel message.

Why do the nations rage? Why this turmoil among the nations? the Psalmist asks [Ps 2:1]. Why, indeed? Perhaps because the brotherhood and peace and justice have not been extended to them. And the raging sometimes comes close to home, as the tenuous relationship between Christianity and the non-white world continues to break down. The heroes of black America, for instance, Rap Brown, Stokely Carmichael, Malcolm X, Eldridge Cleaver,[40] and Mohammed Ali[41] can hardly be considered Christians. The Christian gospel will have to come alive again in a new and entirely different sense for the American Negro, if it is ever to mean anything to him.

But history has a way of playing tricks. Just as the Christianized Jews and the Romans have been shoved aside in Christian history, so now it is the turn of the European-Americans. Before this century is out, even as the Christian Church continues on its way as a dwindling minority in the world, in this same period, the members of the predominantly non-white Third World, for the first time in history, will begin to become the majority in the Christian Church.[42] The barbarian invasion, in reverse.

The call of the nations, or the equality of the nations, as proclaimed in the Bible, is just as startlingly pertinent today in the era of the rich nations and the poor nations, of the third world nations and of the United Nations—as ever it was when it was first proclaimed.

"The loving kindness of God has appeared to all men. God has never forgotten any nation. Each nation goes its own way with evidence of God available to it. All nations can find God. All are called to share in God's kingdom. Through Christ, the Good News is brought to all men. The promise is for all."[43]

So that we make no mistake about just how inclusive this call is, the Apocalypse spells it out in great detail, ". . . the Good News to all who live on the earth, every nation, race, language and tribe" (Apoc. 14:6).[44]

40. Brown, Carmichael, X, and Cleaver were all involved in the civil rights movement and leaders of the Black Panthers in the 1960s.

41. Muhammad Ali (born Cassius Clay) was a three-time World Heavyweight Boxing Champion. He changed his name when he joined the Nation of Islam in 1964, and became a Muslim in 1975.

42. This reversal is documented in Jenkins, *The Next Christendom*.

43. This appears to be a conflation of such texts as Titus 3:4; Acts 17:27; 2:39.

44. "Apoc." Or "Apocalypse" is another name for the Book of Revelation.

As I pass on this message of Peter and Paul and John to the segment of a nation before me, I am overcome with a kind of melancholy.[45] The irony of history is playing itself out, in capsule form, before my very eyes. As I watch these Sonjo men and women, among the fig groves, ponder the implications of this message, I know that they will somehow have to work out their own response to it. And their response, whatever it is, will not have very much to do with me.

As the message passes from us to them, I find myself hoping that they will make better use of it than we did.

All my love,
Father Vince

April 1970

Dear Relatives and Friends,

As spring comes to America, I send along love, greetings and thanks from a grateful guy living on the equator in a country where the only thing that is not changing these days is the weather.

Once upon a time there lived a man named *Khambegeu*. He first appeared as a grown man in the village of *Tinaga*. He began to work wonders, and the reaction to these wonders was decidedly mixed. Opposition to him grew, and he was driven out. He then went to the lush green valley south of *Tinaga*, with its several villages scattered on the hillsides. He continued to work wonders. He cured sick people. He turned water into alcoholic beverage. He walked on the waters. He cured a blind man by applying mud to his eyes. Persecution increased. He fled to yet other villages. He was wounded by the people, the most serious wound being a spear wound in his side. He died and was buried in a cave-like grave. Sometime afterwards, when people went to examine the grave, they found it empty, with only his sandals remaining. It was believed that *Khambegeu* rose, and then ascended out of the valley to a high mountain or to the sun. At the end of the world, he will come back again. *Khambegeu* is God.

45. From here to the end of this letter is incorporated into *CR*, chapter 4, the section "The Nations."

What would you do if you heard a story like that? Anyone who has visited the Sonjo valley, and has been interested enough to listen, has heard this story. I have heard it over and over again. It differs in detail from village to village, but basically it is the same story. And it is the basis for the faith of the pagan Sonjo.

Anthropologists tell us that this story predates the arrival of the first missionaries in the 19th Century. Its origin goes back much further than that. As a matter of fact, it is lost in the beginnings of that intriguing and exasperating thing called African history.

It would seem that here would be an ideal and easy task for a Christian missionary. These people know the whole story of the God-made-man. What could be easier? On the other hand, Europe and America are filled with people who know the Christ-story. But it doesn't mean a great deal to them, doesn't influence their lives overmuch, has ceased to be the vital force that motivates them. It is like a meaningless myth in the center of their lives.

This is a pretty good description of Khambegeu and the Sonjo. Every Sonjo child knows the story of Khambegeu, his life, work, death, and resurrection. But that is about as far as it goes. That Khambegeu died and rose has significance—for *Khambegeu* alone. The fact itself does not shed one iota of light or gentleness over the life of the Sonjo. That life is a bleak life, a short life, a cruel life, a life of utter chance and capriciousness. The Sonjo weep like all those who have no hope [cf. 1 Thess 4:13].

Even though the life of Khambegeu has been transmitted to them down through the centuries, something is missing, just as it is so often missing for a Christian world that knows the story of Christ. The whole significance of that life is missing.

In the case of the Sonjo, we have, I think, the clearest reason for that troublesome question which forever haunts a missionary, which personally haunts this missionary who is writing to you. Why have I come eight thousand miles to these people? Why did I leave a life that was familiar to me, to take up this one that is forever strange? What do I hope to accomplish?

I can never forget a question an atheistic friend of mine from New York asked me years ago, "What are you *doing* out there?" I think I have been trying to answer that question ever since.

What am I trying to bring to these people? What am I trying to do for them? Am I trying to bring them a beautiful philosophy, a satisfying theology, a stirring myth? There is no need for that. They have their own. Am I trying to make them better people, holier people? I have seen too many good and holy pagans to believe that. Am I trying to save them, to bring them salvation? The authentic will of God to save all men could not be so flimsy and arbitrary as to depend for so much on me.

After all these years of working as sincerely as I can and thinking as honestly as I can, I can come up with only one answer to that question. There is only one reason I have come here. There is only one thing I can bring to those people which they do not have. The only reason I have come here is to bring these people *hope*. The only thing I have to offer them, which they do not have, is not theology or mythology or goodness or holiness or even salvation. It is simply *hope*.

I have to say to these Sonjo: "This *Khambegeu* whom you worship—I know him. I make bold to say I know more about him than you do—what he means for you and for me. I, together with all those who believe in him, call him *Christ*. And that resurrection of his has meaning for you and me, for our lives and for our world that you have not even begun to dream about. That resurrection, when he became the Lord, and burst through into a new kind of existence, is like a great hope that has dawned on our world."

It is a strange feeling to analyze your whole missionary life and to realize that it works itself out into being nothing but a precarious line of bearing hope to others. My only work is to be a bearer of hope, a carrier of hope.

But one doesn't have to dwell overlong on the rather forlorn picture of a lone missionary in a foreign field. What about the Church itself of which he is only a symbol? What is the meaning of the Church in Europe or America or in any other part of this jaded, disillusioned and despairing world?

Why is the Church in America? Just try to picture to yourself that vast and indescribably complex thing called the Church in America—all those dioceses and jurisdictions and hierarchies and chanceries and priests and religious and faithful and buildings and resources. Why is it there? Is it there for itself, or for the power and glory of it all? Is it there to make America better, or to make Americans better or holier? Do we really believe that? Is it there to save America, to bring salvation to America? Can we believe even that? Or isn't it there simply and solely—like the missionary—to bring *hope* to America and to the world, the only hope that America and the world really have?

All my love,
Father Vince

May 1970

Dear Relatives and Friends,

I don't think you people will ever know how much of a help you have been to me, how you have enabled me to carry on this work. Know one thing. What I am talking about in this particular letter is not people like you.

The work of bringing the gospel to the Sonjo people is coming towards its climax. We have reached eight villages and a kind of pattern is forming as far as the final stages of preparation are concerned. There are a series of questions emerging which need answering at this time. This is not a test for Baptism for the candidates concerned, but a kind of final dialogue to see that we understand one another. In the course of doing this from village to village, we find ourselves asking each of the prospective Christians a rather obvious question:

"Why do you want to be a Christian? Why do you want to be baptized?" If he answers, "To be saved; to save my soul," or "To go to heaven," we ask a second question: "If you do become a Christian, would you, according to the circumstances and your abilities, feel the obligation to pass on this Christian message, this good news, to others?" If the answer to the second question is as unsatisfactory as the answer to the first, we refuse him Baptism, or defer it, and ask the person involved to think the whole thing over until the next Baptism might come around. We point out that it is probably my fault. Perhaps I have failed to explain well enough what Christianity is. Or it may be that he has failed to understand it.

This might seem a harsh procedure to follow, but we have begun to feel it is a necessary one. There seems to be no other way to prevent a distorted meaning of Christianity from creeping into the community right at the start. It is only in the teaching of an outward-turned Christianity that we have any hope of achieving a Christianity. An inward-turned

Christianity is a dangerous counterfeit, an alluring masquerade—is no Christianity at all.

The salvation of one's own soul, or self-salvation, or self-sanctification, or self-perfection, or self-realization, or self-fulfillment may well be the goal of Buddhism or Greek philosophy or modern psychology—but it is not the goal of Christianity.

For someone to embrace Christianity—or to enter the religious life or the priesthood for that matter—for the purpose of self-fulfillment or self-sanctification or self-salvation is, I think, to betray or to misunderstand Christianity at its deepest level.

And this temptation to look inward is one that affects not only individuals, but also whole Christian communities, parishes, dioceses. In such cases, the spiritual or physical well-being of the Christian community becomes the very goal of the community, the whole reason for its existence. Any ulterior motive for the community's existence is completely forgotten. Indeed, the only valid reason for the community's existence is forgotten.

Christianity must be a force that moves outwards. A Christian, in his community or out of it, must, like Christ, be essentially a "man for others."[46] Not for himself. And the Christian community is basically in existence for others. That is the whole meaning of a Christian community. A Christian community which spends all its resources on a building campaign for its own needs has long ago left Christianity high and dry on the bank. Or all its resources on an education program or youth program, for that matter. A Christian community is in existence "for others," not for "its own."

The universal church is not immune to the same weakness. It is amazing how in every major crisis in world history, the church has the temptation to react in an in-turned way. "Straighten out the calendar of the saints," she says, or, "Purge some of the more outlandish ones on the list." "Reform Canon Law." "Revise the seminary curriculum or structure." "Make new laws about the priesthood or the religious life." "Clean up the liturgy." "Tidy up the sacraments." "Be good and the world will come to you."

And each time the thing that causes the crisis is outside the church. Instead of reaching out and reacting to the crisis where it exists, in a

46. "God in human form . . . man existing for others, and hence the Crucified" (Bonhoeffer, *Letters and Papers*, 179).

realistic way, the church turns inward and cleans its own house. Some of that housecleaning doesn't have very far-reaching effects, and the reforms never really touch the cause of the crisis. After a time, the re-vamped Liturgy grows stale and boring, the Eucharist ceases to be an *an-nouncing* of the death of the Lord, the sacraments become magic again, ecumenism—forgetting its main purpose—"That the whole world may believe"—becomes clubby and suburban, and youth goes its own way.

The ferment and change and revolution are outside; an inward-turned church never seems to realize why its reforms do not affect the world.

The Church has a long history of acting this way. When you read the *Acts of the Apostles*, you would almost think that if the apostles were interested in the salvation of the world, they must have been convinced that the world would come to Jerusalem. This was safe, conservative thinking on their part. After all, Israel, from whom they had sprung, had a very special vocation. The call of Israel was not a mission, a being sent to the nations. Hers was a vocation simply to exist. The nations would come to her. Israel, the Jewish people, has no other mission to the pagan nations than to be the chosen people, to exist. She was not sent forth.

Then, too, Christ himself was a Jew, was circumcised, and, by and large, during his life, followed the Jewish law emanating from Jerusalem. What were the followers of Christ to do? There were some big-named thinkers—Peter, head of the Apostles, John, beloved disciple, James, brother of the Lord, among them—who thought there was nothing else to do except what they were doing. They met in the temple and prayed there. They approved of Jewish sacrificial custom and the paying of the temple tax, and submitted themselves to the judgment of the synagogue. They settled down in Jerusalem and acted as if they were some sub-sect of Judaism. Observation of all Jewish laws, including circumcision, was enjoined on all those who would enter Christianity. What else could they do? Anything else would be sheer heresy.

It would take a radical thinker indeed, a truly revolutionary thinker to see it any other way.

There was such a thinker. His name was Paul of Tarsus, and he proved to be a true troubler of Israel.[47] He went up to Jerusalem and fairly blew up. He resisted those men to their faces [Gal 2:11–13]. He pointed out that their safe, conservative thinking would make Christianity into

---

47. King Ahab called the prophet Elijah a "troubler of Israel" (1 Kgs 18:17).

an in-turned religion, whereas in actuality, it is essentially an out-turned faith, turned out to the world. The church is not Israel. The church has a mission. Christ did not say, "Be good and the world will come to you." He said, "Go out to all the world." Paul told these men that the church would never be Christian if it turned itself in on Jerusalem. It would only be true if it turned itself out from Jerusalem and reached to the ends of the world. It is fortunate that Paul won that argument. If Peter, James, and John had won, Christianity would have deteriorated into an insignificant sect of Judaism. It was Paul who enabled the church to be catholic and—shall we say it?—"pagan-oriented."

And even until now, it is only our contact with the pagan world, and the non-Christian world, that has kept us honest—and true to ourselves. It is when we have turned in on ourselves, and away from that world to which we were sent, that we have become stale and decaying and irrelevant. A church that turns in on itself is no longer a church. A church that turns in on itself will surely die. Many have died in history.

And that alluring siren call, that call of the Lorelei leading to destruction,[48] is being heard once again in our day. "We have reached the end of the era of the foreign missions," it says. "Today, France is the mission. Holland is the mission. Chicago and New York and Los Angeles are the mission."[49] Big-named, respected people are saying this, and, by saying it, are making it the thing to be believed and held and repeated. It would take brave, radical, revolutionary thinkers indeed to go against this rising tide of accepted thought. But God help us, such thinkers had better be found, or Paul's whole battle will have been fought in vain.

And to think it all begins in the mind of a person, standing there in front of you, telling you he wants to be a Christian to save his own soul, and sees no reason why anyone besides a foreign missionary or a paid catechist has the obligation to take the good news to those who have not heard it.

You look up at him wearily and sadly—and send him away.

Sincerely,
Father Vince

---

48. Lorelei was the name of one of the mythological Rhine maidens who lured sailors to shipwreck by their beautiful singing.

49. Cf. the section "Whither mission?" in chapter 1 of CR.

June 1970

Dear Relatives and Friends,

Each day, as I turn on the radio, I hear more of America's troubles.[50] Burdened as you are with troubles, both national and personal, your continuing generosity is all the more remarkable to me. I sympathize with you and I thank you. . . .

As wise as we are in this sophisticated twentieth century, we find it extremely difficult to see the human race in any terms other than American or European, which makes our judgments on the subject about one-fifth valid.

We talk about the *world* entering into the post-Christian age, or the secular age, or the age of atheism, and what we are really referring to is the American-European world. We talk about "man coming of age"[51] and what we really mean are those who have emerged from the University of Chicago. We ignore about four-fifths of the world in our thinking.

It seems a fairly ridiculous stance to sit at the very pinnacle of Greek and Western thought and to pose as the dehellenizing saviors of the future of belief. It may well be that that future lies in truly non-hellenic hands.

When we talk about Christianity, we interpret it from our own point of view alone, which is an extremely ethno-centric interpretation of God's revelation to man. Christianity has been mutilated down through the centuries by the attempts of the Irish and Italians and Germans and Americans to turn it into a tribal religion. The mutilation is no less serious if the attempts today are more sophisticated. Christianity is for the human race, and it must be as wide as the human race to be valid. "Something is lacking to the body of Christ," St. Paul says, and what is lacking has some peculiar relationship to the world that is not Christian. Someday perhaps we might even have an African theologian tell us what the mystical body of Christ really means.

In short, as far as sin is concerned, I think all we are trying in our missionary approach today is to make certain that when the African pagan begins to become conscious of sin, at that moment we will be there to acquaint him with the forgiveness of sin that is available because of

50. In May 1970, four students were shot dead and nine others wounded by members of the Ohio National Guard on the campus of Kent State University (Ohio). The students were protesting the American invasion of Cambodia.

51. Bonhoeffer, *Letters and Papers*, 163, 178.

Christ. The job of a missionary, after all, is not to teach sin, but rather, the forgiveness of sin.

I have seen neurotic, guilt-ridden Africans, but, by and large, they have been christianized Africans, christianized in a way with which our ethno-centric critics might agree, but a way that we, in the midst of these pagans, feel an urgent need to change.

Americans can sometimes be victims of the most incredible culture blindness. I should know. I am one of them.[52]

All my love,
Father Vince

July 1970

Dear Relatives and Friends,

I was really thrilled when one of you, on the biggest day of her life remembered me in such a unique way.[53] That is the way I feel. I am never so conscious of all of you as when I am in the midst of my work.

The word "mission" is used in different ways.[54] In one way it means the act of being sent. And so we say the mission of Christ, the mission of the Church. In another way, it means the plant or establishment where missionaries live. One meaning, the first, is one of the most dynamic, revolutionary ideas imaginable. The second is just the opposite. You would have to have the experience of being sent to a simple, underdeveloped people like the Sonjo, of having the job of preaching the gospel to them, to understand what the mission of the church can sometimes mean, to sense the uncontrollable force you are setting loose. This gospel is their link with the outside, their first step towards development. But as sure as I am that my work is to participate in this mission to the Sonjo, just so certain am I that the development and building up and institutionalizing of the ideas brought in are not part of my work. The one thing I would never do is build a mission in the Sonjo valley. That would be the end of the mission of the church, the end of the revolution.

52. This last paragraph appears at the conclusion of chapter 4 of *CR*.

53. Nora (Donovan's sister) and Michael Koren decided to marry on June 6th, the anniversary of Donovan's ordination.

54. Much of the remainder of this letter is incorporated into chapter 7 of *CR*, the section entitled "The In–Turned Church."

To my way of thinking, in the long history of the African missions, one of the most static and paralyzing ideas in that history has been that of the mission compound. And it is one strictly of our own making. If we go back to Paul or to any other of the early preachers of the gospel, we find that he neither built nor established a mission. He himself was the mission, he and his companions, a mobile mission, a temporary mission in any one place, a team in motion or movement towards the establishment, not of a mission, but of an indigenous church.

Paul founded churches. We found missions. A permanent mission necessarily carries with it the atmosphere of foreignness, of colonialism. The word *mission* should really mean something in action, in motion, in movement. Mission compound, on the other hand, implies that the movement has come to a standstill. In the latter case, it is no longer a centrifugal force reaching out forever as far as it can. It becomes instead centripetal, attracting everything to itself. Instead of symbolizing movement towards another thing (in this case, church), it becomes instead, itself, the end of the line. African resentment at this missionary presence, in some places one hundred years after the initial foundations, is understandable, to say the least. The word missionary is really a misnomer in this context. The command to go out and preach the gospel has become subtly transformed into "Stay here; take care of what you have. Let others come to you." Missionary movement comes to a dead stop.

This missionary malaise in the field itself is only a surface symptom of a deeper malady afflicting the home church, the sending church of Europe and America. And it is here that bishops, priests, theologians and all, who call themselves teachers in our church, are reaching a moment of truth. They must surely realize that they are jeopardizing the biblical authority of their teaching if they go on refusing to acknowledge that the church is set in this world with the sole purpose of carrying the gospel to the ends of the earth.

We lose ourselves in talking about the many works of the church. Actually there is only one work—mission. Mission is not one of the many tasks assigned to the church. It is the only task. It is the meaning of the church, the proper work of the church. There is no other. The church can exist only in so far as it is in mission, in so far as it participates in the act of Christ, which is mission. The church becomes the mission, the living outreach of God to the world. The church exists only in so far as it carries Christ to the world.

The full truth is even stranger and more disturbing than that. So far from the truth is it that mission is only one of the tasks of the church, that the opposite is true. The church is only part of the mission—the mission of God sending His Son to the world. Without this mission, there would be no church. The idea of church without mission is an absurdity.

And as was pointed out, the ideas of mission and revolution are very close together indeed. The biblical vision of the mission of the church is as basically revolutionary as it is possible to be. The mission of the church is indissolubly linked to the end time, to the end of our world as we know it. The gospel must first be preached to all the nations, and then the end will come [Matt 24:14]. If history still continues, it is singularly because the gospel for the world must first be preached to all the nations. From now on, history has no other meaning. The destiny of the world and mankind is dependent on the mission to the nations.

One does not have to dig very deeply to uncover the connection between the mission and revolution, not in theory, but in fact. For the past hundred years, missionaries, the closest collaborators of the colonialists, have been in actuality their deadliest enemies. Just as St. Paul carried with him the germ of the end of slavery,[55] so the missionaries—peaceful, conservative, slow-moving men by nature—have unwittingly carried with them the end of colonialism, and the beginnings of the independence movements throughout the world.[56] Long before communism[57] was born, these men were spreading the ideas of equality and dignity and justice and unity and freedom throughout the world. They were presenting to a people, who scarcely dared dream of it, the prospect of moving forward in a world with unlimited possibilities. They were planting the germs of revolution. The negro revolution[58] is only a grandchild of that larger revolution. The campus revolt of students is only part of it. What is actually involved in the freeing of the women of the third world makes the Women's Lib[59] movement seem like a joke in comparison. We who live in the third world are conscious of a revolution going on around us

55. E.g., Gal 3:28, "In Christ there is neither . . . slave nor free."

56. This is documented by Sanneh, *Translating the Message*, among others.

57. Karl Marx published *The Communist Manifesto* in 1848. Communists came to power in Russia after the Revolution of 1917, and in China in 1949.

58. This was one way of referring to the civil rights movement of the 1960s.

59. "Women's Liberation" was the name given to the movement for equal rights for women in the West during the 1960s.

every day, a revolution that has no equal. This is not the third revolution, or the fourth revolution. This will be the last one.

The walls of history are held apart, the beginning and the end, through the mission of the church. Those participating in this mission of the church—Christians—are messengers of the end time. They are leading the world to its end. They are the true revolutionaries.

There is only one thing for those members of the church to do, who do not want to accept this view, and that is to deny its scriptural basis. I think it is no coincidence that those who most fear this revolution are those who in fact deny this vision, those who have been most unfaithful to this biblical vision of mission. Unfaithfulness to the vision of mission is not restricted to Europe and America.

Where do you see this fear? Where is the evidence of this unfaithfulness to mission? You see it in African priests unwilling to leave their mission compound of Christians, to go to a continent that is pagan— their continent. You see it in African bishops unwilling to send them. You see it in the distribution of the half million priests in the world, with ninety percent of then to Europe and America. You see it in the sending out of the forty-thousand missionaries of the world, with less than one thousand of them assigned to evangelize the four-fifths of the world that is pagan. You see it in the missionary congregations and societies of our day, which have suddenly discovered that their vocation is, after all, to the upkeep of institutions that have sprung up around them in the homeland. You see it in the American church which finds nothing wrong in spending ninety percent of its resources on itself. You see it in the scandal of missionary finances, a subject that would not bear the light of day. You see it in the melancholy fact of the scarcely eighteen percent of the world that has heard of Christ, nearly two thousand years after the Resurrection.

But the mission of God will not be thwarted. The dynamic mission of Christ to the world will go on, *with* the European-American church, if that church chooses to be faithful to that revolutionary vision, and without it, if it does not. In the last analysis, the numbers involved do not count for much.

"Fear not, little flock, for it has pleased your father to give to you the kingdom" [Luke 12:32].

All my love,
Father Vince

October 1970

Dear Relatives and Friends

... Evangelization is not the same thing as convert-making or pros-elytizing. It is not a work addressed to an individual or to individuals. Rather, it is an exposing of a people to the gospel, an opening up of a section of the world to the power and possibilities of the gospel. It is the inviting of sometimes unpredictable responses to the gospel message. It does not consist in predetermining those responses as convert-making does. It is a work which calls for a new attitude towards the gospel, and an almost frightening openness to it. I have seen signs, even in America, that a new day is dawning for evangelism in this sense.

This particular religious congregation [the Spiritans], to fulfill its commitment to evangelization, and because of its limited personnel, will have to take the step all missionary congregations should take. It must point out to American Christians that the missionary obligation of the church is not fulfilled by the work of a few religious congregations. The burden of evangelization falls on all Christians, and on all Christian churches. Vocation directors, instead of addressing themselves primarily to grade school and high school boys and looking to these boys to swell the seminary ranks, will have to address themselves to entire Christian communities, to the mature Christians of these parishes and dioceses, to fill the missionary ranks. And they must be prepared to accept the response that comes from these communities in the form of diocesan priests and nuns and lay people, men and women, college boys and girls, married and unmarried, who are willing and able to participate for some time in the front lines of missionary endeavor.

This is hardly a move calculated to impoverish the home churches. Mission is a two way street. Ecumenism, liturgical reform, the use of the vernacular in the Catholic Church, adaptation—have come from the missions.

All this would mean an end to clerical domination of missionary work, and a vastly different concept of missionary training and forma-tion. (*Priest* and *missionary* should long ago have been separated.) It would also mean a different kind of missionary propaganda and sup-port, with the idea of a sending church supplanting that of a sending religious congregation.

If any religious congregation could help to make such an idea live, even by dying itself in the process, it would not have existed in vain. It might even contribute in a small way to our becoming a missionary people again in all the world.

With all my love,
Father Vince

January 1971

Dear Relatives and Friends,

The years keep rolling by! My warmest greetings to all of you, as '71 starts on its way. I hope this year treats all of you well.

I had finished instructions in four of the Sonjo villages. The other four were nearing completion. I planned to go to the villages, one by one, to ask the people if they wanted to accept Christianity through baptism.

I was excited as I climbed to the village of Ebwe. This was the first village I had come to, the first community that I chose for instruction, the first one to agree to instruction, the first one to complete it. The people had followed instruction for one solid year, one day of every week. The instruction I gave to these people of Ebwe was my most carefully prepared work. I couldn't wait to see them.[60]

I found them all waiting in the square where I had been meeting with them every week. I greeted them and sat down.

"Well," I began, "you have heard everything I can tell you about the Christian faith. You have had a week since I last saw you to think it over and talk it over together. Do you accept what I have told you? Do you believe it all? Do you accept Jesus Christ? Do you want to be Christians? Do you want to be baptized? I'd like to have your answer now."

Chief Saliase answered slowly and clearly, "We have heard what you mean by the Christian faith. For almost a year now we have talked of little else. We have looked forward to your instructions each week. They have been the high point of each week. I speak for everyone here. We

60. The story which follows in this letter is told in chapter 7 of *CR* in the section entitled "Rejection." The village is not named, simply described as "very far from the mission compound."

have listened with great interest. We thank you for coming to us. We think we understand what you mean by the Christian faith. But—we cannot accept it. We cannot accept your Christ or believe in him. We cannot accept baptism. Forgive us. Our answer is, 'No.'"

No! I was stunned. I couldn't believe it. No! I looked at Saliase and then around at the others. They returned my look steadily and calmly. I looked down at the ground, trying desperately to think of something to say. What had I done wrong? What was the weak point in my instruction? Or was it in me? Was I the wrong person to have tried evangelizing those difficult people? A whole year! How could they follow instructions for a whole year, and then refuse baptism? A whole community refusing the Christian message—refusing Christ! Somehow I had failed badly in the mission entrusted to me.

I realized that they were waiting in silence for me to say something. I looked up at them again, even though they were now slightly out of focus.

"Thank you, Chief," I said, not knowing really what I wanted to say. "Thank you, all of you. You have been a very attentive audience and a very intelligent one. You have treated me with great respect and patience. I have disturbed your hour of rest for a year now. I know how much it must have inconvenienced you."

I stood up, with my mind finally coming back into gear. "It's a funny thing. I just realized that I have come here for no other reason than this—to tell you about the Christian faith. That is the only thing I came to bring you—not medicine or schools or tobacco or gifts. I have come a long way just for this. So, if you don't want this, I have nothing else for you, no other reason for bothering you. I won't be disturbing your hour of rest any more.

"As a matter of fact, I have no reason for seeing you at all any more. I will go elsewhere to find if others want to hear the Christian message. We will meet again only in passing. And I do not think that any other missionary will come here after me. It might be that every people has just one chance to hear the Christian message, and that time can pass away. I think, perhaps, yours has passed. Thank you for your patience and kindness and—goodbye."

I hurried away from the square and down out of the village.[61] I scarcely noticed the people who passed me and greeted me on the way.

61. The remainder of this paragraph is omitted from the book.

My mind was somewhere else. I didn't know that day that all the other Sonjo villages would accept Christianity, and that even a new and distinct community in Ebwe, itself, would take up instructions and come to baptism.[62] I knew only that the first Sonjos to hear the Christian message, as a community, had rejected it.

I was not conscious then of the fact—nor did I remember until long after—that Paul himself had shaken the dust from his feet in defiance of the communities that had rejected the Christian message [Acts 13:51], and that Christ had advised his disciples to do the same [e.g., Luke 9:5]. I would not have had the heart to do any such thing, even if I had remembered. I just realized vaguely and dully that my work with those people of Ebwe was finished in a way that it was finished with no other people.

For untouched pagans there always remains that point in the future when they might hear the Christian message, and so they remain a potential field of work for the missionary. Again, if a missionary is running a school, his work with a people is never finished. He is looking to the Christianization of those school children so that tomorrow he will have Christian parents. Then he must continue to look after those Christian parents and their children. There is no end to it.

But there is an end to my work with the people of Ebwe. There are no moves left to make. The only reason I came these thousands of miles was to bring them this Christian message. They have rejected it. My missionary obligation to them is finished.

Perhaps the most important lesson I was ever to learn in my missionary life, I learned that day: that Christianity, by its very essence, is a message that can be accepted—or rejected; that somewhere close to the heart of Christianity lies that terrible and mysterious possibility of rejection; that no Christianity has any meaning of value, if there is not freedom to accept it or reject it.

It is not an automatic thing, coming like a diploma after four or eight years of schooling, nor after one year of instruction. It *must* be presented in such a way that rejection of it remains a distinct possibility. The acceptance of it would be meaningless if rejection were not possible. It is a call, an invitation, a challenge even—that can always be refused. The

---

62. This draws the sting of Elizabeth Isichei's comment on this story as it is told (in abbreviated form) in the book: "Padri not only took it upon himself to deny people the right to change their minds, but also deprived the next generation of the right to choose at all" (Isichei, *A History of Christianity in Africa*, 261).

Christianity of a born Catholic or of a produced Catholic (the result of an automatic baptism following a set period of instructions) which is never once left open to the freedom of rejection, to the understanding that it is a thing freely accepted or rejected—is a dead and useless thing.

Since that day, I have seen those men of Ebwe from time to time, in passing. I look on them as I look on no other people that I have come across in all my missionary years. For me, at least, they are distinct. They are unique. I feel a tremendous respect for them. They taught me something that no other people in Africa have ever taught me.

But it took a long time for that lesson to sink in.[63] The night of that fateful day I went to bed without much stomach for anything else but a cup of coffee. I had long thoughts to think about Christianity and about my vocation within it. And I never remember any other time when the silence and solitude of the African night seemed so complete.

All my love,
Father Vince

February 1971

Dear Relatives and Friends,

Warm and grateful greetings from Africa. When things go well here in my work, they seem even better because I know you are sharing with me in my work, and when things don't go so well, I can bear with it because I know I am not alone.

I stood by the side of the irrigation furrow. The Sonjo are what is known as a hydraulic society. The irrigation furrows are their life stream. The furrows are controlled by a few families, the heads of which are the political and religious leaders of the tribe. Control is exercised over the tribe through these furrows. Life without them would be unthinkable to the Sonjo. They keep the Sonjo healthy and famine out of the valley.

I stooped down and scooped water out of the flowing furrow with a drinking bowl, then stood up and poured the water over the head of the

---

63. The book omits the following two sentences, and inserts instead, "Day after day I found myself returning in thought to that moment at high noon in the hot equatorial sun when I heard *no!* for the first time."

first Sonjo standing in line along the furrow, "I baptize you in the name of the Father and of the Son and of the Holy Spirit."

I was in the midst of the third group of baptisms of adult communities among the Sonjo villages. They stood there, men and women, warriors and teenage girls, their chests and backs glistening with the oil which had been applied rather liberally and was still running down their bodies. Their new names were attached to their toga-like garments. Africans are similar to Old Testament people. A change of name is a dramatic step for them, a change in life.

I unwrapped a bright red cloth and draped it over the shoulders of the first man, "Receive this beautiful cloak; bring it without stain before the judgment seat of Jesus Christ." I picked up a burning ember from a fire that had been lighted nearby and gave it to him. "Receive this burning fire; guard your baptism, let your life among your people shine with the light and warmth of Christ."

Shortly afterwards, when the last girl had been anointed, with the oil dripping down onto her nose and into her eyes, we moved over to the sacred fig tree and squatted down in its comfortable shade around a goat skin that had been spread out to serve as altar. At that point, I became a spectator.

I watched as a teenage girl began the singing in her language and her rhythm asking the mercy of God and Christ. She was too embarrassed and nervous today to do it justice and the singing came out weak and unsteady. I hope she will learn to do it better as time goes on. When she was finished,[64] an old man stood up and prayed for all of us. Not every person, I was assured by the people, has the power to ask blessings from God, only certain ones. This man is one of them.

I was moved as a young elder stood up with the bible and read us a passage from St. Paul. I never heard a worse reading of that particular passage. The man stammered. He hesitated. He made mistakes. It's no wonder. He has never been to school. He learned to read on his own, so he could read at this service.

The sermon was given by another elder. He made no mistakes. He was eloquent. He's always been eloquent. That is why he is the speaker.

Perhaps the most important moment for me came at the collection. I watched as they poured their offerings of maize and millet into a little

---

64. The description which follows is told, with some changes, in chapter 6 of *CR*, in the section entitled "Baptism."

basket and set it down by the goat skin. I doubt if they would realize how significant that act was for me. It was the first sign of an entire direction being reversed. The most difficult part of my job among these people has been to lead them in an "unlearning process", teaching them what a missionary *is not*; what a Christian *is not*. The extraordinary idea these people have of what a missionary is supposed to be, what he is supposed to give them and do for them! No other difficulty here has ever brought me so close to giving up my work among these people as this one. Their idea of a bountiful missionary and his unending generosity—a gravy train with the missionary at the throttle. We have wandered a long way from the Pauline idea of a missionary. I don't think I could ever adequately explain to those of you who have never been in mission lands the excruciating problem this crippling notion presents, an attitude of complete dependence on the missionary for everything, an attitude that would make adult Christianity impossible. Very few things in my life have given me more satisfaction than seeing that little basket of maize and millet placed before the "altar."

Just after this, a young wife stood up and with evident shyness recited the *Sonjo Creed*. They all listened very carefully and agreed that this is what they believe.

At that point, I stopped being a spectator and told them to watch closely what I was going to do. Someday they would have to do it without me and I wanted them to do it correctly. This was tradition that was handed down from the time of the apostles, and this is the way it came to me—that on the night before he died, Jesus took bread into his hands . . . and the cup was the sign of the new testament. The old testament, the old dispensation—the tribal one, the Jewish one, the European one, the Sonjo one[65]—as beautiful and meaningful and valuable as it was, has passed away. This was the sign of the new covenant, the universal one, the one that would last forever.

We sang the only prayer the Lord ever taught us, in a melody that is quickly becoming one of the Sonjo top ten. I have heard it being sung in different villages by Christians and pagans alike.

65. Putting the Jewish scriptures on a par with other "old testaments" develops a theme found, for example, in Karl Rahner's essay "Christianity and the non-Christian Religions," where he makes Judaism one of the "non-Christian" but "lawful religions" in *Theological Investigations*, 121. A more recent writer asks, "What would happen if instead of speaking about Native American spirituality we began speaking of an Old Testament of Native America?" (Charleston, "Old Testament," 72–81).

Then we came to a tense, even a traumatic moment. I passed the bread and cup of wine for all to eat and drink. No male there had ever eaten in front of a female, and had never, never drunk from the same cup as a female. Pagan Sonjo believe that a female pollutes any food or drink she touches, for a male. But this is the tradition I have received . . . one cup, one bread. I have never commented on the way they treat their women, but here at the heart of the minimal tradition I pass on to them, there must be neither Greek nor Jew, black nor white, slave nor free man, male nor female [Gal 3:28]. I could *feel* the emotion in that community as they received. It will have to be a moment they will long remember and think about.

When they had all received, I stood up to talk to them. I looked at the girl singer, at the pray-er, at the lisping reader, and the preacher. I looked at someone else who was unique to my experience, the first pagan priest I had ever baptized. I wondered what was going on in that fine-looking grizzled head of his. I looked at another teenage girl who was smiling at me. I smiled back at her. For a full year, every week, after I had finished my instructions in her village, she went out to her friend who could not attend the instructions, and side by side as they worked together in the fields, she told her everything I had taught the village. Yesterday, she had come with her friend and asked me to see if she was ready for baptism. She was, and she was sitting next to her now, a fellow Christian. I finally was able to speak.

"I have finished my last instruction in your village. I will never come back to teach anyone else here. From this day on, it is you people who must teach all the others who want to be Christians. You yourselves must search them out, instruct them and judge whether they are ready for baptism. It will be your responsibility, not mine. Talk among yourselves to see whether these people are worthy to enter your community. After all, it is you who will anoint then with oil. It is you who will baptize them. It is your church.

"I have seen this morning that you understand the gospel of Jesus Christ. I have heard you preach it, and recite your creed. Guard this gospel. Do not change it for anything. Even if an angel from heaven were to come to preach a different gospel than this—do not listen to him [cf. Gal 1:8].

"When one of you is ready to call this community together, and to hold it together, and to lead it in this baptism you took part, in this morning, and in the Lord's Supper, and in your life outside this supper, then I will leave you and you will be on your own. Learn to stop depending on me—as of today. Start, today, depending on the one you have received—the Holy Spirit. You have the power, now, as a community to reach even to the throne of God, and to truly serve your fellow men, because you are a chosen tribe, a kingly and a priestly people, a nation that has been anointed, a people set apart. Once you were not a people at all. You were a people with a past and no future. Now you are the people of God [1 Pet 2:10; cf. Hos 1:10]."

Some days there is just not much you can say.

All my love,
Father Vince

April 1971

Dear Relatives and Friends,

My continuing thanks to you for your interest and your help. There are times when the work becomes very difficult here. It is at such times that your interest means so much to me.

One benefit arising from bringing the gospel to a pagan people like the Sonjo is the opportunity it affords for considering and coming to a different idea of the church.[66]

It is often said that it is a missionary's job to plant or establish the church. Such a thought can be misleading since it implies a kind of fixed and predetermined idea of the church in the missionary's mind. A missionary's primary job is to bring the Christian message. If he is successful, the church will follow. The church may appear because of his work, but his job is not to preach the church, but Christ.

I would like you to follow with me step by step in an analysis of this process to see if I am desperately wrong, or to see if, perhaps, a different idea of the church does not make eminent sense.

Having explained all that God has done in this world because of his love of human beings; having explained the depths to which this love has gone in the person and life of Jesus Christ, the missionary's job is

---

66. The rest of this letter appears with some alterations in CR, chapter 6, the section entitled "Church."

complete. The rest is up to the people hearing this message. They can either reject the message entirely, or they can accept it. If they accept it, accept as true all that God has done for them, what must they do?

Scripture is pretty clear as to what they must do. First, they must believe in all that God has done, and in Christ. Then they must be sorry that they have thrown this goodness back in God's face in ingratitude; they must be sorry for the part they have played in destroying the world and their fellow men. They must believe the unexpected good news that though they have taken part in this destruction, there is no reason for despair, there is no reason for anyone to remain a failure forever. Because of Jesus Christ, all this can be undone, can be forgiven, and they can begin again, anew. They must signify this belief and sorrow of theirs outwardly through a sign that all can see, that is, they must be baptized. They must not keep all this to themselves. They must go forth and witness to this good news and to Jesus, letting others see the meaning of it all, by their words and by their lives, until the time that Jesus comes again. And this is the final obligation: they must believe that Christ will come again in consummation, and they must work in expectation of that *parousia*.[67]

And that is it. That is the church.

Christ himself explained it very briefly in the first public words attributed to him, "The kingdom of heaven is at hand. Repent and believe in the good news" [Mark 1:15].

We bring the Christian message to a pagan people. They accept that message. Their acceptance, their response, whatever it might be, is the church. They may be a people without prominently visible structures. Or they might be a pagan community with structures and lines of authority clearly drawn. Structured or not, they have a vision of the world and a style of life of their own. They hear the Christian message and accept it. They especially accept Christ with all that he means to that world vision of theirs in all its dimensions, and to their life style. As they now stand, they are the church.

Institutionalized and structured in a way entirely different from ours, or non-institutionalized, non-structured and non-organized, this response of theirs, as strange as it might seem to us, must be recognized as the church, or we are doing violence to Christianity. Tillich says that

67. *Parousia* is a Greek word meaning coming or arrival. In the New Testament, it refers to the return of Christ.

beyond everything else, the church is simply and primarily a group of people who express a new reality by which they have been grasped.[68]

There are possibilities in this concept for the emerging church of the Third World as well as for the badly disintegrating church of the Western world. But one wonders if they will ever be allowed to come to actuality.

"And the churches grew and expanded in numbers daily, and they continued in the teaching of the apostles, in the life of the brotherhood, in the breaking of the bread, and in the following of the Way" (Acts of the Apostles) [Acts 2:42, 47].

Love,
Father Vince

May 1971

Dear Relatives and Friends,

Greetings from an emerging Africa. I wish I could convey to you the gratitude I feel towards all of you, at the times when I realize that in the midst of all your own difficulties you have been largely responsible for enabling this particular missionary to carry out a special kind of task in the church.

You have shared with me in so many steps of my missionary work. I would like you to share in the final step, the step without which all the other steps—all the methods, strategy and planning—would be in vain. It is the most important aspect of all, the end of the quest, the Holy Grail, as it were. It is the gospel that we preach.

I almost despair of explaining, in this short space, how we have come to this particular formulation of the gospel. You must remember that it took years of searching out this message in Scripture and years of presenting it to different peoples. Both elements are important—the gospel and the people. An honesty toward the gospel and a respect for the people for whom you work are the only things which keep you from fanaticism. What I will try to describe is a simple, sincere effort to come to the essence of the gospel message.

68. Tillich, *Theology of Culture*, 212.

It is a question of analyzing not just the four evangelists, but the entire New Testament, because the gospel message is not just what Christ said, but, more important, what he did and what he means. There were some men, the first missionaries, the apostles, who actually preached that gospel, and we have a record of their preaching. Those men took the essence of the Christian message to a pagan world, and began one of the greatest revolutions in history. It would be valuable to know what that message was.

We are not interested so much in what Paul and the other writers wrote to Christians, but rather what they said to pagans. Very practically, what we want to know is what would be required of a pagan, what he would be required to believe before he could be baptized. It is really the gospel to a non-Christian world we are looking for.

We have the record of Paul's preaching to a Jewish audience and to a pagan one [Acts 13:16–41; 17: 22–31]. We also have five other places in Scripture where impartial witnesses give testimony to his preaching [Acts 17:32; 19:40; 23:9, 29; 26:31]. And we have one of his epistles to a newly Christianized people, where he reminds them of what he taught them as pagans [cf. 1 Cor 15:1]. We also have five sermons of Peter to non-Christians [Acts 2:14–36; 3:12–26; 4:8–12; 5:29–32; 10:34–43]. All of these references have to be looked at against the background of the entire New Testament to see that they are in consonance with it.

It would take too much space to reproduce all these references here. I will merely summarize them. But there is one I would like to give in full, because it is Paul's own summary of his preaching: "The loving kindness of God our savior has appeared to all men" (Titus 3:4).

I think the full message can be broken up into three parts:

Part One: The news of the most High God, the kind God, the creator, the immanent God. The human race is one. God has never forgotten any nation. All nations can find God. All are called to share in his kingdom. All who do right are acceptable to God. Salvation is promised to all.

Part Two: Jesus Christ, God and man, went about doing good. Without guilt he suffered and died. The third day he was raised up by God without tasting corruption, and was seen by witnesses. Through his resurrection Jesus is made the Lord. He ascended.

Part Three: What must we do? We must believe and be baptized. The Spirit is promised. We must go forth in the Spirit to witness. We must repent. Forgiveness of sins is now possible through faith in Christ. Judgment is fixed. Christ will come again.

This reminds one of the *Kerygma*[69] that was popular in catechetical teaching several years ago. It is the *Kerygma*, of course, but if you look closely you will notice several differences between this message I am referring to now, and the way that *Kerygma* was used in catechetical programs at that time. I'm not sure that that catechetical program was always entirely honest with the gospel. There were several mysterious omissions and additions in that program.

First, sin does not appear in the first part of this message at all, doesn't appear in fact until Christ and his forgiveness appear. What does appear, however, together with the presence of the High God, is a remarkably strong insistence on the equality and vocation of all nations (races) in the plan of salvation. The Incarnation is there, of course, and so is the cross. The resurrection is there in all its salvific, cosmic and psychological dimensions. What is not there is the rest of the life of Christ. Surprisingly, the teaching and ethics of Jesus are not there. A call to repentance and faith is clearly part of the message. So is the missionary mandate. The institutional church, as we know it, is not there.

I think the whole thing can be simplified into the following message:

The one God in whom we believe is the Most High God, the living God, and creator, the loving and kind God, who regards and guides and loves all nations, and calls all nations to salvation.

This salvation comes through his son, Jesus Christ, completely man and human, who without guilt is put to death by his fellow men, is raised from the dead by God, and through his resurrection becomes lord of heaven and earth.

Having heard this we must face sin, repent of it, receive forgiveness through faith in Christ, signify this by being baptized, spurn all forms of idolatry, and work toward the judgment by witnessing through the Holy Spirit to this good news and to the name of Christ before the nations, as we are waiting for Christ to come again.

I submit that this is the Christian message.

---

69. *Kerygma* is the Greek word for preaching or announcement. In the New Testament, it normally refers to the preaching of the gospel. C. H. Dodd popularized the term in New Testament studies with his book, *The Apostolic Preaching*, which analyzed the message preached by the apostles.

I don't pretend that this is the first time such a claim has been made for it. As a matter of fact it is St. Paul's claim [Acts 26:23]. And Christ himself, after the resurrection, in explaining the scriptures to his disciples that they might understand, describes it clearly in these very terms [Luke 24:46–48].

But we still might ask, "Can this possibly be the Christian message, the news that once turned the world upside down?"[70] We must remember that this is the essence of a message that does not really come from this earth, even though it belongs to the entire earth. To have any meaning on this earth it must become incarnate in particular parts of the earth, in different cultures, in different parts of mankind.

No person exists as a universal man. Nothing has any meaning to him unless it is related to his culture. Religion is no exception. So it is with Christianity. It has no meaning until it takes on the flesh and blood of a particular culture. But once it achieves this incarnation, it comes throbbingly alive.

Having explained this message at length to the Sonjo pagans preparing for Baptism, I also pointed out the obligation of not keeping it to themselves, but of spreading it. They agreed to this, but the people of one village saw a difficulty. How could they be sure of their basic orthodoxy?

They asked if I could help them as they formulated the substance of their belief. So they composed the canon of their beliefs in their own words, and I helped them to the best of my ability to see that it was true to the gospel.[71] The finished product is now used in their mass, with a different person, man or woman, reciting it each week, and the others listening carefully, almost jealously to see if it is indeed what they believe. I suppose you could call it the Sonjo Creed. Maybe you would like to hear it. It goes like this:

> We believe in the one High God, who out of love created the beautiful world and everything good in it. God loves the world, and he loves our tribe as he loves every tribe on the earth. He has promised that he will save the world and all the tribes of the earth. We have known this High God in the darkness, and now we know him in the light. He is not far from us.

70. In Acts 17:6, the apostles are referred to as those who have turned the world upside down.

71. Kohler believes that in fact Donovan was the primary author, rather than the community, though undoubtedly they were involved in the creative process.

We believe that God fulfilled his promise by sending his son, Jesus Christ, a man in the flesh, a Jew by tribe, born poor in a little village, who went about doing good, curing people by the power of God, teaching that the true meaning of religion is love, who was rejected by his people, tortured, nailed hands and feet to a cross and died. He lay buried in the grave, but was not touched by hyenas, and on the third day, he rose again. Now he has the power to rule and save his world and make it new.

We believe that through Jesus we stand together truly before the face of God and need no one else to stand there for us, and that all our sins are forgiven through him. All who have faith in him must be sorry for their sins, be baptized in the Holy Spirit, live as the brotherhood of love, share the bread together in love to announce the good news to others until Jesus comes again. We are waiting for him. He is alive. He lives.

This we believe. Amen.[72]

Here, I think, with the essential message preserved intact, even though clothed in the African garb of the communal and the concrete— is the gospel that we preach.

Love,
Father Vince

July 1971

Dear Relatives and Friends,

In the midst of my work, I am grateful when I remember all of you, and know that I am not alone as I often seem to be, but that you are with me in a very real way.

I would like to speak about money. Maybe you will be put off by this. You will be scandalized by it only if you have never read the letters of St. Paul. He talked about money frequently, and handled a great deal of it for his time. It is interesting to note the difference between the way Paul used money and the way the modern missionary uses it.

St. Paul seemed to feel that the churches he was evangelizing owed him a living; but, although he often reminded those churches of this

72. This creed is reprinted, with some alterations, as "An African Creed" at the conclusion of CR. In March 2008, on the (recorded) NPR program, *Speaking of Faith*, theologian Jaroslav Pelikan read this creed on the air.

right of his, he never availed himself of it. This is the only financial point on which modern missionaries agree with Paul. We don't ask the people we are evangelizing to support us either, probably because these people are poorer than we will ever be.

But we part company with Paul right there. Paul used the money he received for his own support, his own living and working and traveling expenses. We use it for a hundred things besides. We need even more than Paul.

We use our money to buy schools and hospitals for our catechumens, churches for our Christians, supplies for our churches, food and clothing, and many other things for all and sundry.

Paul obviously saw a great danger in giving anything to the people he was evangelizing, a danger of mixed or impure motivation on their part. We have no record that he ever gave his Christians anything. There was no material inducement to believing the gospel in Paul's system—no inducement preliminary to, or subsequent to belief in the gospel. The "rice Christians" of China[73] and the "school Christians" of Africa would have been a mystery to St. Paul. . . .

As we look at all this evidence, we can almost visualize the financial rules by which Paul worked. I would like to try to formulate these rules. As I do, I would like you, reading this, to see if I am doing so honestly and accurately, because the implications for missionaries are tremendous. Here they are:

1. Missionaries have a right to support from the churches which they are evangelizing, but it is better, as Paul did, never to accept anything from these new churches.

2. Missionaries should never give anything material to the churches they are founding.

3. Charity (social works) should be entirely in the hands of the local and regional congregations.

4. A newly founded church should be financially independent as far as ordinary expenses go.

5. The administration of local church funds should never be in the hands of the missionary.

---

73. A term for those who professed Christian conversion in order to receive food from the missionaries. "School Christians" appears to be Donovan's own phrase, formed by analogy.

6. In times of great emergencies (but not for ordinary running expenses), in a spirit of charity and as a sign of unity, one church should help another.

7. Although it is a moot point whether local pastors should be paid salaries, if they are, these salaries should be paid, not from outside, but by the local church.

As we look at these rules, we are numbed by the realization of how far we have strayed from apostolic practice. These people among whom we have been working for the past hundred years will never be truly independent of us. And the dream of a church so missionary and so mobile that it is burdened only by the living expenses of its missionary team is no longer possible among these people. One can only hope that it will yet be possible in that four-fifths of the world which we have not yet evangelized.

All my love,
Father Vince

November 1971

Dear Relatives and Friends,

Happy Holidays to all my friends and supporters. As 1971 draws to a close, this missionary in Africa is grateful once more for your prayers and financial support throughout another year. I wish all of you much happiness and prosperity in 1972.

The Eucharistic celebration was over. The Christians who had gathered together for it seemed reluctant to leave the spot where, for a few fleeting moments, they had experienced a deep and real sense of unity. Now that the celebration was over, there was no sign of it remaining. These people were not dressed like Christians. There was no church, no altar, and no furnishings.

It struck me that if a violently anti-Christian force came into this country bent on persecuting and destroying every trace of Christianity, it would have its work cut out for it here. There are no visible traces, no buildings to tear down, no pictures or statues or tabernacles to violate. Only the kingdom within.

These Sonjo Christians have an interesting way of referring to the Eucharistic celebration. Instead of saying, "going to mass" or "attending mass" or even "offering mass," they say, "making the church." "On Sunday, we will make the church," they tell you. I doubt whether they understand the deep theological significance of what they are saying. They indeed make the church each time they gather to celebrate the Eucharist.

This community is one of eight Christian communities, representing eight of the ten villages in the Sonjo valley. Two more are yet to be added to them. It comes as a shock to realize that, taken together, these communities form one of the young churches talked about so much by Vatican II.

Vatican II indeed had a lot to say about the programs that must be carried out for these young churches[74]—the pledge of continued and increased financial assistance from the richer, Western churches; the fostering of vocations to the priesthood; the training of clergy, the development of the laity; the initiation of social works; religious training and youth work.

I wonder whether there is any other place where I was so disappointed with the wisdom of Vatican II. And I wonder whether there is any other place where the system we are trying to follow here is so criticized and attacked as on this matter of building up the young church.

The program for the young churches, outlined by Vatican II, presents a carbon copy of the mature church in Europe and America. It is almost as if the authors of that program were wishing on us all the difficulties that are tearing the church apart there. Very liberal, progressive, thinking people in America criticize us severely because we hesitate to follow them down that dark path.

Every suggestion we receive from them implies a continued staying on of missionaries for an indefinite time, to carry out these programs for the young churches, as though we had not been here too long already.

One wonders at the sincerity of such a program as envisioned by Vatican II being called for now, after 100 years of not worrying too much about it. If the building up of the young church had been a principle from the beginning, it would not have taken 100 years to complete the program. In truth, a church 100 years old is not all that young. One hundred years after the church was planted in Antioch, it had spread to

---

74. Chapter 3 of "*Ad Gentes*," in Flannery, *Documents*, 835–40.

Europe, was being complained of by Latin writers as being ubiquitous, and was being worried about by the ruler of the Roman Empire.

Our critics insist that we are not giving the correct version of Christianity to these people if we do not build them their churches, write them a catechism, set up diocesan and chancery structures among them, establish seminaries, insure their financial future, and teach them the philosophy of Dewart, the morality of Haring, and the theology of Rahner.[75] In effect, another 100-year plan.

I would think, rather, that the very first principle which must be invoked toward building up the young church is that we do not stay one day longer than is necessary. I think that 90 per cent of our problems with the young churches today stem from a violation of this principle.

The "fostering of vocations" implies a particular concept of the priesthood. I would be more inclined to believe that vocations are not fostered artificially but, rather, found naturally among communities which have accepted Christianity. And the seminary training of priests, the division of the Christian community, into priests' groups, lay groups and youth groups smacks mightily of the Western church, and leads to a rending of the Christian community.

The building up of the young church should begin on the day the missionary first sets foot among a new people. It is a single, undivided work, building up the whole church together or—as the Sonjo would have it—*making* the church. It is not some artificial work, different and distinct from founding that church or running that church, or from the life of that church.

What is it that a Christian community needs in order to live? What are the essential things a missionary must leave with a young church so that it can become mature? What kind of Christianity should be held up as a goal for a young community?

We have seen the American answer of an efficient, organized, financially-sound, regally-ruled, youth-haunted, philosophically-sophisticated Christianity. Would you think us strange if we judged that that was not for Africa?

Love,
Father Vince

75. Leslie Dewart (1922–2009), Bernard Haring (1913–1998), and Karl Rahner (1904–1984) were all popular Catholic theologians. Haring and Rahner were advisors to Vatican II.

January 1972

Dear Relatives and Friends,

Thanks again from a grateful missionary in Africa, not only for your financial support, but also for your prayers and good wishes. Knowing that all of you are interested in my work here in Africa gives me a tremendous lift when the going gets rough.

Years ago, before we missionaries here began to look on the preaching of the gospel message as our most important work, I was examining 100 catechumens prepared for baptism by catechists. The catechumens had memorized all kinds of answers about original sin, mortal and venial sin, sanctifying and actual grace, and the Ten Commandments. But when I asked each one of them who Jesus Christ was, what he did, and what he meant for us, not one of the 100 could answer anything.[76]

That depressing experience has influenced my work in Africa ever since. Now, many years later, as I am faced with Christian Sonjo communities, all recently baptized, the problem haunting me is what to do to these communities, what to give them, so that I can leave them, so they can become a mature, independent church.

Surely the first essential thing I must leave them is something those 100 catechumens long ago did not have—the gospel tradition. These people must be able, as a community and as individuals in that community, "to render an account of their belief," as St. Paul said [? 1 Pet 3:15]. What I must leave them, more than church buildings and seminaries, is the gospel tradition, and the power and the encouragement to begin to see it in their thinking and in their lives.

But this gospel tradition must surely be different from what we ordinarily understand by it. St. Paul brought to the churches he founded a simple teaching and tradition, a gospel to which he often referred: "Brothers, I want to remind you of the gospel I preached to you, the gospel you have received and in which you are firmly established" (1 Cor 15:1, 2). He goes on in a few lines to explain briefly what that gospel was. It wasn't much of a gospel as far as quantity was concerned, but he insisted on it fiercely. It is so simple that Paul, on demand, can simply repeat it in a few sentences.

76. See also letter of May 1965.

What we, on the other hand, consistently think of as the necessary gospel message or doctrine is, so complicated—so heavily overloaded with dogmatic and moral theology and philosophy—that it could not possibly be the same message Paul constantly refers to.

In dealing with these young Christian communities, how many times I have been tempted to pass on to them pet theories of my own, theologies to which I have been attracted. But I have no right to do so. It is not theology which will make them live. It is not a theology to which they must give their assent. They are a people struggling with the basic notions of Christianity, a people reeling under the powerful impact of Christianity on their lives and on their untouched culture. They are in no position to distinguish between the gospel and any philosophy which I might pass off on them as gospel, and as demanding of their belief. I dare not give them anything but the gospel. An externally imposed morality, for example, has done enough damage in the history of the missions.

It is not the teaching of Aquinas[77] or Luther[78] which will bring them peace, nor the theology of Danielou[79] or Rahner, which will save them. We have no such promise. It is only the gospel which saves.

Once they have grasped that gospel and learned to rely on it, they must be shown that it is not a dead letter, that it is a living thing. They must be encouraged to spell out its implications in their lives, to "philosophize" on its meaning—in short, to build up their own theology. Then they will be on the beginning of that long road of freedom—and danger—which is the right of people coming of age. . . .

With mixed feelings, I find myself urging them earnestly to move out, on their own, to strive for that maturity which is their right, and yet, just as earnestly, pleading with them to hold fast to that gospel tradition, begging them to look back from whatever point they reach—and to keep looking back—at the gospel.

77. St. Thomas Aquinas (?1225–1274), author of the *Summa Theologica* and *Summa contra Gentiles*.

78. Martin Luther (1483–1546), one of the leading theologians of the Protestant Reformation.

79. Jean Cardinal Daniélou (1905–1974), a French Jesuit theologian and advisor to Vatican II.

More than any authority of pope or bishop, that gospel is the true source of Christian unity, and this young community will not become an adult and responsible Christian church without it.

Love,
Fr. Vince

March 1972

Dear Relatives and Friends . . .

I have to admit that I was deeply disappointed, to say the least, when I discovered that the Sonjo, the tribe with whom I have been working in Africa, had no word for "thank you" in their language. I would have thought that all tribes and peoples had that concept. Otherwise, how could they express appreciation for kindness and devotion shown to them by their loved ones and family and friends? How could they show gratitude, even to strangers, for any help they might receive? How could they pray?

This last consideration is one with which a missionary must eventually come to grips.[80] He may never have thought of it before. But when he finally brings the Christian message to a people, and brings those people to the acceptance of Christianity, he can no longer avoid it. Pagan prayer leaves a lot to be desired. In every African tribal language that I know of, the concept "to pray" is translated simply as "to ask for." That really doesn't cover the full dimension of Christian prayer. . . .

Missionary theorists, or even active missionaries who never deal directly with pagans, could easily overlook this all-important step in bringing the message of Christianity to a people—teaching them how to pray.

An attitude toward prayer is certainly one of the few things a missionary must leave with an infant Christian community if he wants to depart from them with any hope that they might one day become mature. . . .

The Christian attitude would . . . be the one depicted in the story of the Annunciation, a story of a teenage girl being confronted with a highly improbable and even impossible situation, a situation before

---

80. The remainder of this letter forms the core of the section "A Prayer" in chapter 8 of *CR*.

which she was clearly baffled, and with which she was unable to cope. But instead of closing herself off, she did the opposite. She opened herself up to the presence of God—"fiat"—and suddenly everything was possible to her.

This is precisely what we must do for these recent pagans and new Christians of ours. It is imperative that we open them up to God, to man and to creation. Paganism is a closed and fatalistic system. What we are asking them to believe, in their prayers, is not that the laws of the universe are being suspended, but that creation is open-ended and continuing.

It is a pagan idea to dwell on the possibility or impossibility of God's suspending the laws of the universe, and working tricks and wonders and miracles. I really wouldn't lead any child or adult down that path.

But it is a Christian idea to believe in God, being constantly present and continuing creating, if only we are open to him.

If you stop to think of it (as a pagan, that is), creation itself was impossible, and so were the Incarnation and the Resurrection.

Jesus is portrayed at one time in the gospel as addressing himself to this "impossibility." At the time, he was not talking about God performing wonders, but about the renunciation involved in following the Christ. The "pagan" realists in his audience said that what he was asking was impossible. Jesus answered, "Yes, with men it is impossible, but with God all things are possible" [Mark 10:27]. Almost the identical words the teenage girl of Nazareth heard. It seems to be a theme of the New Testament.

Those who object to teaching newly baptized Christians—or Christian children in Western lands—how to pray are, in reality, asking that these people never be exposed to that attitude of openness, that they never have the opportunity to be opened up.

In prayer, it is not really so much what happens to God that is important, as what happens to us. The crucial question in prayer is not whether God suspends the laws of the universe, or whether he grants what people "ask for," but whether we really open ourselves to him, open ourselves to his creating, saving presence.

As a missionary, I must try to open these people to the presence of God. Holiness for them will not be counted in great deeds done, but simply in remaining open to God and man and creation. I have to tell them, "To be holy means to be open. If God is present to you, all things are possible. There is no limit to what you can become." . . .

Love,
Father Vince

———————————————————————————————————

May 1972

Dear Relatives and Friends,

I want to tell all of you how much I marvel that all of you, with all your worries and concerns, would still care enough to worry about me and remember me. I need the feeling that you are with me these days. Thanks to all of you from a very grateful missionary.

Sitting facing me are several people.[81] One is an illiterate elder; another is a younger elder who can read and write. There is also a woman who is gifted in singing and in explaining the Christian message to non-Christians. Finally, there are a preacher and pray-er.

They are all members of a Christian community, newly baptized. We are sitting under a huge tree, shading us from the hot African sun. We are in the midst of a program so dizzily beautiful and promising—and improbable—that I hesitate to mention its name. I am preparing them to take over their Christian community, so they will be able to function without outside control. Shall I say it? I am training them for the priesthood.

The statement and the situation seem unreal and dreamlike. Perhaps the unreality stems less from the exotic surroundings and people involved in the program, than from the realization that our endeavors here in this line are so very, very different from similar endeavors being carried out in America and elsewhere. . . .

The priesthood of all believers is our main concern. Our training for the priesthood is aimed at the entire Christian community. That group of people sitting facing me under the tree represents symbolically the whole Christian community, each member of which has a function to perform in the community. It is only of secondary importance to us to discover who will emerge as the ministerial priests of that community.

81. The remainder of this letter is the basis for chapter 8 of *CR*, the second half of the section entitled "Eucharistic Community with a Mission."

They are emerging, all right, and we are beginning to see more clearly what their function is. But it is significant that, as they emerge, they are being referred to by other members of the community with a name that is far removed from the name hitherto used for priests in the church. They are not being called elders or priests or pastors. The closest approximation in English to the name being used for them by their fellow Christians is *helpers*, helpers of the Christian community.

In the tribal language this word, *ilaretok*, has a richness of meaning that is hard to capture in English. It describes a person who is entirely essential to a community, to its existence and its life, yet the word carries with it all the overtones and connotations of *servant*. These new African Christian communities seem to want to avoid the continuance of a pagan priesthood. One day African priests may be universally referred to as *helpers*. *Diakonia* may once again be revived in the African Church.

These new African Christians do not conceive of a "priest" as a preacher or prophet or pray-er. Such functions most often fall to someone else in the community. Least of all do they conceive of the priest as the sacramentalist. They are not about to push the priest into a sacramental corner. This would effectively kill the priesthood and at the same time deprive the community, as a whole, of the power of the sacraments.

Rather, they think of the priest as the one (seemingly the only one) who can bring a community into existence, call it together, hold it together, enable the community to function as a community, and enable each member to carry out his or her Christian task in the community. Without this *helper*, the Christian community can neither exist nor function. With him, it becomes a Eucharistic community with a mission.

That person, that *helper*, would be a hyphenated priest in an entirely different sense from, say, a priest-sociologist in America. . . . [T]he African hyphenated priest might be a shepherd or a farmer, who in his own herding or farming community would serve as the person able to call that community into Christian life and action.

There would be no need to search for more meaningful or diversified ministry for him. No question would arise (if he should fail to fulfill his function in that community) as to whether he deserves, because of his anointing, to be placed over some other community which does not even know him. The "priesthood of all believers" should not be used as an empty slogan devoid of all significance for ordinary Christians, as has been the Catholic habit; nor as a negative kind of brake on the deepest sacramental and prophetic meaning of the priesthood of Jesus Christ, as has been the Protestant habit. If only we had the courage to let this force, pristine and untried, loose in the church.

Love,
Father Vince

August 1972

Dear Relatives and Friends,

    . . . [I]t doesn't take the vantage point of 100 years' time, or even that of being in a mission field at the periphery of the church, to look at the situation in America and Europe and to realize that we are not, at the present time, watching merely the recurring of troubles that have plagued the church, off and on, down through the centuries. It doesn't take much of a vantage point at all to realize that, perhaps, what we are witnessing is the dying of the light, the sickness unto death of the Western church.

    One who works in the Third World, that area so fearfully exploited by the Western world, might be expected to rejoice in the demise of the Western church; but such an attitude would indeed be shortsighted. If the Western church goes down, it will, like a giant ocean vessel, drag down in its wake much that surrounds it.

    Almost as an outside observer, I find myself earnestly hoping that the Western church will have the courage to throw off some of the attitudes that are making it difficult to survive, that it will have the courage to cast off the idols of the tribe. There are many idols, but two which are particularly mesmerizing the Western church are individualism on the one hand and love of organization on the other.

    We consistently tend to interpret Christianity either from the individual or [the] organizational viewpoint. The love of organization and power structures have led to our ideas of lord bishops and pontiff popes and national associations of the right and of the left, and to the necessity of keeping the organization together, whether the organization be a diocese, a religious congregation or the Roman Church.

    Individualism has its obsessions also: personal responsibility, personal morality, personal vocation to the priesthood, self-fulfillment.

Individualism on one side, and organization on the other, with little room for community in between.

Besides paying lip service to the idea, how seriously do we consider the possibility that Christianity is essentially directed neither to the individual, nor to the organization, but to the community? . . .

The Western world has made tremendous contributions to the church. Among other things, Americans have taught us what freedom of conscience and tolerance mean. The Germans and the Anglo-Saxons have made a virtual monopoly of their contribution in the field of biblical exegesis. Maybe it is time for the peoples of the Third World to make their contribution to the church. They don't have many scientists or philosophers among them. But they know what community means.

Love,
Father Vince

October 1972

Dear Relatives and Friends,

As an American who has spent a good portion of his life outside of America, I can tell you the rest of the world envies your election process. As you come to the close of the presidential campaign,[82] I can only say I wish I were in America to be a part of it all—the conventions, the campaign, and the election. As I listen to the results of the election on my radio, I will be thinking of each of you, wondering whether you will be elated or dejected. Either way, we do have a chance to cast our votes for the man of our choice. For that we should be thankful.

For a long time we have become accustomed, even here in Africa, to hearing about the accomplishments of women in so many fields that once were reserved to men. Women have shown that they can do job after job as well as, or better than, men. Even on the missions that was true. But out here, we had some reservations, some fears, about pushing that truth too far. We thought perhaps that women on the missions should nonetheless be relegated to the safe jobs, to the security of a hospital institution, to the

---

82. On November 7, 1972, Richard Nixon (Republican) defeated George McGovern (Democratic) in a landslide victory.

ordered serenity of a school, to the more civilized living in a town, to the unhazardous task of sewing clothes for African women.

But along with those reservations, we also dreamed the situation would change someday. I used to look at this mission field of Masailand, some 25,000 square miles of it, with just a handful of men available to try to cover it. I used to wonder if perhaps there were not some women available to help out on the job. Not just for the sake of numbers, but for the specific contribution women could make. Catholic missionary work in many parts of the world, because of its celibate form, presents a kind of one-faceted, one-legged approach to Christianity. I often wondered what kind of effect this had in the minds of the people hearing the message.

Still, how could one expect women to work not only on the frontiers of the church, but on the outskirts of civilization as well, among a warrior tribe like the Masai, in the midst of wild animals, pushed to the ultimate test of isolation? We have found that extreme isolation not only can bring out the strong points in a human being. It certainly will bring out the weakest.

Loliondo Mission, where I am stationed, takes in about a fourth of that area of Masailand. In this mission live a large section of the Masai people, and the entire tribe of the Sonjo. I am working at the evangelization of the Sonjo people, and another priest works among the Masai.[83] Our headquarters is Loliondo, but our fields of work are far apart. For a long time we knew that we needed help.

About a year ago, two Maryknoll nuns volunteered to come and work with us, with their own house and base of operations in Loliondo. The plan was that they were to take over as much of the work among the Masai as they could and, if possible, move in even on the Sonjo work. There were some who doubted that such a plan could possibly work. How could women cope with the barbarous roads, mechanical difficulties and hazardous living conditions of Masailand? How would the Masai, a decidedly male-oriented society, accept women coming to teach them?

The two Maryknoll nuns who came were Sister Julia Kubista and Sister Anne Narciso.[84] Sister Julia had been a mathematics teacher in a

---

83. Fr. Anton (Toon) de Smet.

84. Sr Julia was from West Concord MN. She is presently involved in the Right to Life movement. No biographical information is available about Sr. Anne. In *CR*, Donovan says "they added dimensions to the work that I was not capable of bringing to it" (145).

girls' secondary school in Morogoro, Tanzania. She was an experienced African hand. Sister Anne came fresh from the United States, where she had been trained in community development, and was working at public relations and vocation recruitment.

Julia is a gentle, cheerful, tireless Minnesota girl from Winona Diocese, who startles us with her ability to grasp any new work or situation as though she had been here in Masailand for years. Anne is from the East, from the diocese of Trenton, N.J., and she brings with her a brand of humor and a dimension of warmth previously unknown in our work. She also brings a welcome contact with the modern American church. She speaks in the accents of that church and has already corrected many of our misconceptions about that church. She has a beautiful, clear mind, and she tries to keep our feet on the ground.

I would like to be able to say that Julia and Anne moved into the work slowly. But I can't. Within a few days they were off on safaris. I have to admit to more than a little apprehension the first night I knew they were out in the bush alone. Even being only indirectly responsible for their coming here, if anything ever happened to them, I guess I would never be able to forget it for the rest of my life.

But from the beginning they showed a proper respect for the African bush and, embarrassingly enough, they have been accepted by the Masai, at least as much as we ever were. They moved into areas that were already under evangelization and took over some of the work there. Then they moved into areas where a priest had been neither seen nor known and started there.

During the five or six years that this kind of work has been going on, we have developed notes on the kind of instruction being given the people. Due to the deepening experience with the Masai people, these notes have to be constantly revised. The most recent, up-to-date, most satisfying revision has been made by Anne and Julia. It is a humbling thought that, despite the different men who have been involved in this work off and on down through the years, the final, definitive notes on first evangelization of the Masai will probably be those notes originally conceived of by Anne.

Julia has been elected dean[85] of the Masailand section of the diocese. Whether or not she is the first or only female dean of the Catholic Church, she wears her dignity lightly. But, more important, she has

85. Dean is this context means spokesperson on behalf of clergy in an area.

moved into the program of training the leaders of the existing Christian communities.

We had begun a program of preparing the leaders of the Christian communities to take over as soon as possible all the functions of a community, so they could carry on without us. It is, in effect, preparing them for ordination, on the day the church agrees to take that necessary step.

Julia at first assisted us in this work at several centers in Masailand, but now she is doing more than assisting us in the whole procedure. She is presently in charge of it in the Loliondo area, including even one Sonjo village. This nun is running a mobile major seminary by herself.

I have wondered at times what their Maryknoll colleagues think of these two out in the bush of Africa, a mathematics teacher and a community-development worker, living among a warrior tribe, doing a work that is neither popular nor faddish in the church today.

I don't get to see these two sisters as often as I would like. Their schedule runs seven days a week, mostly in different directions from mine. They evangelize, they bring Christian communities into existence through Baptism, they are continually adapting and bringing up to date the instructions necessary for this work; they are preparing Christian leaders to take over their communities.

When I do see them, they never mention it, but they know and I know that they are doing everything that I am doing, except for the emergency and temporary function of presiding at the Eucharist in the existing Christian communities.

Anne, quoting one of her favorite authors, Father Anthony Padovano,[86] tells us that the difference between a fantasy and a hope is a dream. How nice if that were true because in the early days of this work, when the whole thing seemed impossible of completion, we had another dream—that one day ordinary lay people, married couples, would join us in our work. I think Anne and Julia, besides everything else they have done, have somehow brought that day a little closer.

"These women, Evodia and Syntyche . . . have worked loyally for the gospel, as much as Clement and those other fellow laborers . . . whose names are written in the book of life" (Ph. 4:2, 3).

Sincerely,
Father Vince

86. Anthony Padovano is an American Catholic theologian, President Emeritus of CORPUS (Corps of Retired Priests United for Service), and author of over twenty books.

May 1973

Dear Relatives and Friends,

Early this summer I will be back in the United States for a vacation.[87] I am looking forward to seeing all of you and visiting with you once again. I will never be able to tell you how much your support has helped me these past five years. To say thank you seems so little to do in return, but it is a sincere thank you from the bottom of my heart.

Somewhere after Vatican II, an idea that found its time came into church circles. It spread to both sides of the Atlantic and to the Third World, and developed along similar lines in all of these places. It has been the source of incredible energy and work done in the church, and of most of the major headlines in Catholic papers ever since.

It is expressed in many different ways, but the idea remains the same: The gospel is liberation; mission means aid to the developing countries of the Third World; evangelization is development.[88] It is such a sacred idea that one hesitates to disparage it in any way. But one can't help wishing that, along the way, many more distinctions had been made, and more cautions given in the carrying out of this idea.

A missionary with his main interest in the Third World might look at the problem this way:

1. The gospel is compromised by identifying it with social development.

2. True human development is impossible without the gospel. The gospel is the door to true human development.

One cannot find in the New Testament the blueprint for any socio-economic program. To say this is to say something which is obvious—the gospel cannot be identified with any social, political or economic system. But even though it is obvious, it is something about which we must be reminded from time to time. We must be reminded that it is dangerous to preach the gospel as part of any system. The gospel is compromised by

87. Donovan never returned to Tanzania, but became Director of Vocations for his Order. Marchessault and Herzstein speculate that maybe Donovan felt his work was done now that others had taken up the torch he had lit, but Donovan himself never expressed such a view.

88. CF. the section "Whither Mission?" in chapter 1 of *CR*.

identification with any system. It is more than compromised. It becomes impossible. It is lost through any such identification. . . .

The whole field of development is a delicate, complex one, not suited to the simplistic solutions sometimes offered to it. It is ringed with opportunities and dangers. It can save a people or destroy them. I wonder how many would agree with the working rules we have hammered out so painfully, so cautiously, so carefully, over the years in this area of development:

1. Never identify the gospel with development.

2. Preach the gospel faithfully, to open the door to human development. Without a faithful preaching of the gospel, no development will be possible, and the gospel will be polluted.

3. Having opened the door to development, leave the initiative for further interpretation of what this development means, in any particular culture, with the people themselves.

Beware. Be cautious of our own interpretation. Medicine, education, science, as we know them, are Western. Not only must we not confuse these things with the gospel. We must not force any particular interpretation of development on non-Western people. Otherwise, we might be aborting forms of development, still unknown to us, which can yet spring from that incredibly fertile gospel.

Love
Father Vince

[October 1973]

Dear Relatives and Friends,

Having finished another leg of my missionary journey, it is good to be home again, getting a taste of and catching a glimpse of the life you people have been experiencing while I have been away. Seeing it again makes me wonder all the more at how big and generous you are to be able to support a mission effort far away from home, while living in the midst of such a depressing and anxiety-filled atmosphere. Seeing it all makes me all the more grateful to you.

In the summer a new Provincial was appointed for the Eastern Province of the Holy Ghost Fathers in America.[89] He immediately promised that he would try to reorientate the Holy Ghost Fathers back to their mission vocation. He said he knew that for years I had been stating that we had lost our vocation. He asked me to help him in this reorientation program by accepting the job of Vocation Director for the province, member of the formation committee for all those in training for the missions, and Provincial Councilor.

This was a very difficult decision to make. Missionaries are so scarce for the kind of work I had been involved in. I could never think of giving up that work completely and settling down in America. If I accepted this job, it would not be the normal case of an ex-missionary who had given up missionary work to start a new life. It would rather be the case of a missionary who agrees to work *for a while* on a mission oriented project at home, and then return to the missions.

On these conditions, I have accepted this job. I have cut short my leave which should have extended to January. I will try. I know next to nothing about this kind of work beyond a few general ideas. I also know that I could never become involved in a narrow, simple recruitment program for the priesthood. I could envision a program designed to call different people to different vocations and functions in the church as well as an educational and orientation program for people destined to go to the missions, but I would really welcome any ideas as to how such a job might be fruitfully carried out. That is why I am writing to you. You have helped me so much in the past. Would you be willing to help me again, not financially this time, but with your ideas? I would like to invite you all to a brainstorming session where I might hear any ideas that all of you have concerning what might be done for the church in a job such as I have described to you. We could have a "Sundowner" at the same time as the brainstorming sessions. Would you let me know if you are interested?

Thanks,
Father Vince

I would like to come to the 'Sundowner Brainstorming Session' to be held sometime in November at a date which will be made known soon.
Name................................... Telephone.............................

89. Fr. Philip Haggerty was the provincial superior from 1973–79.

Epilogue

"What Happened Next?"
The Legacy of Vincent Donovan, Thirty-Five Years On

MANY READERS OF CHRISTIANITY *Rediscovered*—and indeed of these *Letters*—ask the question: what happened after Donovan left? Did the churches he began survive? How far do they continue to embody the principles of inculturation that informed his work?

There is no single answer—and no simple answer—to the question. Three snapshots follow, each from a different generation of Spiritan missionaries. The first is the view of Ned Marchessault, who went to Tanzania in 1965, was trained "on the job" by Donovan and continues the same kind of work today. The second is that of Pat Patten, who arrived in Tanzania in 1973 (the year Donovan left) as a seminarian, having been inspired by

Pat Patton standing with a Maasai warrior in front of a Flying Medical Service Cessna 206.

reading Donovan's articles in the *National Catholic Reporter*. He currently runs the Flying Medical Service out of Arusha.[1] The third is that of Bill Christy, who lived with Donovan in the US for a year in 1988 after his novitiate, before going to Tanzania for a two year internship. He returned as a priest in 1992 and was there until 2004, for a total of fourteen years in Tanzania. He is presently serving two aboriginal communities in the Broome Diocese of North West Australia. I visited Ned and Pat in Tanzania in 2006, and Bill in Pittsburgh in 2007. While Ned's analysis is more pessimistic, Pat's and Bill's are more optimistic.

NED MARCHESSAULT

Ned is still involved in parochial ministry among the Maasai, based in Endulen, several hours from Arusha to the east and from Loliondo to the north. He continues to act as priest for a huge area, and visits a number of outstations from his base in Endulen. Having worked for many years in the kind of primary evangelization Donovan writes about, Ned has now handed over that work to lay catechists whom he has trained, but continues to visit the villages and celebrate Mass.

Ned's answer to the question, What happened next? is basically that things did not unfold as Donovan had hoped, though the underlying principles continued to be honored. There were problems both on the Catholic side and on the Maasai side. For example, on the Catholic side, while Donovan's dream was to ordain local leaders as priests to their community,[2] within Catholic tradition that was not a straightforward option. As Ned put it, the vision got "bogged down in the structures of organised religion. I mean, what are you going to do about the Eucharist—just have anybody preside?"

There were unofficial and short-lived experiments with lay leadership of Eucharist-like services. Ned said: "In places where we could only visit at long intervals because of the great number of outstations and the distances involved, we constructed a service that would not need the presence of a priest. This involved cards with stick figures that people could follow for a service of prayer, Scripture readings and eating together."[3]

1. See www.flyingmedicalservice.org.

2. *CR*, 88. Page references in this section are to the twenty-fifth anniversary edition (2003).

3. Ibid., 91n.

This was a step in the direction of so-called "village priests," the natural spiritual leaders of the community who, it was hoped, would be "ordained" for that community.[4] But here too there was a cultural problem. Would their own people acknowledge their authority? In a society which values status, people "didn't want these guys in the village with little or no education [in positions of influence]. That's very strong, you know: the hierarchical aspect of the organization of the church is very important to Africans."

One way to proceed down the path of radical indigenization would have been for the Maasai churches to become independent. Did the Spiritans think about this? Ned was aware that this was one possible way out of the impasse: "nobody outside will accept [village priests and/ or lay presidency], so you're putting yourself in the position of starting your own church." The problems of such an approach, however, made it too daunting to pursue: "Well, the difficulty with that is, then you've got to figure out everything and then you wouldn't have any more time to do anything else. We talked about stuff like that, in the early '70s, late '60s, but I don't think that's a solution."

Later, he added: "We . . . weren't interested in starting our own church. I mean, number one, where would we get our support? How could we even stay here? So we wanted to remain Catholics." As a result, said Ned, "What we did differently was relatively short lived and only very limited."

In spite of this, some Maasai have been trained and ordained in the traditional manner, but they have not, on the whole, pursued an approach to ministry in the tradition of Donovan and the American Spiritans.[5] Neither have they returned to the areas from which they came. This is partly because new clergy feared (justifiably) that they would be inundated with requests for help from family, friends, and others in their home area. Further, the present Catholic hierarchy in Tanzania, though entirely African, is not enamored of the kind of indigenization practiced by Donovan. As a result, there exists today the poignant paradox of white American missionaries encouraging inculturation, and an African hierarchy rejecting it. One could say that the diocese stresses the constants while the missionaries stress the context.[6]

4. Ibid., 108, 114–15.
5. Ibid., 138.
6. Cf. Bevans and Schroeder, *Constants in Context.*

The difficulty has been exacerbated by the cultural conservatism of the Maasai themselves, and this is the second half of the problem with implementing Donovan's ideology. His intention, following Allen, was that each nation and tribe should discover its own way of "being church."[7] Ned's discovery, however, was that:

> Africans in general and Maasai in particular want to know how it should be done. Especially when it comes to religion, because [what matters is] pleasing God or doing what God wants . . . [and learning this] from your grandfather, from the elders, from whoever—and doing it just like they told you to do it. This is what religion is all about—keeping on God's good side and doing things that are pleasing to him. . . . They want to do [church] the way God wants it done and be done with it. I mean, let's not play games with anything as important as our relationship with God.

This leads to the irony that the missionary's desire to do things in the tradition of the local culture is turned on its head when the local culture dictates that things should be done in the tradition of the missionary.

So where are things at today? One answer is that people like Ned continue to exercise missional creativity. His conduct of the Mass (one of which we were able to attend) provides a model for combining fidelity to European tradition (desired by both the Maasai and the national church leaders) with local culture. Though the shape of the Mass was familiar, the service and the sermon (by a Maasai catechist, wearing his red cloak) were in Maasai (the result of Vatican II). Ned wore a black cassock rather than traditional Eucharistic vestments since black is the most sacred color for the Maasai: the colour of God and the colour of the rain clouds.[8] He also had a cow-skin stole, decorated with cowry shells by Maasai women. (Some of those who disapprove of Ned's approach to inculturation refer to him as "the cowry shell priest.")

Throughout the service, Ned held in his hand a bunch of grass, symbol of peace and reconciliation.[9] Then, during the Prayers, people with special concerns came forward, and as he prayed for them Ned sprinkled them with grass dipped in milk, a symbol of life, from a gourd decorated with cowry shells. The singing was haunting, and quite different from other Christian singing I have heard in East Africa. In other

7. CR, 62–64.
8. Rain and God are the same word in Maasai (ibid., 33).
9. Ibid., 94.

words, Ned's incorporation of local elements into the liturgy, though it does not go as far as Donovan had originally hoped, does honor some of the significant symbols of Maasai culture. The constants are modified, but not radically changed, by the context.

Is the process of first evangelization that Donovan pioneered still continuing? The answer is an unequivocal yes: indeed, it has never stopped since its inception in the 1960s. At first, Ned did this work himself: "My first two years in Endulen, I did evangelization in the Maasai villages in this general area, within a twenty mile radius. Then I had the first baptisms of Maasai villages in the Endulen area and these places became Christian communities. After this, I moved to the Ngorongoro crater area, evangelized in various villages and again established centers. Finally, I moved to Nainokanoka on the other side of the crater and did the same thing, evangelizing and eventually establishing Christian communities in that area." The process is almost identical to that described by Donovan. Ned said: "[When] I go directly to work with Maasai villages as villages, I teach the whole group together, elders, women and the whole family, and then make a real effort to have those traditional leaders continue as leaders in the church."

Over time, however, Ned has moved more into a role of training catechists to do it: "Now that I am in my seventies, I am slowing down." He presently has eight of these, all paid—something Donovan was against,[10] but which has become accepted as necessary. These days, once a village decides to accept baptism, they become an outstation of the mission, and Ned adds them to his list of the villages he visits to celebrate Mass.

Although *Christianity Rediscovered* gives the impression that Donovan, following Allen's guidelines, saw a clear distinction between evangelization (the work of the missionary) and pastoral care (the work of the priest or pastor),[11] in fact there are hints in the book that the distinction was not as easy to maintain in practice.[12] Ned confirms that it proved impossible to draw a clear line between evangelization and pastoral care: one led into the other. After he had done initial evangelization, he stayed

10. Ibid., 82–83.

11. Ibid., 24–25, 30.

12. Ibid., 85. Eugene Hillman's essay confirms this: "We . . . teased him, because we were witnesses to his persistent pastoral empathy and compassion. He would graciously modify his best laid plans to keep free of pastoral entanglements whenever people presented themselves to him with needs" (ibid., 162).

in relationship with those communities, not only to lead Eucharist but also to teach.

There has also been a shift in how the missionaries understand the work of mission. Donovan, following Roland Allen, came to feel that the job of the missionary was primary evangelization and nothing else. "The gospel is not progress or development. It is not . . . a school system. It is not a health campaign. It is not a five-year plan" (Letter, May 1973). His fear was that "development," in the form of education or health care or anything else, would activate the "choke law" and would eventually prevent the work of evangelization.[13]

These days, however, education has become a necessity, not least in Ned's work. His rationale is simple and pragmatic: "Well, without education, the Maasai people are going to cease to exist as a people. We need a voice in the decision making process about everything. And if you reject education, well, you're rejecting their survival."

Education is not a value in isolation from the rest of life. It relates to the crucial issues facing the Maasai, such as: "Land, water, decisions about health of both animals and people. Local government, in the sense that people don't get their rights, because outsiders are primarily the ones who are in control. Permanent water continues to be alienated at an alarming rate. In many parts of Maasailand land is being alienated. There are huge seed companies from Holland in central Maasailand."

With financial support of as much as $14,000 per year from friends in the US (mainly retired Spiritan missionaries), Ned has sponsored many Maasai young people to train for different professions so they can help their own people: "We have a girl who just graduated from law school and two boys who are lawyers now. Four of our girls have completed Teacher Training College and two more are in training. Two girls are in medical school and another is about to begin medical studies."

What would Donovan have thought about such effort going into something he considered secondary and even deleterious to true missionary work? Ned was unwilling to speculate. His attitude is that Donovan "gave the basic philosophy and then we re-implemented it as we saw it should."

Ned summarized Donovan's impact like this: "Vince—like most people who are very charismatic, in the sense of people who make an impact on other people, who can kind of grab you and carry you on a

13. Ibid., 75.

mission—he talked beautifully and strongly about things. . . . He gave that initial talk to us in Arusha,[14] he had us all fired up—and it still carries me to this day. It's still the source of the impetus for the kind of work that we do."

What will happen next? Ned believes that once this generation of Spiritans leaves or dies, the vision will die with them. New priests may come in, almost certainly Africans and possibly Maasai in some cases, but it is unlikely that they will share the vision for inculturation.

PAT PATTEN

Pat Patten arrived in Tanzania just as Vincent Donovan was leaving. Like Bill Christy, whose story is next, but unlike the missionaries he followed, his theological preparation was very helpful. Like Bill, he is "a product of Catholic Theological Union and the Chicago Cluster of Theological Schools. . . . I found CTU and the Cluster an outstanding and exciting place to study." He was involved in primary evangelization for ten years—by this time it was being practiced by a good number of Spiritans. He found that: "It was nearly impossible to do a liturgy in a *boma*[15] without one of the guests there, who had never heard about Christianity before, asking us to come to their people and share with them the story. We never had to look for new *bomas* to go to. There were always more invitations than we could possibly handle. This news is so astounding and so transforming that people in the already Christianized west cannot begin to imagine its impact." As a result, "by the time I left Loliondo, I had seventy-two different Christian *bomas* to visit. And if I got to them twice a year, I was happy."

If Ned is overall pessimistic about the future of inculturation among the Maasai, Pat is more optimistic. In part, this is because he is not looking for conventional signs of church. He tells, for example, of a Lutheran pastor who was investigating Donovan's work, but could see no evidence of a traditional church. Pat's response was to ask: "What were you looking for? If you're looking for buildings and people gathering on Sunday,

14. The *Journal* recorded this kind of meeting on June 4, 1967: "The fathers left Arusha after Sunday mass, for a meeting with the assembled fathers to explain our work, the theory and practice." It reported a few days later, "The fathers generally seemed impressed and delighted with the work here, but are hesitant to begin in their own areas."

15. *Boma* is the Swahili word for a Maasai village—a group of huts arranged in a circle, connected by a thorn hedge to form a barrier against wild animals. The Maasai word is *enkang*.

of course you wouldn't find it." The pastor responded, "Yeah, but then how do you mark the difference?" And Pat said, "Well, you mark the difference by the stories that people tell."[16]

In particular, Pat sees evidence that Christian stories are beginning to influence the cultural consciousness of the Maasai. He points out that the West has been deeply shaped by stories such as the parable of the Good Samaritan, or the story of the resurrection of Jesus, and takes them for granted, while for people who have never heard them before they are radical and disturbing: "I've seen people literally, when they heard about the resurrection story, fall off their chairs. I mean, just a big commotion, an old guy just falls off his chair when another Maasai elder is talking, is just relating the Easter story."

His favorite illustration concerns a group of Maasai who brought a badly wounded man of another group—the Ndorobo—to the hospital in Wasso.

> The doctor was able to save the man's life, but then asked the Maasai: "So why did you bring this man?"—because, you know, in Maasai tradition, someone who's that badly hurt will be left outside the village for the hyenas to eat; and this guy was not a Maasai, he was a Ndorobo. . . . And the Maasai elder said, "Well, that's the way the story goes." And the doctor says, "What do you mean? What story?" And the man says, "I'm not sure I remember it right. But it's something like this: there was this guy who was beaten up by thieves and people from his own ethnic group kept passing him by. So we had to bring him."

Such stories are not "just" stories. As they are told, pondered, and discussed in community, they touch the hearers at a deep level and begin to change the way they behave, even to the extent of subverting long-held cultural patterns—in this case, the old conviction that, while you care for your own ethnic group, outsiders do not need to be treated equally.

In terms of worship, Pat's inculturation of the liturgy is more radical than Ned's: "It's very, very interesting how Ned does things, but my liturgies were much looser than his, and it was mostly the community that did the liturgy."

Here is Pat's description of a Mass. It comes as no surprise to find that the telling of stories—stories of Jesus and how they interweave with stories of the village's life—are at the heart of it:

16. Donovan makes a similar observation in the letter of November 1971.

We would start in the evening when the cows were coming in and the elders would gather up green grass. Green grass is a really powerful symbol of forgiveness, and anyone holding green grass, is saying, I'm OK with everybody around here. And if I'm not, I have to go to the person I'm not OK with and get things right.

And so, as the cows were coming in the evening, people would gather the green grass and then, when the cows were milked and everybody was full and at ease, there's a traditional song the women and men sing. They go in concentric circles, counter rotating, singing two different songs that blend fabulously. And then each woman brings a new piece of firewood. All the fires in the households are extinguished, and the warriors start a brand new fire by rubbing fire sticks together.

And then people would start discussing in the group from the circle what story most touched them. And there would be some discussion and then kind of a consensus. And then someone would tell the gospel story and they would tell what happened [in their lives]. And it was not always a success story, it would be sometimes, you know, "We should have been able to do this better," or "It worked partway."

That would be finished then with a communion service, which was done on a cow skin, on which all of their special ceremonies are done, with the *olorika*, the three-legged stool there, and a gourd filled with wine, and a half buffalo horn (they are sliced longitudinally and resemble an artistically shaped plate) with bread on it and everyone would be signed with chalk in the form of a cross on their foreheads. For the Maasai, chalk is a sacred symbol of new birth, of initiation, of new beginnings, and in the evening in the firelight, you would see this vivid white on these black faces.

And then people would share the gourd and the buffalo horn and there would be interspersed the Maasai songs. I don't know if you've heard the chant—they always kind of chant—there is always a verse and a refrain. Someone will lead and sing a verse and then everybody sings the response. And it's a quick back and forth interaction in the singing, not longer drawn out verses, the way we often have.

And then in the end, one of the people from the oldest age groups would stand up and take the fresh milk from the cow and gather up all the grass, put it in the gourd, and then sprinkle everybody heavily with milk as a sign of blessing. And then the women would each take a piece of wood from the new fire and take it back to their homes. Then we would stay there the night and leave in the morning.

This is indeed "much looser" than the fairly traditional Mass I saw Ned do. For Pat, this is justified by redefining what the Mass actually is. The shift becomes clear in Pat's response to the vexed question of who is allowed to celebrate. His response was: "Well, I was just there. . . . The idea was that the Eucharist is something that happens every day, every time you sit down and eat together and you have some kind of consciousness of God there. That is what Jesus was talking about. Most people here don't eat together, and I think the message is, 'Do this in memory of me' is eating together. It's not doing magic with a piece of bread and some wine." If Mass is, at its heart, the simple (though, as Pat pointed out, profound and transformative) act of believers eating and drinking together with an awareness of God, then the question of who presides is hardly central. But this form of celebration, this degree of inculturation, has not become mainstream among Maasai Christians. To quote Ned again, "What we did differently [in liturgy] was relatively short lived and only very limited."

Nevertheless, Pat is not discouraged about the future of the Gospel among the Maasai:

> I can't emphasize enough how much I admire what Ned has done and is still doing, but I don't agree with him on [the question of the future]. Listening to the story transforms people. I think that the change is happening.
>
> We don't realise the impact that one individual has on an-other individual, and I don't think we realise the impact that stories have on our whole view of reality. It works: there are stories that stick with us and they just stay and they change us. So I think—this where I agree completely with Roland Allen and Donovan—the people here will figure their own way. They'll sift out all of our Western deadness, and they'll work it out themselves.
>
> Our vision will probably disappear but hopefully other things that are even better will replace them. . . . The important thing about Christianity is, you never force it. It is so powerful that you never succeed. It always draws you far beyond your wildest imaginations, if you let it. And so you can never im-pose this on people, because you're imposing such pitiful little limits and that's not what it's about. It's about opening up to a universe.

BILL CHRISTY

By the time Bill Christy arrived in Tanzania in 1989, the results of Donovan's kind of evangelization were widespread. He commented that during his years there:

> I never went into a community that hadn't had first evangelization.... Especially because of the Maasai marriage system—they might have been voiceless, they might have been suppressed in their Christianity, they might have been living out their Christianity in different ways than had been passed on to them, but in almost every place that I went, you would find a Christian element in the village.... I would always ... find someone who said, "I was baptized by somebody, somewhere." ... I can think of no area currently in Maasai land that would not have one or two baptized persons ... living in the community.

Often, according to Bill, it was the women who were the natural evangelists, taking the gospel with them when they married and left home, and beginning Christian communities, perhaps as small as two co-wives, or a mother and children, in their new village. Sometimes such isolated believers would travel large distances to meet with other Christians, even across denominations.

I asked Bill whether first evangelization as he experienced it was the same as Donovan had described it in *Christianity Rediscovered*. One change in approach has come about because of political changes rather than a change in missionary principles. In 1967, the socialist government instituted a policy of "villagization," demarcating the whole country into villages, which can be huge and include many *bomas*. The centre of such a village would usually be a civic meeting point such as a school, a shade tree, or a water point. This then would be the point at which the missionary would meet with the Maasai rather than the *boma*, and the group being evangelized would therefore be far larger than the extended family of the *boma*.

Often too the initiative for evangelization would come, not from the missionary as in Donovan's time, but from the villages. A few baptized people in one village would invite Bill to come and teach them, and then Christians from the next village would discover that he was there and ask to join in. Then, said Bill, "I would go and greet the elders and get their blessing so I could begin teaching." One implication of this description, of course, is that the line between *kerygma*, the gospel message, and *didache*, the regular teaching of believers, has once again been blurred. This is inevitable in a situation where a proportion of the population is already baptized.

Sometimes Bill would visit market centers and meet the people, and further invitations would result because people would approach him and say, "Oh, we want the Church in our village"—perhaps for the sake of social development, or because of the phenomenon of "spirit possession." This is clearly a different world from that which Donovan inhabited: "the church" now is already a known quantity and (in some cases at least) its presence desired for what it is perceived as being able to contribute to the community.

In terms of liturgy, Bill's approach was closer to Ned's than to Pat's. His principle was always "addition, never subtraction." In other words: "You could add whatever you wanted to the Roman rite. You were standing on thinner ice when you subtracted things from the Roman rite."

As with Ned's practice, there were specific Maasai elements that he added. For example, this is how he described the ordination of the first Maasai-speaking Spiritan, John Laizer:

> One goal was that a person who was not Christian could enter into this ritual, observe this ritual, and maybe not understand all the elements of it, but definitely see the significance of what was going on.
>
> With the permission of the local bishop (well, we didn't ask him until that morning!), we incorporated many facets of Maasai inculturation into the ordination ritual. To begin with, as he came in, he was escorted by his older sister, the woman who escorted him in to his circumcision. She carried over her arm the cow-skin on which John had been circumcised. Just as she had accompanied him years ago for his circumcision, she now came in carrying the cow-skin, the same way as she had done then.
>
> When the Bishop called him for election—"Those to be ordained to the priesthood, come forward: John Laizer!"—she stood up with him to escort him to the altar, just as she had escorted him for his circumcision. But, as he started coming down the aisle, he was stopped, and the Maasai elders addressed the Bishop and said, "This man is a warrior; he is a Morani, and as such is unable to take on the role of presbyter". So, they sat him on the stool, blessed him with grass and milk, and kind of symbolically cut his hair (usually it's shaved for the ceremony, but they just took part of his hair and cut it) and said, "Now he is ready to be presented." So he was presented.

His sister continued to walk him forward. The rite was all in Swahili, not in Maasai—the Bishop is not a Maasai speaker. But she came forward and put down the cow-skin, and the Bishop came forward and put the Bishop's chair on the edge of the cow-skin. So, as the Bishop ordained him, John was kneeling on the cow-skin on which he had been circumcised. And then, when it came time for prostration and the litany, the chair was moved aside and it was on that same cow-skin that John was prostrate for the litany. And then the ordination continued.

So, there was nothing that was subtracted from the Roman rite, but symbols were added so that even John's relatives, who were not Swahili-speaking, who were not Christian, could see immediately the significance: they saw the elder sister; they saw the cow-skin; they saw the blessing with the milk and the grass; they saw the hair-cutting; they saw him kneeling before the Bishop; they saw him prostrate on that same cow-skin he had been circumcised on. So, they might not understand the elements of Catholic Christian ordination to ministry, but they knew something significant had happened in his life that day.

The reference to the bishop indicates a continuing suspicion or perhaps nervousness on the part of the church hierarchy towards inculturation. I asked Bill how he accounted for this attitude. He repeated what I had heard from Ned among others—that there is a natural conservatism among Africans. But he added that African clergy and bishops live with a sense of being "suspect," since they have not been Christians for long—they may even be first-generation Christians—and they want to prove their true Catholicity to the wider church. There is also the related reality than they are often dependent financially on the goodwill of the western church, and do not want to endanger that. Spiritans, including indigenous Spiritans, were free of those pressures.

In one significant way, Bill has gone beyond Donovan. When Donovan began to teach the Christian story to the Maasai, he basically "translated" the story into Maasai terms: Jesus is a warrior; "Christ" means "the one rubbed with oil by God Himself"; he "carried a tuft of grass" as he rode into Jerusalem, and so on (letters, November 15 and December 20, 1960). This is parallel to the liturgical changes Ned and Bill made to traditional forms of service, whether Mass or ordination—adding Maasai elements to the conventional structure.

However, there is little evidence that Donovan in his teaching made direct use of either Maasai or Sonjo mythology. It is true that, in leading his first Mass among the Sonjo, Donovan says, "The old testament, the old dispensation—the tribal one, the Jewish one, the European one, the Sonjo one—as beautiful and meaningful and valuable as it was, has passed away" (Letter, February 1971). Yet he does not seem, from his writings, to have ever used this "old testament" in the way that Christians have traditionally used the Jewish scriptures—as a source of theological insight which has a direct relationship to the Gospel.

Bill Christy, however, did take this step:

> For the first six months that I would be with people, I was basically teaching Maasai theology—which excited them. It also increased my knowledge, because everyone would say, "You left out this point!"
>
> First of all, when you come into a village in Maasai-land, as a European on a motorcycle who speaks a smattering of Maasai, you are the cinema, the attraction. So you are going to get every man, woman and donkey on the first day, because you are the show. Now, if you sit down and begin to tell them their own stories, they are immediately engaged. They are immediately thinking theologically. They're thinking of themselves and of their history and of their relationship with God. . . .
>
> So the first story was always about the leather ladder that stretched from heaven to earth, from which God gave the first Maasai all blessings. And the hunter-gatherer, the Ndorobo, came in and, jealous of the blessings that God had given to the Maasai, shot the arrow into heaven. Because heaven was just right here—you could touch heaven. Heaven was just above the heads of the giraffes. Oh yes, the giraffes used to speak with God. The tallest of the giraffes was able to stand up on a hill and talk to God in heaven.
>
> And, oh yes, the dog! The dog was the only creature that could travel up and down this ladder between heaven and earth. And the whole story about how God had reserved the lamb. It was the one gift that God wouldn't give to the Maasai. And how the dog brought news of this hidden gift to the people. And the people asked for this gift, and the gift came down.
>
> So you would be in this raucous—sometimes it was hard to keep control of the meeting, because everyone is adding in their own parts of the story. I'm quickly taking notes on anything I didn't know!
>
> And we would end that, and I would say, "You know, from the very beginning, God wanted this connection between heaven and earth. And it was only through our own human actions, the

action of the Ndorobo firing the arrow into heaven, that drove God away. But that wasn't God's desire. God's desire was to be close. God's desire was to have the leather ladder connecting heaven and earth. And so, I'm going to be back next week and I'm going to start telling you a little bit about the new ladder that God has created that spans this breach between heaven and earth."

So I'm teaching for maybe two, two-and-a-half hours in a Maasai village for the first time, and I might spend five minutes on Christianity.[17]

One reason Bill's experience could be so different was undoubtedly the nature of his preparation for overseas service. By the time he went to study at Catholic Theological Union, there were courses in cross-cultural ministry, something previous generations of Spiritans lacked (and later complained about). There was a new emphasis on the work of the Holy Spirit in every culture, legitimizing the study of anthropology and fostering new respect for a people's mythology and religion. Missionaries of Donovan's day had to learn these things from painful personal experience. Students at CTU also undertook practical cross-cultural placements, such as "going out to Lakota reservations in Rosebud, South Dakota, and experiencing sweat lodges and Lakota traditional religious practices." Obviously the specifics of Maasai culture were different from those of the Lakota, but the preparedness for culture shock created a whole different mindset among new missionaries.

What then is the usefulness of *Christianity Rediscovered* to a new generation of missionaries? Bill says:

> I take Donovan's book as a parable, not a manual. If you try to follow *Christianity Rediscovered* as a textbook or a manual of missiology, then you're going to be trapped. It was good for one time and one place and one person. That's why the subtitle is that it is an epistle. Taken in that way, it has to find new meaning in every generation, and in every situation. As a parable, you found the central truth of it, then modified that to every different situation. Right now, there's been a request for me to go back on mission. This time I'm being called to go to the Aboriginal Church in West Australia. Now, I'm going to take *Christianity Rediscovered* as a parable to the Western deserts of Australia if—God be praised—this goes through. And it will have as much

17. In Paul's speech to the Athenians (Acts 17), nine verses are devoted to interaction with the Athenians' religion and culture, and only one verse to Jesus, who even then is not named.

meaning—as a parable—as anything that I did in Maasai-land with a book about Maasai.

CONCLUSION

The influence of *Christianity Rediscovered* has been remarkable. The book went through twenty reprints before its second (twenty-fifth anniversary) edition came out in 2003. It is referenced in works on missiology from many traditions—for example, Elizabeth Isichei's *History of Christianity in Africa* (1996); Bengt Sundkler's *A History of the Church in Africa* (2000); George Sumner's *The First and the Last* (2004); Stephen Bevans and Roger Schroeder's *Constants in Context* (2004); Michael Pocock, Gailyn Van Rheenen and Douglas McConnell's *The Changing Face of World Missions* (2005); and Dorothy Hodgson's *The Church of Women* (2005). It is also referenced in books on topics other than missiology, such as John Stott's *The Contemporary Christian* (1998), Mary Stewart Van Leeuwen's *My Brother's Keeper* (2002), and Stanley Hauerwas and Samuel Wells' *Blackwell Companion to Christian Ethics* (2004). The examples run into the dozens.

I believe, however, that more significant than the interest from historians of mission, theologians, and anthropologists is the interest in Donovan's work among contemporary western practitioners of inculturation. Two examples stand out.

Brian McLaren is a leader of the emerging church[18] movement in the USA and around the world. At its core, this movement is seeking to communicate the gospel, and to be the church, in and for a postmodern world. Influenced by such writers as Lesslie Newbigin, it understands that the Christian church in the west is engaged in a cross-cultural missional exercise, just as much as any "overseas" missionary. This is clearly an endeavor parallel to that which Donovan undertook in a very different culture, and, not surprisingly, emerging church leaders have found inspiration in him.

One of McLaren's most influential books, *Generous Orthodoxy*, has a chapter called "Jesus: Savior of What?" which opens with a summary of *Christianity Rediscovered*. McLaren calls Donovan's book, "one of the most important mission-related books of the twentieth century, a

---

18. This is also called the emergent church, but since Emergent is an official organization in the USA and UK, it seems safer to use the more generic term.

treasure too few have discovered."[19] He goes on to draw explicit parallels between the mission of the emerging church and Donovan's work: "Donovan found himself caught between the 'heathen Masai' and a very confident, well-oiled religious machine. That in-betweenness forced him to rethink the whole meaning of what Christians call 'salvation,' much in the same way my experience among 'unchurched postmoderns' has affected me."[20]

This introduces a section where McLaren muses about how to redefine words like salvation and judgment, and evangelical terms like "personal savior." He concludes, "like Vincent Donovan, I think we need another song." Like Donovan, he is trying to rescue the gospel from the ways it has become inculturated in Western culture, in order to release its power in a new culture where it is not known.

The emerging church movement is not without its critics, of course, from both right and left. It makes mistakes, as McLaren is the first to admit. But the impulse to inculturation is a perennial one, and in this particular expression of it, Donovan's has become the voice of a pioneer and prophet.

The second example concerns a contemporary movement in the Church of England, called Fresh Expressions, supported by the Archbishop of Canterbury, Rowan Williams. The website explains: "A fresh expression is a form of church for our changing culture, established primarily for the benefit of people who are not yet members of any church." The terms "forms of church," "changing culture," and "for the benefit of people who are not yet members of any church" alert the reader to a similarity of vision to that of *Christianity Rediscovered*. The movement is inspired in part by the fact that between 30 percent and 40 percent of the population of the UK do not have significant contact with any church, and are unlikely to attend a conventional church, however welcoming and "seeker friendly." When the Fresh Expressions website was first created, people were invited to post information on their fresh expressions of church: over 700 did so.

This is a serious attempt to translate the gospel, and traditional forms of church, into the language and culture of contemporary Britain, with all its diversity. It is now possible to be assessed for ordination, to be trained, and ordained specifically for "pioneer ministries" of this kind.

19. McLaren, *Generous Orthodoxy*, 91.
20. Ibid., 92.

A new structure, the Bishop's Mission Order, enables bishops to give approval to a fresh expression of church in their diocese. Unlike the situation in Tanzania, in Britain a significant number of bishops support this move towards inculturation.

What is interesting is that many leaders in the Fresh Expressions movement look to Donovan as an example of the kind of inculturation they are attempting. The book which provided much of the initial impetus for Fresh Expressions was a best-selling church report (a phrase which would normally seem like an oxymoron) called *Mission-Shaped Church*. There the authors (a group of eleven) explicitly refer to Donovan as a model for what they are doing. They say: "Britain at the start of the third millennium is predominantly a consumer society. The missionary challenge is to embody the Church within it, while also challenging the consumerist pattern." They then summarize the story of *Christianity Rediscovered* and comment: "Vincent Donovan saw the process of inculturation as having the potential to create a pointer to God's future."[21] It is a process they are seeking to emulate, albeit in a new cultural context.

Donovan's friend and colleague, Eugene Hillman, suggests that the limited success of Ronald Allen's methodology among the Maasai was because the apostle Paul, on whom Allen based his ideas, was working mainly in cities, among people of a similar culture and language to his own, and he could normally begin by preaching in the Jewish synagogue. None of these advantages was present for missionaries to the Maasai.[22] For the emerging church movement and for Fresh Expressions, however, at least the first two factors are in place: much (though not all) of their growth is in cities, and they share, to a large extent anyway, the language and culture of those to whom they minister. It will be interesting to watch these movements in the coming years, and see how far their passion for inculturation can be worked out, and with what effects on the church.

The generation of Vincent Donovan and his contemporaries is passing away, and the challenge is for a new generation of missionaries and missiologists to work with their legacy, and to apply their insights, their passion and their commitment in a new century. The need for inculturation has not gone away. The need for Christians to respect and learn from those they seek to evangelize is more urgent than it was then.

21. Cray, *Mission-Shaped Church*, 91–93. It is now available as a PDF online, free of charge at www.cofe.anglican.org/info/papers.

22. Personal conversation, May 2008.

And the need to discern what the good news of Jesus Christ is for any given culture is a task every generation of Christians has to undertake—not only in East Africa but anywhere in the world, not least (as Donovan himself points out) in North America. And in those respects, Vincent Donovan remains a challenging and generative guide.

The words Donovan wrote of Roland Allen are a fitting final tribute to his own work: "I do not think he would have expected us, or wanted us, to come to the identical conclusions on every point that he himself reached. . . . But the main and general insights and questions of this remarkable man are as valid today as they were when they first stunned and disturbed the church of his day."[23]

23. *CR*, 25.

Bibliography

Bevans, Stephen B. and Roger P. Schroeder. *Constants in Context: A Theology of Mission for Today*. Maryknoll, NY: Orbis, 2004.

Bonhoeffer, Dietrich. *Letters and Papers from Prison*. 2nd ed. London: SCM, 1956.

Bosch, David. *Transforming Mission: Paradigm Shifts in Theology of Mission*. Maryknoll, NY: Orbis, 1991.

Charleston, Steve. "The Old Testament of Native America." In *Lift Every Voice: Constructing Christian Theologies from the Underside*, edited by Susan Brooks Thistlethwaite and Mary Potter Engel, 69-81. Maryknoll, NY: Orbis, 1998.

Christy, Bill. "History of the American Spiritan Mission in Africa." Unpublished paper, n.d.

Cray, Graham, ed. *Mission-Shaped Church: Church Planting and Fresh Expressions of Church in a Changing Context*. London: Church House Publishing, 2004.

Dodd, C. H. *The Apostolic Preaching and Its Developments*. New York: Harper & Row 1964.

Donovan, Vincent J. *Christianity Rediscovered*. Twenty-fifth anniversary edition. Maryknoll, NY: Orbis, 2003.

Flannery, Austin P., ed. *Documents of Vatican II*. Grand Rapids: Eerdmans, 1974.

Gallagher, Vernon. *Six Weeks in Tanganyika*. N.p., 1964.

Gray, Robert F. *The Sonjo of Tanganyika: An Anthropological Study of an Irrigation-based Society*. Oxford: Oxford University Press, 1963.

Groop, Kim. *With the Gospel to Maasailand: Lutheran Mission Work among the Arusha and Maasai in Northern Tanzania 1904-1973*. Åbo, Finland: Åbo Akademi University Press, 2006.

Hillman, Eugene. *Polygamy Reconsidered*. Maryknoll, NY: Orbis, 1975.

———. *Toward an African Christianity: Inculturation Applied*. New York: Paulist, 1993.

Hodgson, Dorothy. *The Church of Women: Gendered Encounters between Maasai and Missionaries*. Bloomington: Indiana University Press, 2005.

Hood, Hugh. *The Camera Always Lies*. New York: Harcourt, Brace, & World, 1967.

Isichei, Elizabeth. *A History of Christianity in Africa from Antiquity to the Present*. Grand Rapids: Eerdmans, 1995.

Jenkins, Philip. *The Next Christendom: the Coming of Global Christianity*. Oxford: Oxford University Press, 2002.

Kohler, Girard. *East-West Newsletter* 34.1 (2006) 11–14.

Kollmann, Paul. *The Evangelization of Slaves and Catholic Origins in Eastern Africa.* Maryknoll, NY: Orbis, 2005.

Koren, Henry J. *Spiritan East Africa Memorial 1863–1993.* Bethel Park, PA: Spiritus, 1994.

Kurtz, Laura S. *A Historical Dictionary of Tanzania.* London: Scarecrow, 1978.

Loliondo Mission Journal, The. (Unpublished typescript journal.)

McLaren, Brian D. *A Generous Orthodoxy.* Grand Rapids: Zondervan, 2004.

Neill, Stephen. *A History of Christian Missions.* Harmondsworth: Penguin, 1964.

Rahner, Karl. *Theological Investigations,* Vol. 5. Baltimore: Helicon, 1966.

Sanneh, Lamin. *Translating the Message: the Missionary Impact on Culture.* Maryknoll, NY: Orbis, 1989.

Spindler, Marc R. "Libermann, Francois Marie Paul." In *The Biographical Dictionary of Christian Mission,* edited by Gerald H. Anderson, 399. Grand Rapids: Eerdmans 1998.

Tillich, Paul. *Theology of Culture.* New York: Oxford University Press, 1959.

Vähäkangas, Mika. "Ghambageu Encounters Jesus in Sonjo Mythology: Syncretism as African Rational Action." In the *Journal of the American Academy of Religion* 76.1 (2008) 111–37.

Watschinger, Herbert. *Don't Give up Hope: A Life in Service of the Maasai.* Np, nd.

Index